Poetic Identity in
Guillaume de Machaut

Poetic
Identity in

Guillaume de Machaut

Kevin Brownlee

THE UNIVERSITY
OF WISCONSIN PRESS

Published 1984

The University of Wisconsin Press
114 North Murray Street
Madison, Wisconsin 53715

The University of Wisconsin Press, Ltd.
1 Gower Street
London WC1E 6HA, England

First printing G_1 f_r 4-98

Printed in the United States of America

For LC CIP information see the colophon

ISBN 0-299-09200-3

PQ
1443
.G5
B7
1984

To my beloved parents,
Roland H. and Frances S. Brownlee

Contents

Acknowledgments   ix

I   INTRODUCTION: MACHAUT AND THE CONCEPT
     OF *POÈTE*   3

II   POET-NARRATOR AS LOVER-PROTAGONIST: EARLY POEMS   24

        Introduction / 24
        Le Dit dou vergier / 24
        Remede de Fortune / 37
        Le Dit de l'alerion / 63

III POET-NARRATOR AS LOVER-PROTAGONIST: *LE VOIR-DIT*   94

        Introduction / 94
        Le Voir-Dit: Part 1 / 95
        Le Voir-Dit: Midpoint Sequence / 123
        Le Voir-Dit: Part 2 / 127

IV   POET-NARRATOR AS WITNESS-PARTICIPANT   157

        Introduction / 157
        Le Jugement dou roy de Behaingne / 158
        Le Dit dou lyon / 171
        La Fonteinne amoureuse / 188

V   CONCLUSION: RAMIFICATIONS OF MACHAUT'S
ACHIEVEMENT   208

Abbreviations Used in the Notes and Bibliography   217

Notes   219

Selected Bibliography   255

Index   263

Acknowledgments

This study is a revised version of my Princeton University doctoral dissertation. I would like to express my deep sense of gratitude to Professor Karl D. Uitti, my teacher and mentor at Princeton, under whose guidance the dissertation was written. His inspirational seminars and writings have profoundly influenced my ideas.

For their careful critical reading of the dissertation I wish to thank Professors Alan Deyermond, Robert Hollander, and François Rigolot. In addition, I am very grateful to Professor Douglas Kelly for his helpful suggestions and encouragement. Dr. Lawrence Earp kindly shared with me his profound knowledge of the musical and codicological aspects of Machaut studies. I am indebted to Professor Peter F. Dembowski for his meticulous reading of the manuscript and for his many insightful criticisms, which have been of great help in the preparation of the revisions.

My colleagues at Dartmouth, Stephen G. Nichols and John D. Lyons, have generously provided advice and support at crucial junctures. I am grateful to Dartmouth College for having funded my research at important stages. I would like to thank Professor John Plummer for his help in connection with manuscript M. 396 at the Pierpont Morgan Library.

My wife, Marina, has been a constant and essential source of intellectual companionship throughout the enterprise represented by the present study, to which her contribution has been immense.

Note

All translations from Old French are my own. My primary aim in the case of Machaut is to provide comprehensible and literal English prose renderings of his (largely untranslated) fourteenth-century French verse. The elaborate syntax, extensive wordplay, and stylistic elegance of the original are thus of necessity only faintly reflected. I have not translated passages in modern French or material cited in the Notes.

Poetic Identity in
Guillaume de Machaut

I. Introduction: Machaut and the Concept of *Poète*

The last fifteen years have seen the advent of a new kind of scholarly interest in and approach to the late Middle Ages in France (motivated in large part by the seminal work of Daniel Poirion).[1] The fourteenth and fifteenth centuries, previously viewed either as a period of "decline" vis-à-vis the Renaissance of the twelfth century or as an extended gestation period for the Renaissance of the sixteenth century, are now finally being considered on their own terms — as a time of intense literary activity characterized by consistent and wide-ranging innovation.

In this context Guillaume de Machaut assumes a role of central importance, for he has long been regarded as the greatest poet as well as the greatest composer of fourteenth-century France. The full import of his innovative self-presentation as author figure, however, is only beginning to be recognized. What is at issue is nothing less than the first adumbration of such fundamental modern literary notions as "poet" and "book." Self-consciously expanding the parameters of the earlier vernacular literary tradition in France and in particular building on the *Roman de la rose*, Machaut created his new poetic identity by conjoining the clerkly narrator figure of Old French (OF) hagiography and romance, the first-person lyric voice of the *grand chant courtois*, and a new conception of the professional artist — in part a development of thirteenth-century scribal activity in "editing" and organizing codices. An extraordinary expansion of the range of the lyric-based, first-person

3

poetic voice was thus brought about, which allowed for great generic and linguistic diversity while providing a unifying element. A new set of literary possibilities came into being which was to have important consequences until the time of Villon and beyond.

Before going on it is necessary to consider briefly the historical dimension of Machaut's status as professional artist, since this status was such an important component of his new conception of poetic identity. Machaut's own formation was that of a *clerc*[2] but his patrons and protectors came from the highest ranks of contemporary courtly society.[3] Born around 1300 in Champagne, Machaut had by 1323 entered the service of John of Luxembourg, king of Bohemia, one of the most admired rulers of his age, a model of both *chevalerie* and *courtoisie*. In his capacity as "clerc, secrétaire et familier"[4] to King John, Machaut accompanied his royal master on campaigns in Silesia, Poland, and Lithuania in the 1320s and 1330s. In 1337 he received a canonicate in Reims (as a result of papal favor prompted by King John), and by 1340 the poet was installed as canon in the cathedral city, though he continued in King John's service until the latter's death in 1346 at the battle of Crécy. The poet remained linked to the family of his former patron through Bonne of Luxembourg, King John's daughter and, from 1332, the wife of the dauphin, Jean de Normandie (the future Jean II of France). After Bonne's death in 1349, Machaut attached himself to King Charles II of Navarre, a relationship which lasted until 1357, when King Charles's unsuccessful intrigues against the House of France prompted the poet to leave his service. From 1359 on we see Machaut in close contact with the French royal family, especially Bonne's two sons Charles de Normandie (the future King Charles V) and Jean de Berry, who emerge as two of Machaut's chief patrons during the final decades of the poet's life. During the 1360s Machaut was associated with Pierre de Lusignan, king of Cyprus (d. 1369), for whom he wrote the *Prise d'Alexandrie*. In 1371 Amédée de Savoie and Jean de Berry each purchased luxury manuscripts of Machaut's works,[5] completed, most likely, under the master's personal supervision shortly before his death in 1377.

Machaut's enormous artistic output may be divided into three broad categories: narrative verse, lyric verse, and musical compositions. (Indeed, this division is to be found in all the major manuscripts.)

There exist two excellent editions of the complete musical works: that of Friedrich Ludwig (4 vols., 1926, 1928, 1929, 1954) and that of Leo Schrade (2 vols., 1956).[6] Detailed studies of Machaut's musical corpus are provided by both Ludwig and Schrade, as well as by Armand Machabey and Gilbert Reaney.

The single edition of the complete lyric poems is that of Vladimir Chichmaref (1909).[7] Daniel Poirion's *Le Poète et le prince* (1965) contains the definitive literary study of Machaut's achievement as a lyric poet and explains his pivotal position in the development of the late medieval courtly lyric.

A particularly privileged locus for an investigation of Machaut's self-presentation as poet is found in his narrative verse, both because of its extent and its variety. Eight of the ten long narrative *dits* have been edited with scrupulous scholarship by Ernest Hoepffner (3 vols., 1908, 1911, 1921), and Louis de Mas Latrie's edition of the *Prise d' Alexandrie* (1877) is still serviceable. While the only published edition of the *Voir-Dit* (by Paulin Paris, 1875) is demonstrably flawed,[8] Paul Imbs's promised critical edition of the work is eagerly awaited. The four short dits all exist in excellent editions: the *Dit de la harpe* was edited by Karl Young (1943); the *Dit de la fleur de lis et de la Marguerite* by James Wimsatt (1970) and by Anthime Fourrier (1979); the *Dit de la Marguerite* and the *Dit de la rose* by Fourrier (1979).[9] Poirion treats Machaut's narrative works selectively and insightfully in Chapter 5, Section 1 of *Le Poète et le prince,* suggestively exploring the problematics of "poetic selfhood" in the fourteenth century. In 1974 there appeared the first study entirely consecrated to Machaut's dits, William Calin's *A Poet at the Fountain: Essays on the Narrative Verse of Guillaume de Machaut.* Calin's work performed a great service to Machaut studies by calling attention to the real literary merit and importance of Machaut's narrative poetry, thus remedying the relative neglect to which this key part of Machaut's artistic achievement had previously been relegated. The scope of Calin's study is comprehensive: each chapter contains an essay on one of Machaut's ten long dits, while an excursus treats the shorter dits and the *Prologue.* Calin's approach is avowedly (and fruitfully) heterogeneous:

his stated intention "apart from explication, is to explore Machaut's work for archetypal patterns, comic modes, parody, levels of meaning, realism, narrative point of view, and aesthetic values. A concluding chapter aims at a more synthetic view of Machaut's work, traces his development as an artist, and discusses his place in the history of French literature" (p. 20). Calin's work has served as an important preliminary to subsequent scholarly treatment of Machaut's dits. His consideration of narrative structure is particularly relevant to the present study of the nature and complex ramifications of Machaut's innovative concept of poetic identity.

Douglas Kelly's groundbreaking *Medieval Imagination: Rhetoric and the Poetry of Courtly Love* (1978) represents a new departure in Machaut scholarship. Mainly (though not exclusively) concerned with Machaut's narrative verse, Kelly begins by situating the poet in the OF courtly tradition extending from the *Roman de la rose* to René d'Anjou and Charles d'Orléans. The primary focus of Kelly's treatment of Machaut (largely confined to Chapters 5 and 6) is the latter's "conception of *fin'amors*," which Kelly views as involving a radical departure from preceding courtly doctrine. While Machaut's earliest dits made use of a "standard" presentation of courtly love (in which desire was a defining element), beginning with the *Remede de Fortune* a kind of "sublimation" is effected; *desir* is replaced by *esperence* in such a way as to detach the love experience from dependence on the *dame*. The condition of hope becomes emotionally and imaginatively self-sufficient and fin'amors a kind of sublime solipsism. The true *amant* is thus freed from the power of Fortune since his love does not depend on external events (e.g., his success or failure with a particular dame) but is, rather, a purely internal experience.

Kelly goes on to consider the rhetorical consequences of Machaut's sublimation and idealization of courtly love: "a more impersonal, abstract Image becomes appropriate to the representation of the lady [whose] qualities exist in a realm outside any materiality save their representation in the lover himself" (p. 149).

Kelly is thus primarily concerned with Machaut's concept of love as doctrine (even as a kind of ideology) and with Machaut's innovative rhetoric of the imagination as growing out of this doctrinal position. Both Kelly's approach and his conclusions have important implications (as will be seen) for the study of Machaut's concept of poetic identity that I propose to undertake.

This study involves two distinct but mutually defining parts: first, a general consideration of the nature of Machaut's self-presentation as poet (found in Chapter I); second, a detailed consideration of the way in which Machaut's poetic identity may be said to function in certain of the individual works that, collectively, make up his *oeuvre* (found in Chapters II, III, and IV). In order to carry out this detailed investigation most effectively, I have confined myself to Machaut's seven long narrative *dits amoureux*.

Before going on to consider Machaut's poetic identity on its own terms, however, it is first necessary to establish the historico-linguistic background for Machaut's innovations.[10]

To a considerable extent the modern notion of "poet" derives from fourteenth-century developments, for it is during the fourteenth century that a new relationship between the individual who produces poetry and the text resulting from this activity is first adumbrated. In fact, it is only in the fourteenth century that the semantic field of the very term "poète" in French is expanded to include vernacular, contemporary poets. Previous centuries used the term only with reference to the classical *auctores*. The earliest examples of this expanded usage that I have been able to find come from the *Ballades* written by Eustache Deschamps in connection with the death of Guillaume de Machaut.[11] In his ballade "A dame Péronne, après la mort de Machault,"[12] Deschamps portrays himself as requesting that Péronne (the Toute-Belle of Machaut's *Voir-Dit*) accept him as *ami* in place of his dead master. The ballade begins as follows:

> Après Machaut qui tant vous a amé
> Et qui estoit la fleur de toutes flours,
> Noble poete et faiseur renommé,
> Plus qu'Ovide vray remede d'amours,
> Qui m'a nourry et fait maintes douçours,
> Veuillés, lui mort, pour l'onneur de celui,
> Que je soie vostre loyal ami.

[After Machaut who loved you so much, and who was the flower of all flowers, noble poet and renowned maker, truer remedy of Love than

Ovid, who raised me and did me many kindnesses, may it please you, since he is dead, that, for his honor, I be your faithful lover.]

It is interesting to note that Deschamps seems to feel that the term *poète* requires a gloss, "faiseur" ("maker, creator"), a term already in use to designate vernacular poets. Deschamps is, it appears, aware of the linguistic innovation involved in using the term *poète* to refer to Machaut. In his second ballade "Sur la mort de Guillaume de Machaut" (dated 1377),[13] Deschamps uses the term in a context that links the classical poetic inspiration of the *auctores* with the contemporary vernacular master:

> La fons Circé et la fonteine Helie
> Dont vous estiez le ruissel et les dois,
> Ou poetes mistrent leur estudie
> Convient taire, dont je suis moult destrois.
> Las! c'est par vous qui mort gisez tous frois,
> Qui de tous chans avez esté cantique.
> Plourez, harpes et cors sarrazinois,
> La mort Machaut, le noble rethorique.

[It is fitting that Circe's fountain and the spring of Helicon, of which you were the stream and the canal, and at which poets study, be silent — which makes me very sad. Alas! It is on account of you who lie dead and cold, who were the canticle of all songs. Weep, harps and Saracen horns, for the death of Machaut, the noble rhetorician.]

Again, Deschamps's use of the term seems to be deliberate and to involve an intentional expansion of its field of meaning. As Jean de Meun linked Guillaume de Lorris and the Latin elegiac poets in the *Rose*, so Deschamps links auctores and Machaut. This connection is rendered explicit in the first text cited above when Deschamps utilizes the same generic term in order to designate *both* Ovid and Machaut (and by extension himself, self-depicted as Machaut's successor). The idea of *auctor* thus is, as it were, built into, fused with, the idea of *poète* in its expanded sense. What had been implicit in Jean de Meun, I repeat, becomes explicit in Eustache Deschamps.

That Deschamps should take Machaut as an *exemplum poetae*

is no accident. This is the way in which Machaut conceived of himself. The complex poetic identity he constructed may be regarded as the real innovation — even though Machaut did not explicitly apply the term *poète* to himself. Building on the *Rose*, Machaut established a new kind of poetic identity, 'greatly expanding the range of the lyric voice, and thus authorized the new sense of the term *poète* as applied to him by Deschamps.

This becomes clear when we examine what might be termed the literary antecedents of the concept of the vernacular *poète* as they appear in the OF tradition. Let us turn then to a brief survey of the different generic and poetic functions of the first-person voice in the various eleventh-, twelfth-, and thirteenth-century textual corpora most relevant to a reading of Machaut.

The clerkly narrator figure is an essential component of both OF hagiography and OF romance narrative but operates differently in these diverse generic contexts.[14]

The vernacular saint's life, in order to function (poetically and otherwise) may be said to *require* the clerkly narrator figure. He serves both as authoritative witness to the hagiographic story he tells and as a mediator between his *matière* and his audience, a kind of officiant without whom the saintly paradigm ceases to exist as such (i.e., ceases to be relevant to a contemporary audience). The OF *Vie de Saint Alexis*[15] provides an excellent example of this functioning. The narrative opens with a kind of prologue in which the clerkly narrator establishes an explicit link between himself, his medieval audience, and his ancient subject matter. This link is a genealogical one: he will tell of "nostre anceisour" (v. 12) [our ancestors], the Christian Romans. The idea of clerkly witness to the saint's life is built into the story (and, indeed, the genre) itself. In the OF *Alexis*, the saintly protagonist writes down the story of his life just before he dies. This document ("la chartre," v. 284) is found on his body by the Pope and read to the assembled multitude of the faithful by a clerc. In this way the hagiographic paradigm provides a built-in model (and authorization) for its telling and transmission. At the end of the *Alexis*, the clerkly narrator effects a fusion of matière, self, and audience into a potentially universal Christian community: "Aiems, seignour, cest saint ome en memorie, / Si li preioms que de toz mals nos tolget" (vv. 621–22) [Let us have, my lords, this holy man in our memory, and let us pray that he remove us from all evil]. It is the creation (the perpetual re-creation, each time the saint's life is read and experienced) of this Christian community that results from the working of the poem. The clerkly narrator figure is essential to this process — for he belongs to his audience but is not identical to them (his clerkly learning sets him apart) and he belongs to his matière as well. By putting his clerkliness (including his poetic craft) at the service of the religious truth of his story, the clerkly narrator figure makes the saintly paradigm work for a contemporary audience.

In twelfth-century OF romance narrative, the clerkly narrator functions in a different way; his identity is modified in the context of different generic requirements.[16] Many of the traits of the hagiographic narrator are maintained, but as romance develops into a genre which celebrates poetic process as such (rather than using poetic processes and poetic craft to celebrate a truth, religious or political, external to a given poem), the clerkly narrator's poetic role and function change as well. Already in the romances of Wace, the identity of the clerc as the transmitter of the values of civilization is articulated quite explicitly.[17] The topos of *translatio studii* linked to that of *translatio imperii* is employed to bestow immense value and prestige on the (poetic) activity of the clerc. The process of reading and writing (the essence of clerkly activity) is viewed as a continuum by means of which cultural values remain alive. Indeed, Benoît de Sainte-Maure in the prologue to the *Roman de Troie* affirms that, without collective cultural memory (perpetuated by clerkly activity) men would all live like beasts.[18]

Already evident in Wace, however, is a certain distancing of the narrator from his matière, which represents a radical departure from the attitude, the identity, and the poetic function of the clerkly narrator of hagiography. Wace periodically intervenes in his story to express a certain detached, critical perspective, attributing, for example, a particular narrative event to hearsay evidence for which he (qua narrator) does not bear responsibility.[19] A strengthening of the narrator figure results: while he serves to link his audience and his subject matter, he cannot be entirely identified with either. Rather, his identity resides in his clerkly learning and his literary craftsmanship.

The possibilities inherent in this strengthened clerkly narrator figure are further developed by Chrétien de Troyes in terms of, in accord with, the generic requirements of the new kind of romance he created. A further dimension of literary self-consciousness is thereby attained — and celebrated as such. Thus in the prologue to *Erec et Enide*[20] the narrator presents himself, gives himself an identity, largely in terms of his poetic craft. It is he who has made the "molt bele conjoincture" (v. 14) [most pleasing structure]. In the prologue to *Cligés*,[21] the poet-narrator's identity again resides in his literary production.[22] He first describes himself in terms of his past works. His identity is above all that of a poetic craftsman. The separating of the translatio studii from the translatio imperii that we find in this prologue, and the valorization of the former at the expense of the latter that we find in all of Chrétien's romances, further demonstrate the way in which the narrator figure has here become a specifically romance construct. The opening of *Yvain*[23] shows how the convention of the romance narrator figure lends itself to the creation of irony. The high-flown description of Arthur's court as a model of courtoisie that we find in the opening lines of the work (vv. 1–41) is almost immediately undercut by the very uncourtly behavior of the members of the court. The narrator figure, then, is not only not identified with his matière (or with his audience), but is unreliable — not a source of any truth lying outside the poem, but one of a number of romance constructs whose mutual interaction (poetically speaking) is what is important. It is indeed this which may be said to constitute the "working out" of the poem itself. In the *Lancelot*[24] we have the establishment of a parallel between the clerkly (i.e., poetic) service of the poet-narrator and the chivalric service of his protagonist. Chrétien serves his dame as Lancelot serves his (though the latter is of course, and this is part of the point, subsumed into the former). In the *Perceval*[25] we find a new seriousness in the way the narrator figure functions, determined in part by the new seriousness that is to be found in the romance as a whole.

The lyric *je* of the "grand chant courtois"[26] is quite different from the narrator figure of OF hagiography and romance. Again, however, the identity of this je figure is determined by (and determines — there is certainly a kind of dialectic at work here) generic constraints. It functions poetically within the context of the courtly lyric as genre. This functioning as well as the nature of this first-person voice may be succinctly illustrated by means of what Karl Uitti has termed the "lyric triangle construct." This lyric triangle involves three related, in fact mutually defining, elements. First, there is the poetic ego, the je. Second, there is the love experience — highly conventional, but deeply felt by the je, who is simultaneously poet and lover, for whom there is no significant temporal discrepancy between loving and writing. Third, there is the "song" — including all aspects of poetic craft from diction and technique to music. These three elements of the lyric triangle are indispensable to each other. The poetic je of courtly lyric, unlike the clerkly narrator figure of romance, defines his identity (within the context of the poem) by means of reference to his "personal experience." The experience itself forms the stuff, the matière, of the lyric poem. The song then becomes at once the form of the poem and of the experience. There is thus a complete fusion of loving, writing poetry, and ego. A lyric poet like Conon de Béthune, Thibaut de Champagne, or the Chastelain de Couci is, in a very important sense, identical with his song and with his love.

In the *Roman de la rose* of Guillaume de Lorris we have a transformation of the narrative je of courtly romance whereby it is conflated with the lyric je of the grand chant courtois.[27] Guillaume effects his transformation through a brilliant structural innovation — that of narrative *dédoublement*. A twenty-five (or more)-year-old narrator tells the story of his own love-experience when he was twenty. Narrator and protagonist are thus the same "person." It is as if Lancelot were to tell his own story from a more mature narrative perspective. Guillaume's narrator-protagonist configuration allows him to combine the perspective of the clerkly narrator figure (including his authority and sapience) with the lyric perspective of the first-person love experience. At the same time the lyric triangle construct that is implicit in this configuration provides a kind of self-authentication by means of lyric: Amant's experience authenticates Guillaume's poetry. In Guillaume's section of the *Rose,* then, thanks in part to the transformation of the lyrico-narrative je he effects, thanks to his narrator-protagonist configuration, we have romance procedure combined with lyric matière and structure.

Jean de Meun continues and expands Guillaume's narrator-protagonist configuration.[28] He maintains the dédoublement, keeping Guillaume as lover-protagonist, but making himself into the poet-narrator. This continuation/transformation is overtly presented as such at the midpoint of the conjoined poem,[29] in the course of Amors's long address to his troops. First, Guillaume is explicitly named as Amant, the lover-protagonist: Amors asks that Guillaume be helped in his quest to win the rose. Next, Jean is explicitly named as the poet-narrator who is to finish the romance: Amors asks that Jean be helped to *write* more easily, speaking of the poet-narrator in the future tense by means of a temporal construct of great complexity and subtlety. Because he is continuing Guillaume, however, Jean employs je to refer both to the lover-protagonist and to the poet-narrator. A new kind of first-person voice, a new notion of poetic identity emerges, implicit in Jean's attitude towards his matière. In effect, Jean qua poet is singing someone else's love experience in the first person. Jean thus situates himself with respect to his story in a way which transcends the conflation of clerc and *trouvère* so brilliantly effected by Guillaume. While Jean is never identified as a lover, neither can his literary activity properly be identified as clerkly. Rather, his is a love service that is exclusively poetic.

A further elaboration of Jean's new notion of poetic identity occurs in the final sequence of the poem (the taking of the rose, vv. 21, 316–21, 750). Here we seem to have a fusion of the two je's: lover-protagonist and poet-narrator win, make love to, and pluck the rose together, *by means of poetry,* for the entire sequence is recounted in terms of metaphor and symbol, in such a way as to valorize the language of metaphor and symbol (i.e., poetic discourse) which does not require any separable gloss in order to be completed. It is important to note that the courtly diction of Guillaume de Lorris has, as it were, been *dépassé,* subsumed into a more universal and open-ended poetic discourse that is presented and celebrated as such at the end of the *Rose.* This new kind of poetic discourse implies nothing less than a new concept of poetry, closely linked to the new kind of poet figure that emerges from Jean de Meun's transformation and continuation of the narrator-protagonist configuration of Guillaume de Lorris.

In the works of Rutebeuf we find a different kind of transformation of the lyrico-narrative je. Rutebeuf's persona may best be thought of as a "poetic voice"[30] which serves to unify a generically diverse body of poems into an oeuvre. The same basically lyric voice is put to a multiplicity of uses, undergoes a wide variety of generic permutations, yet is itself a unity. Thus the lyric narrator-protagonist of the "Griesche d'été," the "Mort Rutebeuf," and the other "poems of misfortune"[31] is closely linked to Rutebeuf the polemicist who rails against the mendicant friars, chastises the University of Paris for inactivity, or implores the great lords of Christendom to become crusaders. The same poetic voice functions in hagiographic narratives, the *Vie de Sainte Marie l'Egyptienne* and the *Vie de Sainte Elysabel* as well as the *fabliau*-like *Sacristain et la femme au chevalier* and the *Miracle de Théophile*, a masterpiece of hagiographic theater.

Amidst this striking variety of genres and dictions, tones and themes, the presence of a single poetic voice is established by means of common linguistic and rhetorical devices: extensive *annominatio*, elaborate paronomasia, the *figura etymologica* on the name Rutebeuf, etc. What might be termed a poeticization of technique is effected here, for the je that calls itself Rutebeuf is, to a large degree, identical with a characteristic manner of exercising his poetic craft, of deploying his technical mastery. At the same time the essentially lyric quality of Rutebeuf's persona is always in evidence, visibly exploited both as construct and as literary convention: it is the "personal experience" of the poet figure that, in different ways according to the requirements of the different genres in which he writes, guarantees the truth and the significance of his *matière*.

When viewed in the context of the OF literary tradition, Guillaume de Machaut's concept of poetic identity appears as a development of suggestions latent in Rutebeuf and Jean de Meun. On the one hand, Machaut's concept of the vernacular *poète* involves the explicit unification of a generically and linguistically diverse corpus of first-person poems into a single oeuvre. On the other hand, the attitude of Machaut's poet figure towards his first-person matière underscores its essentially *literary* character. For Machaut, love service and poetic service are conflated in such a way as to present the poète's fundamental lyric "experience" as the activity of poetic composition.

The nature of the relationship between Machaut's innovative concept of poetic identity and its OF literary antecedents becomes fully evident, however, only after a direct consideration of Machaut's self-presentation as poète. Such a consideration must begin by taking into account his presentation of his vast and heterogeneous artistic production as a unified and coherent body of work, as an oeuvre. For not only is this kind of presentation made possible by his concept of poetic identity, it serves as one of the most important defining elements of that identity.

In both the *Voir-Dit* and the *Jugement dou roy de Navarre* Machaut consistently portrays himself as above all a professional writer, for whom the activity of composing poetry and music is closely linked with the physical aspects of the writer's craft: the transcription and circulation of manuscripts and the business of patronage. Indeed, one of the most striking aspects of Machaut's self-presentation as poet in the *Voir-Dit* is his explicit concern with the supervision of the arrangement and copying of editions of his collected works — i.e., with the making of codices.[32] This activity is thus presented as an inherent part of Machaut's poetic activity — of his poetic identity. The poet no longer simply composes verses, songs, or dits, but, in addition, concerns himself with the transcription of his various works — with their codicological existence. The arrangement of codices — in the thirteenth century largely the business of scribes (who often exercised considerable editorial, even literarily significant, roles)[33] — becomes with Machaut the business of the poet himself. Indeed, the notion of organizing a codex is transferred by Machaut into the organizing of an oeuvre. We have moved one step beyond the accomplishments of the thirteenth-century scribes to something approaching the modern idea of the "book."

This explicit expansion of the realm of the writer's activity — of the poet's activity qua poet — is of the utmost significance. For, by depicting himself as supervising the transcription and arrangement of his own complete works, Machaut has done nothing less than to raise the codex to the level of literary artifact, making if function as an inherent part of his poetic production.

This implication is confirmed by manuscript evidence. In each of the major manuscripts one notes an evident concern with the arrangement and ordering of the whole, which was almost certainly the result of Machaut's personal supervision. Codex A^{34} "opens with an original index on 2 unfoliated pages bearing the superscription . . . 'Vesci l'ordenance que G de Machaut wet quil ait en son livre'" [Here is the order that G. de Machaut wants his book to have].[35] That our author was indeed presenting his *oeuvres complètes* as such is further confirmed by the *Prologue*. Written near the end of the poet's life, this is not the prologue to any individual work of Machaut but to his collected, complete works, which are thus presented as a unified oeuvre.[36]

Not only does the existence of a global prologue of this sort make even more explicit the poeticization of the codex, but it serves to inform our reading of Machaut's oeuvre in a very important way. For Machaut's *Prologue* does more than serve as a formal unifying element. It involves the explicit establishment of the poetic voice that will be speaking in all the works that follow. It is the character of this poetic voice — what might be called Machaut's "global" identity as poète — that allows an extremely diverse collection to be presented as a unity, as an oeuvre.

Since it is in the *Prologue* that Machaut's global poetic identity is most explicitly established, I would like to turn now to a detailed examination of this text.

The *Prologue* is composed of four ballades, each preceded by a brief prose introduction. There follows a sequence of 184 lines of rhyming octosyllabic couplets.[37] (It is important to note that the form of the *Prologue*, combining lyric and narrative verse patterns, appears as, in the words of Ernest Hoepffner, "un raccourci de toute l'oeuvre du poète."[38]) In the first ballade (as indeed throughout the *Prologue*) the dignity and importance of the poetic vocation are strongly affirmed. Nature invests Guillaume (who is explicitly named) with his poetic mission: "Je, Nature . . . Vien ci a toy, Guillaume, qui fourmé / T'ay a part, pour faire par toy

fourmer / Nouviaus dis amoureus plaisans" (vv. 1–5) [I, Nature
. . . come here to you Guillaume, I who have formed you apart
(from others) in order to have you form new, pleasing love songs].
Nature then gives the poet "Scens," "Retorique," and "Musique"[39]
—his poetic means or technique ("la pratique"). In the second
ballade, Guillaume accepts his poetic vocation explicitly and
wholeheartedly. This vocation involves following "le bon commandement" (v. 2) [the good command] of "dame" Nature. In the
third ballade Amour comes to Guillaume to give him his "matere"
(v. 3). Service of Amour is presented as involving above all the
process of poetic composition: Amour gives Guillaume ". . . grande
sustance / Dont tu porras figurer et retraire / Moult de biaus dis"
(vv. 17–19) [great substance from which you can shape and derive many beautiful poems]. In the fourth ballade, Guillaume
thanks Amour and reaffirms his "poetic commitment": ". . . ces
fais que j'ay a ordener, / Pour lesquels arriere tous mis / Seront
autres, puis qu'a ce sui commis" (vv. 14–16) [this activity which
I have to arrange, for the sake of which all others will be put
aside, since I am committed to this]. As was the case with Jean
de Meun in the *Rose*, Machaut's service to Amour consists more
in writing well than in loving well.

In the narrative sequence of 184 lines that follows, we have both
a commentary on and expansion of the ceremonious taking up
of the poetic vocation depicted in the ballades. The poet-narrator
claims that no one has ever served Amour better than he will.
Then he restates the equation of love service with poetic service
and reaffirms his commitment to both. He lists the specific genres
in which he will write (vv. 11–16) and the different kinds of rhyme
he will use (vv. 151–56). We have here what could be called an
explicit poeticization of poetic technique, i.e., the incorporation
of poetic technique into the very economy and stuff of the poem.
Technical mastery becomes one of the characteristics of the poet
figure who is presented to us here, hence the importance of "retorique": "Retorique versefier / Fait l'amant et metrefier, / Et si fait
faire jolis vers / Nouviaus et de metres divers" (vv. 147–50) [Rhet-
oric makes the lover versify and metrify and thus it causes pretty,
new verses in diverse meters to be made]. Finally, poetic activity
is depicted as joyous activity, as celebration (vv. 49–55, 77–86).

As such it is exalted, being associated with the highest kind of celebration, the angels' music of praise before God: they "loent en chantant" (v. 118) [praise by singing]. David and Orpheus are praised by Machaut as archetypal poets analogous to the angels in their "chants." With line 138 we have a celebration of poetry carried, as it were, to the second power; a poet making poetry about a poet making poetry: "Cils poetes dont je vous chant" [This poet about whom I sing to you]. The reference is to Orpheus and the use of the term "poetes" is significant. The sense of the Greco-Latin *poeta* as "maker, contriver" (cf. Deschamps's "faiseur") as well as "poet" in the modern sense seems to be particularly relevant to the poetic identity that is established in Machaut's *Prologue*. The emphasis is on the act of *making* poetry (more explicitly, making verses — hence the importance of technical mastery) rather than on the experience of the lyric poet. Thus, Machaut's concept of poetic identity allows for (implies, even) a multiplicity of experiential perspectives from which poetry can be written, a variety of poetic stances. Yet all of these can remain in the first person, since they can all be placed within the context of serving love through poetry.

What emerges, then, from the *Prologue* is a carefully constructed poetic persona: a complex first-person poet-narrator whose identity serves to unify the vast corpus to follow. The clerk, the lover, and the poetic craftsman are conflated into a single but multi-faceted poetic voice. This is the poète figure: acutely aware of the dignity of his calling, highly conscious of his technical expertise, glorying in the breadth and diversity of his artistic production. Machaut's poet figure is no longer bound by the lyric convention which requires him to sing his own love experience only. Since it is poetic activity (which includes music) that is presented by Machaut as constituting his service to ". . . li dieus d'Amours, qui mes sires / Est. . ." (vv. 3–4) [the god of Love, who is my lord], the service of the poète is different from that of the lyric poet. Though the latter is, as it were, included in the former, the purely "lyric stance" becomes only one of a number of possibilities open to him. This potential diversity of expression is consequently one of the defining, and new, characteristics of the vernacular poète.

By establishing the figure of the poète, the *Prologue* thus provides the diverse sections of Machaut's corpus with a principle of unity built into the body of the work itself. In addition (and this provides a further measure of unity), the *Prologue* situates the poète figure within the particular poetic tradition of the *Roman de la rose* in such a way as to embody the principles of continuation and transformation that are inherent in that tradition.

It is highly significant that Guillaume receives his poetic mission from dame Nature, and "li dieus d'Amours," acting as necessary complements to each other. These are the same two figures whose combined effort in the *Rose* had made possible the taking of the castle, the winning of the rose, and thus (in a sense) the writing of the poem.

Further, Guillaume's taking up of his poetic mission is depicted as his entering the "trés dous service" (v. 7) of "li dieus d'Amours." Again, there is a significant correspondence with (as well as departure from) the *Rose*. First, there is a structural transformation: the midpoint of the *Rose* has become the *Prologue* to Guillaume's oeuvre. By midpoint I mean both the midpoint of Guillaume de Lorris's section of the poem (where Amant enters the service of Amors) and the midpoint of the conjoined *Rose* texts (where Amant reenters the service of Amors). Second, it is Machaut the poet, *not* Machaut the lover, who enters Amour's service. It is as if the twenty-five-year-old poet-narrator of Guillaume de Lorris or the narrator figure in Jean de Meun were to undergo directly the ceremony of entering into the service of Love that they describe Amant undergoing. In Machaut's *Prologue* the lover-protagonist of the *Rose* is conflated with the poet-narrator and a new poetic identity emerges — that of the poète.

The fact that this identity may be seen as deriving from the *Rose* provides it with a very important kind of authorization in terms of the values of the OF literary canon. Further, this explicit link with the *Rose* establishes a poetic point of reference that will continue to operate throughout Machaut's diversified corpus. Time and again in his varied oeuvre, Machaut utilizes the *Rose* as a source of poetic constructs; he does so on every level. In the *Prologue*, this process of poetic exploitation is itself poeticized.

That Machaut viewed the *Rose* as embodying an entire poetic tradition, in whose context he sought authorization for his own artistic endeavor, is, I think, sufficiently clear from even a preliminary consideration of the *Prologue*. But if Machaut conceives of himself as being, in a very important sense, a poetic descendant of the *Rose*, he is equally conscious of the fact that his own work represents a kind of fragmentation of the *Rose*. With Machaut, we no longer have a self-consciously encyclopedic but structurally unified single poetic work (a poetic *summa*, as it were). Rather, in his case we find a series of separate works that are presented as though, together, they formed a unified oeuvre.

Utilizing the *Rose* as authorization, while departing from it in a radical way, Guillaume de Machaut developed a new kind of poetic identity which is much closer to the concept of *poeta* as used, say, by a Petrarch, than to any of the terms previously employed by OF writers in speaking of themselves or their poetic activity.[40] It is, I think, this exemplification of the concept of the poeta that explains why Deschamps should apply to Machaut the term *poète*. It is also Machaut's self-presentation as poeta that approaches, for the first time in medieval French literature, our modern notion of "poet."

Perhaps the single most important result of Machaut's concept of poetic identity involves a widening of the range of contexts in which the poet could portray himself qua poet, an increase in the range and number of poetic stances open to him — all under the general rubric of serving love through poetry. Even a cursory consideration of the corpus of Machaut's narrative poetry reveals a striking variety with regard to narrative stance. Though all ten of Machaut's long dits are recounted in the first person, a series of different narrator-protagonist configurations is employed. The kind of poetic identity that Machaut has established in the *Prologue* not only authorizes all of these permutations in narrative structure but allows them to be considered components of a unified whole.

The narrative stance most frequently employed by Machaut depicts the poet-narrator as lover-protagonist. This configuration is found in the *Dit dou vergier*, the *Remede de Fortune*, the *Dit de l'alerion*, and the *Voir-Dit*. Not only does Machaut achieve an extraordinary degree of variety within the limits of this narrative construct, but he exploits it in what appears to be a progressively more elaborate manner. This progression culminates, in a sense, with the *Voir-Dit.*

A further example of the transformations of the lyric je made possible by Machaut's concept of poetic identity may be found in the three dits in which the poet-narrator figures as witness-participant, no longer the protagonist in the story he recounts: the *Jugement dou roy de Behaigne,* the *Dit dou lyon,* and the *Fonteinne amoureuse.* In effect, what we have in these three dits is the poet-narrator singing the love-experience of someone else, but in a first-person context—the whole being conceived of always as part of the poète's service to Amour. Again, a progressively more elaborate exploitation of this narrator-protagonist configuration may be discerned.

In addition, Machaut exploited three other narrative stances, which serve as a further illustration of the greatly expanded range of possibilities open to the kind of poetic identity he created. In the *Jugement dou roy de Navarre,* the first-person narrator-protagonist is presented as much more a poet than a lover. Not only is he named Guillaume de Machaut within the context of the dit itself (the only one in which this occurs), but he is depicted (and treated by the other characters) as a professional writer. In the *Confort d'ami,* the poet-narrator is presented as a kind of "authoritative adviser," speaking in the first person to the imprisoned king of Navarre, Charles le Mauvais. In the *Prise d'Alexandrie,* Machaut's last narrative poem, he adopts the narrative posture of an "epic chronicler" and recounts the life of the great fourteenth-century crusader, Pierre de Lusignan, king of Cyprus.

The remarkable variety of first-person narrative possibilities to be found in Machaut's collected works can be explained by means of the general consideration of his poetic identity that we have undertaken in the present chapter. A fuller understanding of this identity requires a detailed examination of the way in which Machaut's concept of the *poète* may be said to function in the various dits, considered both as individual works and as components of the larger poetic entity that is the oeuvre.

In the chapters that follow I will give this kind of detailed examination to the seven dits in which Machaut's most frequently employed narrator-protagonist configurations are to be found: poet-narrator as lover-protagonist and poet-narrator as witness-participant. Two factors determine this choice. On the one hand, these seven poems share a certain broadly conceived generic affinity: they are all dits amoureux. As such they constitute the largest subgrouping of Machaut's narrative poems that can be studied together coherently in the context of the present investigation. The *Jugement dou roy de Navarre*, the *Confort d'ami*, and the *Prise d'Alexandrie* will not, therefore, be subject to individual analyses, but will be treated very selectively. [41]

Second, confining myself to the dits amoureux allows for an examination of what I see as a developmental dynamics in Machaut's work. The progressions involved in Machaut's repeated use of a given narrator-protagonist configuration function as part of an oeuvre which explicitly calls attention to its "ordenance" (see p. 16, above). Thus the order in which I treat the various poems within each of these categories is based on the organization of MS *A*. While recognizing that no definitive chronology for the dits can be established on the basis of present evidence, I think it likely that this codicological organization reflects order of composition, as Hoepffner argues. [42]

My treatment of the individual dits involves, in each case, a double focus (with specific terminology and orientation varying according to the requirements of the individual poems themselves). First, I examine in detail the identity of the narrator figure. This examination involves both an analysis of narrative structure and a consideration of the relationship between the narrator of a particular dit and the global poète figure of the oeuvre as a whole. My approach derives from the work of Uitti, Kelly, and (to a lesser degree) Gérard Genette. [43]

Second, I undertake a linguistic analysis of Machaut's employment of first-person narration in each individual dit. This analysis makes extensive use of Harald Weinrich's opposition between "narrated" and "commented" tenses, as set forth in *Tempus — besprochene und erzählte Welt*. [44] Weinrich's dichotomy resembles in several important ways Emile Benveniste's distinction between *histoire* and *discours*.[45] Both Weinrich and Benveniste associate "narrative" (or histoire) with the past, past perfect, and conditional tenses, while "commentary" (or discours) is linked to the present, the present perfect, and the future. In applying this theoretical binome to particular texts of Machaut I attempt to elucidate the complex relationship between narrator figure and poète on a linguistic level.

Finally, the nature of Machaut's concept of poetic identity necessitates a study of the poetic uses to which he puts his sources and analogues, that is, a comprehensive examination of his creative reworking of various elements (from the most broadly conceived generic constructs to highly particular examples of imagery and vocabulary) of the OF literary tradition in which he situates himself. In this investigation it is Machaut's transformations of the *Roman de la rose* that, necessarily, receive the greatest emphasis and the most extensive treatment.

II. Poet-Narrator as Lover-Protagonist: Early Poems

Introduction

The narrative stance employed in the *Dit dou vergier*, the *Remede de Fortune*, and the *Dit de l'alerion*[1] involves the poet-narrator as lover-protagonist. In each case we have a first-person account in which the narrator's own love experience forms the central matière. Yet within the context of this narrative stance, a striking variety prevails, a variety which is both explained and authorized by Machaut's concept of poetic identity (as established most explicitly in the *Prologue*) and which, at the same time, serves as an extended illustration, even manifestation, of that identity.

The present analysis will center on the identity of the narrator figure in each of the three early poems under consideration. On the one hand, this will involve for each dit a detailed examination of narrative structure, which may be viewed as simultaneously deriving from and serving to define the narrator's identity. On the other hand, the nuanced relationship between the narrator figure and that of Machaut the poète will be considered in detail. Indeed, this relationship is central both to the poetic function of each individual dit as such and to the function of the individual dit as part of the larger poetic entity in which it participates — the oeuvre.

Le Dit dou vergier

The *Vergier* is the first of the dits in MSS *AFGVgJKDM* (see Chapter I, n. 34) and serves in many ways as an opening signal, an important informing element, for the entire corpus of Machaut's narrative poetry. Further, in MSS *AFG* (those which, as we remember, Hoepffner considers to be the best and most complete; see Chapter I, n. 37) the *Vergier* follows directly after the *Prologue*, where it is mentioned explicitly, its *incipit*, as it were, serving as the *Prologue*'s last line: "Et pour ce vueil, sans plus targier, / Commencier le *Dit dou Vergier*" (vv. 183–84) [And thus I want to begin the *Poem of the Garden* without delay]. This presentation of the *Vergier* (combined with its position in the manuscripts) is quite significant. First, it involves a striking (and strategically placed) instance of the incorporation of what had previously been scribal activity into the activity of Machaut's new and expanded poet figure. The ordering of the various works in a codex thus becomes part of the poet's concern qua poet. This is all the more striking in that the *Vergier* was almost certainly Machaut's earliest narrative poem while the *Prologue* dates from the last period of his life.[2] The juxtaposition and explicit connection between these two poems (each presented as constituting sections of the larger entity, Machaut's complete works) thus serve to poeticize the codex, to present Machaut's collected artistic output as constituting a unified oeuvre.

In addition, one of the defining aspects of the identity of the poète figure, the author of the oeuvre as a whole, results from this connection between the *Vergier* and the *Prologue*. The unnamed first-person voice that narrates the *Vergier* is strikingly different from the first-person voice (explicitly identified as "Guillaume de Machaut") speaking in the *Prologue*. The link between the two poems, however, presents the narrator figure of the *Vergier* as a permutation of the global poète figure, author of the oeuvre as a whole. The first-person narrator-protagonist of the *Vergier* thus appears as distinct from, but subsumed by, the identity of Machaut the poète. This configuration may be seen to function in all of Machaut's narrative poetry. Indeed, each of the narrative poems may be viewed as a variation on this basic construct, derived from and authorized by it. At the same time, this extended series of different, highly varied, first-person narrations can be seen as a coherent whole—the oeuvre of the poète.

When read in conjunction with the *Prologue* (i.e., as part of

Machaut's oeuvre) the *Vergier* thus serves as an important opening signal with regard both to Machaut's identity, his self-
presentation as poète, and to the transformation of the codex
through the concept of oeuvre that is an essential part of that
identity. In addition, the *Vergier* may be regarded as an important
opening signal in another way, for it situates Machaut's poetic endeavor self-consciously in the tradition represented by the *Roman
de la rose*, thus strengthening and making more explicit the poetic
kinship with the *Rose* that we have already seen established in
the *Prologue*. At the same time the *Vergier* (like the *Prologue*)
emphasizes the process of transforming and fragmenting the *Rose*,
which Machaut's narrative corpus will involve.[3]

The *Vergier* does not begin with a formal prologue but plunges
immediately into a first-person narrative. The introductory section of the dit (vv. 1–154) serves to establish the identity of the
narrator figure and the setting (narrative as well as literary) for
the rest of the work. This is accomplished, however, indirectly,
emerging from the story line as it unfolds.

On a beautiful April morning,[4] the narrator awakens and, after
walking through an idyllic garden, arrives at the entrance to the
vergier:

> S'entray ens pour moy deporter,
> Pleins d'amoureuse maladie,
> Et pour oïr la melodie
> Des oisillons qui ens estoient
> Qui si trés doucement chantoient.
>
> (vv. 18–22)

[Thus full of love's sickness, I entered the garden to divert myself and
to hear the melody of the birds inside who were singing so sweetly.]

The narrator is incapable of enjoying the various delights of the
vergier, however, because he is completely absorbed by the memory of his beloved lady, who does not return his love. The pain
caused by this thought is so intense that the narrator falls into
a trance, during which he has a vision:

Einsi fui transis longuement
Sans avoir joie ne tourment,
Fors tant qu'une joie me vint
D'une vision qui m'avint
Si trés plaisant, a grant merveille,
Qu'onques mais ne vi sa pareille.

(vv. 149–54)

[Thus I was unconscious for a long time, without feeling joy or pain, except for the joy brought to me by a vision—which was so very agreeable that I never saw its like.]

The introductory section of the *Vergier* has thus established, within the context of the story line, the narrator's identity as lover in terms of a personal, though highly conventional lyric experience. At the same time, numerous verbal and structural reminiscences of the opening of the dream-narrative of the *Roman de la rose* call attention to the presence of the poète figure and serve to differentiate him from the narrator. It is the poète who establishes the *Rose* as literary model for the *Vergier*. Equally important, he does so in a way which serves to emphasize the fact that this model is undergoing a process of transformation. First, this section of Machaut's poem is significantly shorter than the corresponding section of the *Rose*. A substantial abbreviatio (presented as such) has been effected. Second, Machaut's narrator-protagonist enters his vergier fully awake, not in the context of a dream. This involves a reversal of the narrative structure of the *Rose* in that the vergier of the dit serves to frame the *vision*, whereas in the earlier work, the dream-vision had, in effect, served to frame the vergier. Yet more than a simple structural reversal has been effected here. The fact that the *Vergier* involves not a dream ("songe") but a trance ("transissement") and a vision ("vision") is significant precisely in that it represents a deliberate departure from the terminology employed in the *Rose*.

The fact that the *Rose* as literary model is thus radically transformed from the outset of the *Vergier* has important implications for the identity of the poète figure as he is implicitly presented in his text, for the identity of the narrator figure, and for the relation between the two. The poète appears as above all a literary craftsman whose personal love experience neither generates nor structures the text. He is differentiated from (indeed, may be said to contain) the narrator, whose identity resides in his personal love experience and nothing else. In large part because of the highly visible presence of the *Rose* as transformed literary model, the narrator of the *Vergier* takes on the status of a literary convention — a transformation of a character from an earlier work. For Machaut's narrator may be viewed quite simply as a recombination (on a vastly reduced scale) of various elements of the narrator-protagonist of Guillaume de Lorris. There is an important difference, however. Machaut's protagonist is already a disappointed lover when the narrative begins. His experience of love antedates the opening of the story line of the *Vergier*. Not only is the love experience of Machaut's narrator thus invested with an extra dimension of literariness, but it appears limited and static by comparison with its model. The characterization of the narrator figure by means of a kind of personal love experience — and his consequent differentiation from the poète figure — will be exploited repeatedly as the dit unfolds.

The vision itself constitutes the largest (and central) section of the dit (vv. 155–1210). It is divided into seven parts in which narrative segments alternate with direct speeches by the God of Love.

The first narrative segment of the vision (vv. 155–246) opens with a description of what the narrator actually sees: a blind, winged "créature" sitting in a tree, holding a "dart" in one hand and a "brandon" in the other, and surrounded by six youths and six maidens who honor him as their lord (vv. 155–92). Overcoming his initial fear, the narrator approaches the company and, emboldened by the créature's courteous return of his greeting, asks a series of questions concerning the créature's identity and "la signefiance toute" [the entire meaning] of his accouterments and attendants. The narrator's interlocutor agrees to answer all his questions and the first direct speech of the vision ensues (vv. 274–376), with the as-yet-unnamed god discoursing first on the universality of his power before going on to develop at length the topos of Love as the great leveler.[5] The speech concludes as the speaker reveals his name: "Dieus d'Amours me fais appeller" (v. 376) [I am called the God of Love].

In the second narrative segment of the vision (vv. 377–400), the narrator, recognizing the God of Love as "mes sires," [my lord] kneels before him and requests help in his own unhappy love affair. Amour, however, interrupts the narrator, saying that he will respond to this particular request for help at a later and more fitting time. For the present, Amour does not wish to concern himself with the personal love experience of the narrator, but rather wants to discourse to him on the love experience in general:

> Lors ne me volt plus escouter,
> Pour ce qu'il me voloit compter
> De tous les autres l'ordenance
> Et de lui la signefiance.
> (vv. 397–400)

[At that point he no longer wanted to listen to me, because he wanted to explain to me the position of all the others as well as his own significance.]

We thus have an explicit rejection of the first-person narrator's love experience as narrative matière, a playful devalorization of "personal love experience" by the God of Love himself.

The second direct speech of the God of Love (vv. 401–1070) begins as Amour completes his answer to the narrator's original question by explaining the signefiance of his various emblematic attributes and accouterments. He concludes by naming the six youths and six maidens who serve him: Voloir, Penser, Dous Plaisir, Loiauté, Celer, and Desir; Grace, Pitié, Esperence, Souvenir, Franchise, and Attemprance. These are the twelve "nobles vertus" who make Amour's power possible.

It is important to note that Amour does not resort to allegorical discourse to explain the signefiance requested by the narrator. Rather, a single metaphoric system is consistently maintained and exploited as such, not translated into the terms of another system. Both this metaphoric system itself (a highly conventionalized reworking of Ovidian amatory imagery) and the implicit rejection of allegorical discourse should be seen as deriving from the *Rose*.[6]

The God of Love next discourses to the narrator on the nature of the love experience in general. This discourse takes the form of a narrative, a dramatization in which the various personification characters of Amour's entourage play the major roles. The narrator himself does not participate at all, but serves rather as spectator, as addressee. This configuration, of course, represents a striking (and somewhat playful) departure from the *Rose* and is meant to be perceived as such.

The general, impersonal perspective of Amour's narrative is evident from the outset:

> Je te di tout premierement
> Que, quant li homs nouvellement
> Entreprent l'amoureuse vie,
> Il couvient, quoy que nuls en die,
> Que Franche Volenté contreingne
> Son cuer, par quoy l'amer empreingne.
> (vv. 631–36)

[First of all, I tell you that when a man undertakes the amorous life for the first time, it is necessary (no matter what anyone says about it) that Free Will constrain his heart so that love take hold.]

The protagonist of the story that follows is not the narrator but this generalized "homs" who becomes transformed into a generalized "amant" or "ami" (both terms are used). Fran Voloir and Dous Penser preside at the awakening of love in this archetypal character. Plaisance intensifies the experience, allowing Desir to attack the amant, who, by this point, manifests all the conventional symptoms of Ovidian lovesickness (vv. 695–717). Souvenir then goes to the lover's aid, making him remember his lady. Finally, Esperence comes to comfort the amant and gives him the courage to approach his dame and make "la requeste" (v. 784). The six personification characters who are the amant's enemies react immediately, speaking in turn against his request, which they characterize as "outrages et folie" (v. 801) [outrage and madness]. These six adversaries (Dangier, Cruautez, Durtez, Doubtance, Honte, and Paour) are quickly confronted by Amour's six maidens in an extended debate which ends in a complete victory for the latter who make their defeated opponents swear never to be "a nul loial ami contraire" (v. 1029) [opposed to any true lover].

After this triumph, the six maidens, accompanied by Amour's six youths, bring the ami before the God of Love himself. They plead on his behalf that he be given "la joie qui est nompareille" (v. 1049) [the ultimate joy]. Amour, convinced of the amant's worthiness, grants this request with the proviso that honor always be properly maintained. After this happy ending to his story, Amour concludes his second speech by telling the narrator that everything has been revealed to him:

> Or t'ay je dont tout descouvert,
> Que je ne t'y ay riens couvert,
> De ceuls que vois en ma presence,
> Qui tuit me font obeïssance,
> Les noms, la force, la servise,
> Et si t'ay dit toute la guise
> De moy, et comment li amis
> Est de joie par moy saisis.
>   (vv. 1063–70)

[I have thus revealed everything to you, and have concealed nothing from you, concerning the names, the power, and the function of those you see before me, who all obey me. And I have told you all about my own procedure and how I seize the lover with joy.]

The most extensive treatment of the love experience as such in the *Vergier* does not at all derive from the first-person narrator. Indeed, the protagonist of Amour's narrative (which may be seen as a variation in miniature on the central story line of the *Rose*) is made to contrast with the narrator as lover in several significant ways. First, we see the development of his love experience from beginning to end. Second, this ami (unlike the narrator) is able to express his feelings to his beloved. Third, his love affair has an explicitly successful outcome.

These contrasts serve to emphasize the split effected by the *Vergier* between lyric experience and its narrative treatment.[7] Indeed, this split is reflected in the very structure of the vision as a whole — in a way which suggests an opposition between the personal lyric love experience of the narrator and an impersonal, non-lyric, doctrinal love experience, recounted by Amour and associated with a generalized, archetypal amant figure. The pattern of repeated alternation between narrative segments (focusing on the narrator as lover) and direct speeches by the God of Love (concerned with a disembodied, theoretical treatment of the love experience in general) functions, ultimately, to undercut the value of the personal, lyric love experience of the narrator both as experience and as narrative matière.

This process of playfully undercutting the lyric love experience is done in a manner which calls attention to the presence of the poète figure and differentiates him yet more sharply from the first-person narrator. For it is above all by means of an adept and elaborate exploitation of literary references (emanating from the poète) that this process takes place: a multi-faceted transformation (and reduction) of one of the constructs central to the *Rose*. In the *Vergier* the God of Love appears to the narrator not in order to receive him into his service and actively intervene to bring his love affair to a successful conclusion (as in the *Rose*) but to function as a secondary narrator who recounts the love experience of someone else. Amour himself is made to delyricize the love experience, i.e., to place it in a third-person context, while using diction, topoi, even characters deriving from the *Rose*.

An implicit opposition is thus suggested between the narrator as lover and the poète as literary craftsman.[8] At the same time there is a displacement of the lyric love experience from the structural and thematic center of the work (as in the *Rose*) to the periphery. The central focus in the *Vergier* is on a literary process — the fragmentation and transformation of the *Rose* — and thus on the literary activity of the poète, who contains the reduced lyric je of the narrator figure.

The third narrative segment of the vision (vv. 1071–150) opens with the narrator renewing his plea for help in his own love affair. In addition, the God of Love is requested to explain why the narrator always loses all courage in the presence of his dame and becomes unable to speak and declare his love for her. This use of the *amant couart* topic to characterize the narrator serves to distance him both from the generalized amant figure of Amour's discourse and from the poète.[9]

Amour's reply begins in indirect discourse. First (vv. 1105–40) he advises the narrator to be loyal and discreet and to remember all the other virtues associated with Amour. By following this (eminently courtly) advice the narrator will achieve *joie*, his lady will be softened, and love's pains assuaged. Next (vv. 1141–50) Amour explains why the narrator loses countenance in the presence of his beloved. He starts this explanation by shifting to a general perspective:

> Lors me dist qu'il n'est nuls vivans
> Qui soit amis, s'il n'est doubtans;
> Car on doit sa dame doubter.
> (vv. 1145–47)

[Then he told me that there is no lover alive who is not fearful; for one must fear one's lady.]

As Amour proceeds to consider the narrator as a particular case of the universal love rule he has just enunciated, the text shifts from indirect to direct discourse, and the third speech of the God of Love (vv. 1151–95) begins. Amour explains to the narrator that, as is the case with all lovers, in the presence of the lady "tu as doubte / Que tu ne doies faire ou dire / Chose qui ta besoingne empire" (vv. 1154–56) [you are afraid of doing or saying something that will harm your suit]. An elaborate description (in terms of personification characters) of the origin of this "doubte" ensues, following which Amour announces that he has answered all the narrator's questions and that they are about to part: "Maintenant plus ne t'en diray. / Tu demourras: je m'en iray" (vv. 1189–90) [I now have nothing more to tell you. You will remain here; I will leave].

The fourth and final narrative segment of the vision (vv. 1195–1201) serves as a transition. As Amour flies away from the tree in which he had been seated, he shakes its branches and cold dew falls on the narrator's face, causing him to awaken from his trance:

> Elle me fist tout tressaillir,
> Si qu'a moy me fist revenir
> Et mist hors dou transissement
> Ou j'avoie esté longuement.
> (vv. 1207–10)

[It (the dew) made me start so that I came to myself and left the trance in which I had been for a long time.]

Hoepffner sees this transition as characteristic of Machaut in that it involves "traits empruntés à la vie réelle, de petits détails propres à donner à ses inventions le caractère de quelque chose de vrai, de vécu."[10] Hoepffner thus considers that Machaut has "improved" on his model. It would seem rather that Machaut is again transforming his model for his own purposes, in this case to cause vision and "reality" to intermingle in such a way as to stress the literary quality of the former as well as the primacy of the poetic work as container of visions.[11]

The Epilogue (vv. 1211–93) presents the narrator alone in the vergier after his vision has taken place and thus completes the narrative frame for the vision initiated by the Introduction (vv. 1–154). The Epilogue falls into two distinct parts. The first (vv. 1211–22), employing narrated tenses exclusively, tells how the narrator, when he realized that he was alone, was initially frightened but quickly remembered the advice that the God of Love had given him.

The second part of the Epilogue (vv. 1223–93) involves a tense shift — to Weinrich's "commented world" — and constitutes an extended lyric sequence, situated at the time of writing (i.e., detached from the preceding narrative). The je who speaks here must be viewed as an expanded version of the narrative voice that we have encountered up to this point in the work. He handles an extensive repertoire of thematic and linguistic conventions of contemporary vernacular lyric poetry with consummate skill.

The narrator affirms that he has "mis en Amours mon vivre" (v. 1226) [given (his) life to Love] and that he is completely devoted to his dame whom he "aim, pris, serf et tien chier" (v. 1245) [loves, esteems, serves and holds dear]. (This repeated use of the present tense is noteworthy.) He is "envers Amours . . . si tournez" (v. 1256) [so inclined towards Love] that he will never cease to love and serve his dame "com vrais amis loyaus, parfais" (v. 1265) [as a true, loyal, perfect lover], awaiting "le don qui m'a esté promis / Dou dieu, se je sui vrais amis" (vv. 1287–88) [the gift which the god promised me, if I were a true lover].

If there has been no improvement in the narrator's situation as a lover (he has not been helped by Amour in this respect), there has been a significant change in the verbal expression of the narrator's love experience, as evinced in the sustained lyric sequence with which the dit concludes and which may be seen as a lyric poem generated out of the didactic advice of the God of Love to the narrator.

It is significant in this concluding lyric sequence that the presence of the poète becomes most highly visible, and in such a way as to stress the text's existence as verbal artifact. For these concluding lines contain a series of examples of annominatio, piled one on top of the other, compounded until the very presence of this figure seems to become thematized. The first annominatio is on *partir* (vv. 1229–38). The second, on *chier* (vv. 1239–45). The third, on *tourner* (vv. 1254–62). The fourth, on *faire* (vv. 1265–68). Last, and most significant, comes an extended annominatio on *fin/finer* (vv. 1269–82). Not only is there thus a play between the (final) position of this particular annominatio in the series and one of its most important semantic components (*fin* = end), but this same semantic component becomes detached from the particular passage that produced it and applicable to the dit as a whole which is nearing its formal end. This suggestion is elaborated in a particularly witty and self-conscious manner when the narrator (ostensibly speaking of his love) says within ten lines of the end of the poem: "Einsi jamais ne fineray, / Car plus chier a definer ay" (vv. 1281–82) [Thus I will never finish, for I would rather die]. We have here an exploitation of the annominatio on *fin* as a signal of closure for a particular poem,[12] which serves particularly to heighten our awareness of the presence of the poète figure (in contradistinction to the narrator) and of the dit's existence as verbal object, as poetic artifact. At the same time the semantic content of lines 1281–82 suggests a je larger than the formal boundaries of the particular poem, who will not finish as the poem finishes, who contains the poem. This suggestion is confirmed and amplified in the very last lines of the dit:

Pour c'en doubtance et en cremour
Vueil ma douce dame obeïr,

Servir, celer, et sans partir
Vivre en son amoureus dangier.

Ci fenist le Dit dou Vergier.
(vv. 1290–94)

[Thus in fear and trembling I want to obey, serve and conceal my sweet lady and to live, continually, under the power of her love. Here ends the Poem of the Garden.]

The *explicit* has been incorporated into the body of the poem itself. The codicological existence of the dit is thus made part of the dit's existence qua poetic entity. Not only is the organization of the codex thereby incorporated into the realm of the poet's activity, but this particular dit is implicitly presented as constituting only one part of a larger poetic entity — the *oeuvre*. This use of codicological material for poetic effect is all the more extraordinary in that the *Vergier* is chronologically Machaut's earliest surviving narrative poem. It is doubtless this early innovation that authorizes the (chronologically later) incorporation of the incipit of the *Vergier* into the last line of the *Prologue.*

When we consider the structural importance of the concluding lyric sequence, it becomes clear that the advice, the intervention of Amour, has not led to any narrative development of the personal love experience of the narrator (certainly not to any amatory success on his part) but rather to a more densely patterned and richly nuanced verbal expression of this experience, which thus takes on the status of literary subject matter; it has led to a poem rather than an experience. This final exploitation of a lyric matière visibly derives from a kind of intervention of the poète, more intensely present here than anywhere else in the dit. The personal love experience embodied by the narrator is thus made to appear as literary subject matter for the poète.

Indeed, this seems to be the central point both of the transformation of the various narrative constructs of the *Rose* and of the poeticization of the codex through the incorporation of the explicit into the body of the text. The narrator is not helped as lover, but the dit is written. A playful devalorization of "personal love experience" as such has been effected, while the value of the literary activity of the poète in the service of Amour has been both demonstrated and affirmed.

Remede de Fortune

In the *Remede* the identity of the narrator figure is much more elaborately developed than in the *Vergier*. The poem begins with a formal Prologue (vv. 1–44) which serves to establish one of the two major elements of this complex identity as well as to inform our reading of the dit as a whole. In the Prologue the narrator adopts a clerkly stance and diction, discoursing authoritatively on the general subject of learning:

> Cils qui vuet aucun art aprendre
> A douze choses doit entendre:
> La premiere est qu'il doit eslire
> Celui ou ses cuers mieus se tire
> Et ou sa nature l'encline;
> Car la chose envis bien define
> Qu'on vuet encontre son cuer faire,
> Quant Nature li est contraire.
> Aimme son maistre et son mestier
> Seur tout; et ce li est mestier
> Qu'il l'onneure, oubeïsse, serve;
> Et ne cuide pas qu'il s'asserve,
> Car s'il les aimme, il l'ameront,
> Et s'il les het, il le harront:
> Pourfiter ne puet autrement.
> Doctrine reçoive humblement;
> Mais bien se gart qu'il continue,
> Car science envis retenue
> Est et de legier oubliée,
> Quant elle n'est continuée.
> Soing, penser, desir de savoir
> Ait, si porra science avoir.
> Et l'entreprengne en juene aäge,
> Eins qu'en malice son corage
> Mue par trop grant congnoissance.
> (vv. 1–25)

[He who wants to learn an art must apply himself to twelve things: first, he must choose what his heart prefers and what his nature inclines him toward, for when one acts against one's heart and against Nature there's a fast end to things. Let him love his master and his calling above all; and he must honor, obey, and serve them; and let him not believe that he is enslaving himself, for if he loves them, they will love him, and if he hates them, they will hate him: this is the only way he can benefit. Let him receive instruction humbly; but let him take care to persevere, for knowledge half-heartedly retained is quickly forgotten when it is not reviewed. Let him be careful, thoughtful, and eager to know—so that he will be able to obtain knowledge. And let him begin at an early age, before his heart is wickedly transformed through too much experience.]

This general perspective is maintained as the narrator proceeds to elaborate on the topos "one learns best when he is young" (vv. 26–40). The Prologue concludes with the narrator (shifting for the first time from third to first person) explicitly identifying himself as an authority, the auctor (and guarantor), for all that has just been affirmed:

> Car chose ne puet si forte estre,
> S'il vuet, qu'il n'en deveingne mestre,
> Mais qu'il vueille faire et labeure
> Ad ce que j'ay dit ci desseure.
> (vv. 41–44)

[For nothing is too difficult for it (human understanding) to master if it wants to—provided it is willing to work at and to accomplish what I have described above.]

Clerkly authority is thus "lyricized," i.e., situated in a first-person voice in the process of composing poetry. As we shall see, the conflation of clerkliness with lyric structure is central to the identity of the narrator figure of the *Remede*, who may be viewed as derived from, but contained by, the global figure of Machaut the poète.

The theme of education (how to learn) set forth in the Prologue will be of primary importance for the entire dit in several ways simultaneously. On the level of plot the dit may be seen as a lyrico-narrative *ars amandi* (cast in the first person and telling a story). On an extradiegetic level the dit may be seen as an *ars poetica*. The authoritative first-person voice speaking in the Prologue has implicitly linked these two didactic aspects of the dit while he has presented himself as teacher, as master (*magister*).

The first major narrative segment (vv. 45–801) of the *Remede* opens with a transition passage (vv. 45–134), in which the auctor-narrator of the Prologue presents himself and his past experience as a particular example of the general precepts of learning that he has just set forth. At the same time, but implicitly, the dit itself (as poetic text) is presented as exemplary.

A temporal structure, loosely based on that at the beginning of the *Roman de la rose,* is employed:

> Pour ce l'ay dit que, quant j'estoie
> De l'estat qu'innocence avoie,
> Que juenesse me gouvernoit
> Et en oiseuse me tenoit,
> Mes ouevres estoient volages.
> (vv. 45–49)

[Thus I have said that when I was in the state of innocence, when I was ruled by youth and lived in idleness, my behavior was flighty.]

The time gap thus established between narrator qua narrator (situated in the present — the time of writing) and narrator qua character (situated in the past — the time of the narrative) is never made any more precise than the opposition between youth and maturity found in this passage. Indeed this very temporal imprecision will be exploited (at times playfully) as the dit progresses.

The narrator begins his story by recounting how when he was young and innocent he fell in love. To the standard courtly diction and imagery used to describe this experience is added an extended series of learned references presented in a particularly latinate syntax (vv. 107–27) to form an elaborate rhetorical figure: the inadequate lover. With this commingling of clerkly and courtly diction we have a linguistic manifestation of the fusion of the two major aspects of the narrator figure's identity.

The tense structure used to describe the love experience is significant, for it involves a conflation of the present time of writing and the past time of the narrative (thus of the narrator qua nar-

rator and the narrator qua character) not at all hinted at in the
Prologue:

> Car ç'a esté m'amour premiere,
> Et si sera la darreniere . . .
> . . . Amours le me firent faire
> Qui m'i donnerent ligement,
> Quant je la vi premierement;
> Si que siens sans riens retenir
> Sui, que qu'il m'en doie avenir,
> Et seray, com je vivray,
> Ne jamais autre n'ameray.
>
> (vv. 81–82, 128–34)

[For this was my first love and will also be my last. . . . Love who gave
me to her faithfully made me (fall in love) when I saw her for the first
time. Thus I am entirely hers, no matter what may happen to me, and
I will remain so for as long as I live, nor will I ever love another.]

With this conflation of tense systems, the second major element
of the identity of the narrator figure — a lover in the courtly mode
— is fully established. An initial clerkly posture and language are
thus conjoined with a lyric stance and diction. The *Roman de
la rose*[13] provides the model for this kind of complex first-person
narrator-protagonist, and this use of the *Rose* as a visible literary
analogue is itself incorporated into the presentation of the narrator figure of the *Remede*. His *literary* genesis is emphasized as
he is implicitly differentiated from the poète, whose textual presence is thereby strengthened.

Shortly after the narrator's declaration of love and self-
presentation as courtly lover, comes an extended description of
the dame as teacher, in which an elegantly arranged and rhetorically elaborate catalogue of moral and amatory virtues serves (on
a more purely textual level) as a poetic *tour de force*, a superla-
tively executed display piece: the *louange*[14] (identified as such in
v. 349). Protagonist, lover, and narrator are thus, as it were, fused
together, and subsumed by the implicit presence of the poète.

In the ensuing narrative sequence (vv. 357–430) the narrator
recounts the development of his love experience and links it to

his poetic experience. For an important, indeed crucial, aspect of the narrator's identity as lover is his self-presentation as love poet. This may be seen as a self-conscious elaboration of the narrator-protagonist configuration of the *Rose* that serves as a model for the *Remede*.[15] In addition, the narrator's identity as love poet will function to differentiate him from Machaut the poète in the service of Amour.

Within the context of the story line, the narrator served his dame long and well, but secretly, since her presence always caused him to lose countenance. The conventional symptoms of Ovidian love sickness (vv. 387–95) are combined with the amant couart topos (esp. vv. 371–76) within the framework of courtly love service. This love service seems to be synonymous with poetic activity:

> Et pour ce que n'estoie mie
> Toudis en un point, m'estudie
> Mis en faire chansons et lais,
> Balades, rondiaus, virelais
> Et chans, selonc mon sentement,
> Amoureus et non autrement;
> Car qui de sentement ne fait,
> Son ouevre et son chant contrefait.
>
> (vv. 401–8)

[And because I was never in the same situation, I put my effort into making songs and lays, ballades, rondeaux, virelays, and music according to my amorous feelings, and not otherwise; for he who does not work according to his feelings counterfeits both his poetry and his music.]

Not only does the narrator thus list the various forms of lyric poetry into which his love experience is transformed, he goes on to give an example: a lay (vv. 431–680) whose thematic content serves to epitomize his amorous condition at the time of writing: although the poet-lover considers the state of loving (and writing love poetry) to be its own reward, he still wants his dame to know of his love, but fears a possible refusal so much that he does not dare to declare his feelings to her.

On another level, the striking technical excellence of the lay,[16] the most demanding of the fourteenth-century *formes fixes*, may be seen as an indication of the presence of the poète in the very text of the dit. The sense of this presence is intensified when the lay is considered in light of the didactic Prologue and the sequence in which the dame is presented as teacher: a lyric poem has been, as it were, generated from doctrine through the artistry of the poète.

Finally, on the level of plot, this lyric poem functions to advance the narrative in which it is embedded. In the final sequence (vv. 681–800) of the first major narrative segment, the dame discovers the lay, has the poet-narrator read it to her, then asks him the name of the author. Unable either to admit that he wrote it (since this would involve confessing his love) or to lie to his dame, the narrator is overcome with fear and embarrassment and cannot speak a word. Without taking leave he flees her presence (v. 752), sighing and weeping, until he arrives at "un trop biau jardin / Qu'on claimme le Parc de Hedin" (vv. 785–86) [a very beautiful garden called the Hedin Park]. Unable at first to penetrate the "haus murs" [high walls] with which the garden is "enclos . . . et environnez" (vv. 790–91) [enclosed and surrounded], the narrator finally discovers "un petit guichet" [a little gate] through which he enters the *plaisance* (v. 801).

This narrative sequence involves an obvious inversion of the joyous Amant approaching the enclosed garden of Deduit in the *Rose*. Indeed, the presence of the earlier poem as a transformed literary model seems to be explicitly signaled by the rhyme words "mensonge" / "songe" in vv. 747–48, inverting the order in which they appear in the first two lines of the *Rose*.[17] The narrator-protagonist of the *Remede* thus finds refuge in an overtly "literary" setting, constructed in such a way as to highlight both its own artifice and the presence of Machaut the poète as its creator. All of this may be viewed, in an important sense, as preparation. For the narrative events that are going to be situated in the garden will be seen to involve, above all, the transformation and fragmentation of literary models, in particular the *De Consolatione Philosophiae* of Boethius.

The second major narrative segment of the *Remede* (vv. 802–3043) takes place entirely in the Parc de Hedin and may be seen as falling into five parts. The first of these (vv. 802–1480) begins as the narrator, after brooding on his recent behavior, decides to hold Amour responsible for his own *meffait*. A series of general reflections on the changeable nature of Amour and Fortune (vv. 872–96) leads to an explicit and highly stylized account of the process of transforming "experience" into lyric poetry:

> Et en ce penser ou j'estoie
> Je m'avisay que je feroie
> De Fortune et de mes dolours,
> De mes pensers et de mes plours,
> Un dit qu'on appelle complainte,
> Ou il averoit rime mainte,
> Qui seroit de triste matiere.
> Si commensai en tel maniere.
> (vv. 897–904)

[And while I was having these thoughts, it occurred to me to make a poem called a complaint on the subject of Fortune and of my own sufferings, thoughts, and tears. It (this poem) would have many rhymes and a sad theme; and I began in the following way:]

Poetic activity is thus thematized in a way which highlights (as had the introduction to the lay, discussed above) the specifically lyric framework of the poetry in question; it is presented, within the context of the story line, as generated by the narrator-protagonist's personal love experience. Yet the evident artificiality of this process serves to reduce the first-person narrator-protagonist to the status of a literary device. By implication, the intercalated lyric *complainte* derives from the experience, not of the narrator, but of the poète. And, as we shall see, this experience is to a very large and very visible degree a literary one.

The complainte itself (vv. 905–1480) opens with a long discourse on the nature of Fortune in general (vv. 905–1192), presented in a clerkly, didactic tone, exclusively employing commented tenses. The arbitrariness and inconstancy of Fortune are described in detail by means of standard medieval thematic and imagerial topoi, and Boethius is cited explicitly as auctor (v. 982). It is only after extensive elaboration that this clerkly treatment of Fortune in general is related to the particular situation of the narrator:

Einsi m'a fait, ce m'est avis,
Fortune que ci vous devis.
Car je soloie estre assevis
   De toute joie.
Or m'a d'un seul tour si bas mis
Qu'en grief plour est mué mon ris,
Et que tous li biens est remis
   Qu'avoir soloie.
Car la bele ou mes cuers s'ottroie,
Que tant aim que plus ne porroie,
Maintenant vëoir n'oseroie
   En mi le vis.
Et se desir tant que la voie
Que mes dolens cuers s'en desvoie,
Pour ce ne say que faire doie,
   Tant sui despris.
               (vv. 1193–208)

[It is my opinion that Fortune, whom I describe to you here, has treated me in just this way. For I used to be provided with every joy. But now, with a single turn, she has put me so low that my laughter is changed to bitter weeping and all the good I used to have is taken away. For now I would not dare to look directly at the face of the beauty to whom my heart gave itself and whom I could not love more than I do. Thus, I desire to see her so much that my piteous heart becomes distracted, and I am so miserable that I don't know what to do.]

From clerkly we have passed to courtly diction, from an impersonal (almost *auctor*) stance to a personal one, from didactic to lyric. (Though, it must be stressed, this lyric moment is integrated into the unfolding narrative of the *dit*.)

   Immediately following this lyricization of the discourse on Fortune comes an extended sequence dealing with Amour (vv. 1209–408), which opens in the lyric mode that will predominate throughout the remainder of the intercalated poem:

Amours, Amours, ce m'as tu fait
Qui m'as fait faire le meffait
Qui toute ma joie deffait!
             (vv. 1209–11)

[Love, Love you have done this to me: you made me commit the misdeed which undoes all my joy.]

This lyric complaint is, however, based on, generated from, the narrative situation of the narrator-protagonist established before his entry into the plaisance. Thus, after stating that he will die if, as a consequence of his "meffait," he is deprived of the presence of his dame, the narrator proceeds to accuse Amour of treating him unfairly. He has performed loyally in the service of Amour and has been badly rewarded (vv. 1353–68). A meditation on his present unhappy state, void of "esperence" (vv. 1369–419), is followed by a gloomy reflection on the future (vv. 1420–40) and a reiteration of the unfortunate fact that his dame remains unaware of his love and suffering (vv. 1441–64). The complainte concludes with a final exclamation against the cruelty of Fortune and Amour, coupled with a restatement of the lover's devotion.

The second part of the second major narrative segment (vv. 1481–2109) opens as the narrator, having finished his complainte, describes his amorous suffering in a way which conflates past and present, combining young protagonist and mature narrator into a single lover who speaks of the ". . . grans doleurs et des meschiés / Dont j'estoie et sui entichiés" (vv. 1485–86) [great suffering and misfortune with which I was and am tormented]. The lover-protagonist ends by falling into a trance as a result of all he has suffered, and in this state he notices an unknown "bele dame" (v. 1503) seated next to him. She appears to him to be of supernatural origin, for her presence exerts a comforting effect over the suffering lover; indeed the lady is described as a doctor (vv. 1533–43, 1576–78, 1603–4).

The simultaneous exploitation of two literary models may be seen at this point in the text. First, we have an inversion of the narrative framework of the *Rose* similar to that found in the *Vergier*: the configuration of dream-vision (of the lover-narrator) containing a garden is transformed into a configuration of garden containing a dream-vision. Second, the construct of complaint on the inconstancies of Fortune followed by the appearance of a consoling superhuman female figure (compared to a doctor) recalls the opening scene of the *De Consolatione Philosophiae*.[18]

The visibly literary construction of this narrative situation heightens the presence of the poète in his text and serves to differentiate him from the narrator. At the same time, it invites us to read the entire central section of the dit as a reworking of Boethius. Even before she is named, the lady in the *Remede* thus appears as, in some sense, a transformation of Lady Philosophy. The full significance of the Boethian subtext will only become apparent as the dit progresses.

The bele dame proceeds to "comfort," to "console" the narrator by means of defending Amour against the accusations made in the narrator's complainte. A playful kind of textual self-consciousness is involved here as the bele dame is implicitly presented as a "reader" responding to the narrator's intercalated lyric poem. In addition, the formal opposition between lyric and narrative verse is stressed at the same time as the two are integrated into, contained by, the larger generic structure of the dit. Both of these suggestions are developed as the lady (vv. 1701 ff.) argues that Amour has in fact granted the request made earlier in the narrator's lay, that his love be discreetly revealed to his dame. The visible signs of Ovidian love sickness combined with the inability to speak openly of his feelings have demonstrated to his discerning lady that the narrator is a "loial amant."

In conclusion (vv. 1935–76), the as-yet-unnamed lady tells the narrator that the only sign of the true lover that he lacks is "Esperence." She then promises to give him her help and take him under her protection. As if to guarantee her promise (and her power), the lady proposes to sing a "chanson roial":

> Mais pour toy un petit deduire
> Et pour tes maus a joie duire,
> Te vueil dire un chant nouvelet;
> Car chose plaist qui nouvele est.
> (vv. 1973–76)

[But in order to divert you a little and turn your woes into joy, I want to (sing) you a new little song, for new things are pleasing.]

The narrator now briefly intervenes (vv. 1977–84), stressing his position within the story line as audience and reemphasizing the fact that the lyric piece to follow is a "chant nouvel" (v. 1984).

The thematic content of the lady's *chanson roial* (vv. 1985–2032) is directly related to the ongoing narrative progression in which it is embedded: true lovers are joyous and content with their condition; they should not ask for more; Amour rewards his own.

Again, the simultaneous opposition and interrelation between lyric and narrative (heightened in retrospect by the ironic reading of the chanson roial suggested at the very end of the dit) serves to signal the presence of the poète figure. This presence is intensified by the fact that, for the first time in the course of the *Remede*, a character other than the first-person narrator-protagonist (i.e., the bele dame) has expressed herself within the context of the story line by means of an intercalated lyric poem — which the text repeatedly calls attention to as such. The poet-narrator is thereby differentiated from the poète, whose identity as the global author who has composed *all* the intercalated lyrics becomes increasingly visible in the very poetic organization of the dit. Both the (first-person) narrator and the (third-person) bele dame in their capacity as lyric poets are thus reduced to the status of fictional constructs emanating from, and contained in, or by, the poète. The relationship poète/text is implicitly presented as underlying a sophisticated narrative configuration in which characters are depicted as poets. The increased distance between narrator and poète has important implications for the depiction of poetic inspiration in the dit. An opposition seems to be suggested between, on the one hand, the highly conventionalized process by which lyric poems are generated out of the narrator's love experience and, on the other, the more all-inclusive, more literary, but lyric-based, process of poetic inspiration and composition of the poète. The stance of lyric poet thus seems to be presented as something contained by the poète's larger identity.[19]

After having finished her song, the bele dame bends down over the narrator and speaks to him encouragingly (vv. 2039–93). It is important to note, however, that she begins by asking his reaction to her song (vv. 2041–46), then explicitly praises it herself: "Se ce n'estoit pour moy vanter, / Je diroie de mon chanter / Que c'est bien dit" (vv. 2047–49) [If it weren't self-praise, I would say that my song is a good one]. This represents on the part of Machaut the poète a playful insistence on the intercalated lyric as such and on his own identity as its author. The bele dame goes on to advise the narrator to give up his "merencolie," (v. 2060) then renews her offer to help. A particularly vernacular quality seems to have become incorporated into her speech as a result of her repeated use of proverbs (e.g., vv. 2081–82, 2087–89).[20] This functions as a means of underlining, on the level of diction, the bele dame's distinction from her Latin model, Lady Philosophy.

After finishing her speech, the lady takes a ring from her finger and places it on that of the narrator (vv. 2094–96), which causes him to awaken completely from his trance. This narrative construct may perhaps be seen as a reference to, and elaboration of, the end of the *Vergier*, where cold dew awakens the narrator from a dream-vision in a garden. As such, it would involve an implicit comparison of the two dits, placing both in the context of the oeuvre of the poète. This suggestion is perhaps strengthened when one recalls the utilization and transformation of this same narrative construct in the expanded lyric context of the *Fonteinne amoureuse*. In all these cases the starting point is an inversion of the dream-vision/garden structure of the *Rose*.

The third part of the second major narrative segment (vv. 2110–347) constitutes almost the exact midpoint of the dit and involves the revelation of the identity of the bele dame who had appeared to the narrator-lover.

Upon awakening from his trance the narrator, addressing the bele dame directly for the first time, asks who she is. The lady responds by explaining that she is "li confors des amans" (v. 2151) [the comfort of lovers] in a highly rhetorical speech (vv. 2148–92), characterized especially by extensive use of anaphora that repeatedly stresses the first-person singular pronoun which has yet to be assigned a proper name as antecedent. We thus have an elaborate verbal preparation for the self-naming that is to follow, as the bele dame explains her identity in terms of her relationship to lovers:

> Je les aide; je les conseil;
> Je sui de leur estroit conseil;
> Je les deffen; je les deporte;
> Je les secour; je les conforte.
> (vv. 2153–56)

[I help them; I advise them; I am their counselor in difficult situations; I protect them; I delight them; I assist them; I comfort them.]

Not only does the high level of rhetorical patterning found in the bele dame's speech serve to call attention to her language as poetic discourse and thus to the presence of the poète figure in the text, but the fact that this speech contains an elaborate and self-conscious revelation of identity at the midpoint of the dit visibly exploits one of the structural conventions associated with romance[21] in a way which highlights still further a self-consciously literary (and playful) authorial presence.

The bele dame goes on (vv. 2193–284) to explain how she comforts lovers, by means of an extended simile in which her effect on amorous hearts is compared to that of the sun on the earth in spring. The clothing imagery used in this connection is reminiscent of that found in the description of springtime at the beginning of the *Rose* (vv. 55–66). Again, the presence of the poète seems to be particularly visible here, at the midpoint of the dit, signaled this time by the transformed intertextual reference. Next, the level of the simile is elevated when the bele dame goes on to compare herself to Nature (vv. 2252–72), in what seems to be yet another reminiscence of the *Rose*. Having finished the description of her identity in general terms, she reaffirms her status as a character in the particular story line of the *Remede*:

> Et pour ce que je te savoie
> Desconforté et nut de joie
> Et qu'a conforter sui tenue
> Les amans, suis je ci venue.
> (vv. 2273–76)

[I have come here both because I knew that you were discouraged and deprived of joy and because I am committed to comforting lovers.]

The bele dame ends the progressive revelation of her identity by explicitly naming herself for the first time in the dit: "Esperence sui appellée" (v. 2286) [My name is Hope].

The fourth part of the second major narrative segment (vv. 2348–816) opens as the narrator requests that Esperence teach him how to defend himself against Fortune (vv. 2353–402). Her extensive reply (vv. 2403–816) constitutes the "remede de Fortune" of the title and is based almost entirely on Books 2 and 3 of Boethius's *De Consolatione Philosophiae* with regard both to the substance of the argument employed and to the formal structure of dialogic discussion.[22] It is significant, however, that Esperence begins her speech with a reference to the earlier complainte of Amant, the lover-protagonist, thus situating the Boethian material to follow in a new, lyrico-narrative context. Attention is thereby called to the fact that the *Consolatio* as a literary model text is being transformed, reworked for the purposes, and within the context, of the *Remede*.

After a disquisition on Fortune's two faces (vv. 2407–40) — an *amplificatio* of a brief passage in *Consolatio* 2, 1 and 3 Pr.— Esperence goes on to demonstrate to the narrator that the favors of Fortune are by definition unreliable and cannot lead to happiness (a line of reasoning based on *Consolatio* 2, 4 Pr.). Arguments and images taken from Boethius continue to predominate as Esperence explains to the narrator that Fortune has not acted badly towards him, but simply according to her nature (vv. 2519–92; cf. *Consolatio* 2, 1 Pr.). Next Esperence argues that Fortune has on balance been favorable to Amant (vv. 2593–702; cf. *Consolatio* 2, 2 and 4 Pr.). She goes on to explain that Fortune, in accordance with her nature, has only lent her goods to Amant whose desire to retain them is in contradiction with Fortune's fundamentally changeable character (cf. *Consolatio* 2, 2 Pr.). Esperence next advises Amant on the proper attitude to adopt, insisting that ". . . tu ne prises une prune / Desormais les biens de Fortune . . . / Car plus qu'oiselès sont volens" (vv. 2737–38, 2742) [you not value Fortune's goods as worth anything, for they are more flighty than little birds]. A brief discourse on the evils of avarice (vv. 2743–72, based on *Consolatio* 3, 3 Pr., and 3 Metr.) is followed by praise for the virtues Souffissance and Pacience which can protect man from the vagaries of Fortune and put him on the road to Bonneürté, the supreme good (vv. 2773–96, based on *Consolatio* 2, 4 Pr., and 3, 9 Pr.). The fact that this entire didactic sequence is so closely modeled on Boethius[23] makes all the more striking the fact that Esperence concludes by placing her entire "remede de Fortune" into an amatory context:

Je ne vueil mie que tu penses
Que d'amer te face deffenses;
Eins vueil et te pri chierement
Que tu aimmes trés loiaument;
Qu'amy vray ne sont pas en compte
Des biens Fortune, qui bien compte,
Mais entre les biens de vertu.

(vv. 2797–803)

[I do not want you to think that I am forbidding you to love; rather, I desire and warmly request that you love with great faithfulness; for true lovers, if one understands correctly, are not beholden to Fortune but to virtue.]

An inversion of Boethius, a reorientation of Boethian material for the poetic purposes of the *Remede*, has been effected, which may be seen as emblematized in the transformation of Lady Philosophy into Esperence. The arguments of Books 2 and 3 of the *Consolatio* when utilized in the *Remede* do not lead to the elevated metaphysical and ethical conclusions of the original. Rather they are used to affirm the value of courtly love service by a character who personifies belief in its value. The fact that first the presence then the inversion of a Boethian subtext are so clearly signaled serves to emphasize these literary processes as such, as well as the *Remede*'s status as nonmimetic literary artifact. Once again the poetic organization of his text serves to highlight the presence of the poète, the global author figure whose "experience" and activity are fundamentally literary.

Esperence concludes her speech by returning to the narrative situation of the *Remede* (vv. 2817–49), speaking now more as a character in this particular dit than in a general didactic vein. She announces that she is about to leave, but reaffirms her promise to help Amant whenever he needs her, advising him to put aside his timidity and pursue his beloved. Before disappearing, Esperence announces her intention to sing a second lyric poem, giving Amant instructions on how to "use" it:

Mais ensois de ma clere vois
Te diray une baladelle,
De chant et de ditté nouvelle,

> La quele tu emporteras,
> Et en alant la chanteras,
> Afin que tes cuers s'i deduise,
> S'il a pensée qui li nuise.
>
> (vv. 2850–56)

[But I will first sing to you, with my clear voice, a baladelle with new music and words, which you will carry off, singing it as you walk along in order to delight your heart should it be troubled.]

This intercalated lyric is thus explicitly differentiated from the narrative progression at the same time as it is thematically integrated into the unfolding story line. This textually self-conscious presentation again serves to heighten the presence of the poète as author figure. Simultaneously, a final suggestive parallel is established between Esperence and her Boethian model whose didactic discourse involves repeated alternation between "argument" and "song" (most explicitly treated in *Consolatio* 3, 1 Pr. and 4, 6 Pr.).

The baladelle (vv. 2857–92) gives Amant such pleasure that he immediately begins to learn both the melody and words by heart. While he is absorbed in this activity, Esperence vanishes (v. 2919).

The fifth and last part of the second major narrative segment (vv. 2920–3043) opens as Amant realizes that Esperence is gone, then returns to the task of memorizing his lesson:

> Et par maniere de memoire
> Tout le fait de li et l'istoire,
> Si com je l'ai devant escript,
> Estoit en mon cuer en escript
> Par vray certein entendement
> Mieus cent fois et plus proprement
> Que clers ne le porroit escrire
> De main en parchemin n'en cire.
>
> (vv. 2939–46)

[Her entire visit and teaching, just as I have written them out above, were written in my heart by means of memory and true understanding one hundred times better and more accurately than any clerk would be able to write by hand on parchment or wax.]

This passage involves a high degree of textual self-consciousness achieved in part by means of a play on the distinction between the first-person lover-protagonist—a character in the unfolding narrative (the "mon cuer" of v. 2942)—and the first-person poet-narrator, who seems at this point to overlap with the poète, the author of the *Remede* as a whole (the "je" of v. 2941). This distinction is emphasized by the repetition of "escript" in the rhyme position (vv. 2941–42) and by the opposition between the literal and figurative meanings of the word. The poète has written down the preceding passage (concerning Esperence) which is thus presented as a poetic text—as *écriture* in every sense of the word. The reader is confronted by the physical dimension of the text's existence—words written by a clerk's hand on parchment calling attention to themselves as such and playfully shown to "contain" the figurative "writing" on the heart of the lover-protagonist. The comparison employed therefore serves to highlight its own artifice and that of the "experience" of the protagonist, which is implicitly presented as a poetic fiction by means of the very rhetorical opposition of this experience to the written word.

Having successfully memorized Esperence's lesson, Amant, feeling stronger and more self-assured, begins to walk towards the *guichet* by which he had earlier entered the garden. For the first time he becomes aware of the joyous birdsongs to which he had been deaf before the visit of Esperence. This sequence (vv. 2981–92), with Amant delighted by birdsong only on his way *out* of the garden, seems to involve a reversal of the narrative construct found at the beginning of the dream in the *Roman de la rose*. Again, the stress on the *Rose* as subtext and the process of transformation of literary model serves to highlight the presence of the poète in the text of the *Remede*. Further, the courtly convention of birdsong as a metaphor for lyric poetry (also elaborately exploited in the *Rose*) is artfully developed. On hearing, and being moved by, the birdsong, Amant becomes a bird (i.e., a lyric poet) himself:[24]

> Si m'abelli tant leur dous chans
> Qu'ensois qu'il fust soleil couchans,
> Je m'en senti a volenté

> De cuer, de corps et de santé
> Tant pour la douce ramenbrance
> Que j'avoie en bonne Esperence,
> Comme de ce que je pensoie
> Que briefment ma dame verroie.
> Et pour ce qu'estoie au retour
> De vëoir son trés noble atour,
> Tantost fis en dit et en chant
> Ce ci que presentement chant.
> (vv. 3001–12)

[Their sweet song pleased me so much that before the sun set I felt as good as could be in heart, body, and health. This was as much because of my sweet memory of good Hope as because of my thinking that I would soon see my lady. And since I was returning to see her very noble person, I immediately produced in words and music the following song.]

The sweet songs of the birds lead him to think that he will soon see his dame, which in turn leads him to sing a "balade" (vv. 3013–36). Again, the explicit presentation of a conventionalized lyric inspiration and poetic production serves to differentiate the poet-protagonist from the poète. Similarly, as with the other intercalated lyrics of the *Remede*, the balade's formal separation from its narrative verse setting is emphasized at the same time as it is thematically integrated into the story line: its primary motif being the lover's hope ("espoir") [v. 3017] of seeing his beloved. Amant continues to walk as he sings until he arrives back at the guichet, through which he leaves the garden (vv. 3043–44).

The third (and final) major narrative segment of the *Remede* (vv. 3044–4256) tells the story of Amant's love affair after his departure from the garden, and may be seen as falling into five episodes. The first of these (vv. 3044–348) begins as the narrator, coming into sight of "le lieu ou ma dame demeure" (v. 3052) [the place where my lady lives], becomes paralyzed by fear and timidity. Esperence reappears to give him encouragement, renewing her promise of help and support, and advising him to approach his dame with confidence. After Esperence has left, Amant, now reassured, kneels in the direction of his dame's chateau and addresses a *prière* (vv. 3205–348) to Amour and Esperence. This intercalated lyric (the only one in the *Remede* without musical accompaniment) begins with an affirmation of Amant's devotion to the service of Amour, couched in quasi-religious terms. Amant then asks forgiveness for having earlier complained of love's pains, thus presenting the prière as, in part, a palinode to the complainte in a way which suggests a structuring function for the lyric set pieces.

The next episode (vv. 3359–516) begins as Amant comes upon an elegant and noble company dancing in a charming *parc*. The scene is, of course, reminiscent of the *querole* of Deduit's troops in the *Rose*, and its literary genesis stresses the presence of the poète and the fictionality of the narrator. At the same time this displacement of the querole from inside to outside the vergier may be seen as a significant reversal of the model provided by the *Rose*. As Amant sees his dame among the dancers (v. 3381) he begins to feel helpless and afraid, but remembers Esperence and her advice "que j'avoie escript en mon cuer" (v. 3391) [which I had written on my heart]. He approaches the group and is recognized by his dame who invites him to join. After having danced for a brief time, Amant is requested by his beloved to sing:

> Je li respondi sans demour:
> "Ma dame, vo commandement
> Vueil faire; mais petitement
> Me say de chanter entremestre.
> Mais c'est chose qui couvient estre,
> Puis qu'il vous plaist." Lors sans delay
> Encommensai ce virelay
> Qu'on claimme chanson baladée.
> Einsi doit elle estre nommée.
>   (vv. 3442–50)

[I answered without hesitation: "My lady, I want to carry out your commandment; but I hardly know how to handle a song. However, because it pleases you, it must be done." Then I began without delay (the following) virelay, which is properly termed a "chanson baladée."]

This introduction to the intercalated lyric conflates the first-person voice of Amant the poet-narrator and the first-person voice of the poète concerned with matters of poetic terminology (vv. 3348–50).[25] Shortly after the *virelay* (vv. 3451–96) — a flawlessly courtly declaration of love and devotion — is sung, the dame announces that it is time to return to her *manoir*, and the dancing stops.

The next episode (vv. 3517–870) begins as the dame takes Amant aside and asks for an explanation of his earlier behavior with regard to the lay. The long reply of Amant (vv. 3551–714) involves a retelling in miniature of the entire plot of the dit, beginning with the birth of his love and emphasizing the "experiential" basis of his lyric poetry. The lover-protagonist is thereby differentiated from the poète, whose implicit presence in the text at this point is further emphasized by the very process of what might be called "narrative doubling." Amant (qua protagonist) is now recounting to his dame what he has already recounted (qua narrator) to the reader at the beginning of the dit. It is the act of narration as such that is thereby emphasized — and the existence of the *Remede* as structured narrative. In addition, a kind of implicit textual self-referentiality (and self-authorization) is set up as the "truth" of what the lover-protagonist recounts to his dame is guaranteed by the fact that it has already been recounted from a different perspective (i.e., that of the narrator/reader) and vice versa.

Amant's embedded secondary narrative concludes by rejoining the situation that had motivated it in the diegetic "present" of the primary narrative. He thus shifts (vv. 3683 ff.) from narrated to commented tenses to make his first direct declaration of love — an impeccably courtly avowal prompted by the insistence of Esperence. Amant ends his speech by commingling his identity as lover and as love poet when he invokes his lyric poem (i.e., his virelay of vv. 3451–96) as a guarantee of the truth of his sentiment:

> Et s'il vous plaist, ma dame chiere,
> A resgarder la darreniere
> Chansonnette que je chantay,
> Que fait en dit et en chant ay,
> Vous porrez de legier savoir
> Se je mens ou se je di voir.
>
> (vv. 3705–10)

[And if you will kindly look at the last little song that I sang, whose words and music are my own, you will easily be able to know, my dear lady, whether I am lying or telling the truth.]

Significantly, the dame's first response is to question Amant about his identity as a lyric poet, asking if he really composed the lay himself (vv. 3723–28), before going on to question him about his love for her and the truth of the episode with Esperence that he has just narrated. Amant, after reaffirming the truth of all his statements, reformulates his declaration of love, stressing that he speaks only in the name of Esperence. The dame replies that she will obey Esperence (whom she praises at length) and accepts Amant as her lover, granting to him "loiaument de m'amour l'ottroy" (v. 3844) [the loyal offer of my love].

The next episode (vv. 3871–4114) begins as the dame breaks off her conversation with Amant in order to maintain the secrecy of their newly declared love. It is only after an elaborate round of courtly festivities that the couple is again able to speak together in private.

After they renew their love vows (vv. 4029–52), the dame asks Amant about the ring he wears and, on learning that it comes from Esperence, proposes an exchange of rings to her overjoyed lover. As this is taking place, Esperence suddenly appears (v. 4078 ff.) to preside over the ceremony and give her blessing to the union, acting as witness and authority.

Amant now parts from his lady after a final amorous glance and is so filled with joy at the way in which Esperence has fulfilled her promise that he composes a rondelet (vv. 4107–14) whose lyric inspiration is made part of the narrative progression, generated directly from his love experience. This is the last intercalated lyric poem in the *Remede* and coincides with the apex of the narrator's amatory success within the context of the story line.

The final episode (vv. 4115–256) of the third major narrative segment opens as Amant, confident and happy in his new love, goes off to participate in various noble (courtly, even chivalric, rather than clerkly) activities (vv. 4116–38). The learning motif first enunciated in the Prologue is restated now as the narrator tells how, with respect to these activities, he observes:

> . . . il failloit que j'aprenisse,
> Car qui n'aprent en sa juenesse,
> Il s'en repent en sa vieillesse,
> S'il est tels qu'il le sache entendre:
> Car trop noble chose est d'aprendre.
>   (vv. 4128–32)

[it was necessary that I learn, for he who does not learn in his youth repents in his old age, if he is able to understand the situation: for learning is a very noble thing.]

This evocation of the authoritative, didactic stance of the Prologue may perhaps be seen as a signal of the approaching end of the dit. It is also a reminder of the complex identity and diction of the narrator figure, a conflation of clerkly and courtly elements.

On returning to his dame (v. 4139), Amant is greeted with indifference. She appears "changie" (v. 4152) and seems to be attempting to ignore him. All his former joy vanishes at this reaction and Amant falls into painful doubt and "grant merencolie" (v. 4161) [great melancholy]. He is unable to arrive at a satisfactory or unambiguous interpretation of her behavior: ". . . je ne pos onques le voir / De la mansonge concevoir" (vv. 4169–70) [I could not tell truth from lie]. When he seeks an explanation, demanding that she tell him outright if she has ceased to love him, the dame assures him he has no reason to worry and excuses her previous coldness on the grounds that it was a ruse to deceive the *médisants*:

> Car je le fais pour le millour
> Et pour mieus celer nostre amour,
> Car qui en amours ne scet feindre,
> Il ne puet a grant joie ateindre.
>   (vv. 4197–200)

[I did it with the best intentions and to better conceal our love, for he who does not know how to dissemble in love cannot attain great joy.]

Amant intensely desires to believe his dame, but the episode closes somewhat ambiguously.[26] Amant maintains the same verbal attitude towards her as before, but all he has is the "hope" that he is loved. At the same time (v. 4219 ff.) a shift in tenses occurs (from narrated to commented) as Amant speaks of himself and his love in the present time of writing. Although he has suffered much since the incident just described, "Nompourquant je me vos tenir / De tous poins a fermement croire / Qu'elle disoit parole voire" (vv. 4226–28) [Nevertheless, I want to hold fast to the firm belief that she spoke the truth]. The inherent ambiguity of this final love situation is heightened by what appears to be an elaborate attempt on the part of Amant to convince himself to believe his lady. His arguments seem doctrinaire and abstract, ending in a kind of maxim about lovers in general: "Et aussi qui aimme sans blame / En tous cas doit croire sa dame, / Einsi comme il vuet qu'on le croie"[27] (vv. 4243–45) [Thus he who loves blamelessly must in all cases believe his lady, just as he wants to be believed]. Again, the didatic, clerkly tone of the Prologue seems to be in evidence as the dit comes to a close, linked to (and contrasted with) the first-person lyric protagonist recounting his own story:

> Si que pour ce je la crëoie,
> Et qu'il m'iert vis qu'en amité
> Me disoit pure verité,
> Que j'estoie en sa bonne grace.[28]
> (vv. 4246–49)

[And because of this I believed her and was of the opinion that she lovingly spoke pure truth and that I was in her good graces.]

The authenticity of the poet-protagonist's love experience within the context of the story line seems to be put into doubt, or at the very least, rendered problematic. The final verbal attitude of courtly devotion that the narrator explicitly adopts thus takes on an artificial, conventional *literary* aspect. At the same time, the temporal framework maintained throughout the dit seems to break down as the lover-protagonist (ostensibly a youth) and the poet-narrator (ostensibly an adult) appear to fuse:

> Or doint Dieus que jamais ne face
> Chose de quoi perdre la puisse,

> Et qu'amie et dame la truisse,
> Einsi com je li suis amis.
> (vv. 4250–53)

[God grant that I never do anything to lose her and that she remain my lover and lady, just as I am her lover.]

The Epilogue (vv. 4257–98) involves a kind of final expansion of the narrator figure in which the two major elements of his identity — authoritative clerc and courtly lover/poet — are presented in sequence as they had been at the beginning of the *Remede*, but significantly modified by the (now completed) unfolding of the dit itself. The first section of the Epilogue (vv. 4257–71) contains the poet-narrator's anagram signature, introduced as follows:

> Mais en la fin de ce traitié
> Que j'ay compilé et traitié
> Vueil mon nom et mon seurnom mettre,
> Sans sillabe oublier, ne lettre.
> (vv. 4257–60)

[At the end of this treatise which I have compiled and composed, I want to place my full name, leaving out neither syllable nor letter.]

The reference to the *Remede* as a "traitié" stresses the clerkly, didactic side of the identity (and discourse) of the narrator figure, initially (and most elaborately) established in the Prologue. Further, the use of the term "traitié" points to a deeper level of didacticism inherent in the *Remede*: its self-presentation as an ars poetica (to be discussed in greater detail below). This crucially important aspect of the work involves a configuration of poète/text/reader that seems to by-pass the narrative subject matter of the dit, i.e., the first-person story of the protagonist's love experience. It is thus not surprising that the je of line 4258 speaks explicitly as the author (compiler, maker) of the poetic artifact which is the *Remede*. The voice of the narrator seems to overlap with that of Machaut the poète at the moment when their common name is being revealed.

The final part of the Epilogue (vv. 4272–98) presents the second major component of the narrator's identity: poet-lover in the service of Amour. The exclusive employment of commented tenses signals the final and complete fusion of the young je-protagonist and the mature je-narrator, brought about, it would seem, by the writing of the dit:

> Et pour ce que je suis es mains
> De loyal Amour que j'aim si,
> Li fais hommage et di einsi:
> "Bonne Amour, je te fais hommage
> De mains, de bouche, de corage,
> Com tes liges sers redevables,
> Fins, loiaus, secrez et estables,
> Et met cuer, corps, ame, vigour,
> Desir, penser, plaisence, honnour
> Dou tout en toy avec mon vivre,
> Com cils qui vueil morir et vivre
> En ton service, sans retraire."
>
> (vv. 4272–83)

[And because I am in the hands of loyal Love, whom I love so much, I do him homage and speak as follows: "Good Love, I do you homage with my hands, mouth, and heart as your indebted, loyal servant—refined, faithful, discreet, and firm. I place entirely in your keeping my heart, body, soul, strength, desire, thought, enjoyment, and honor along with my life, as one who wants to live and die steadfastly in your service."]

In this concluding declaration to Amour, the poet-narrator goes on to cast the dit as a whole as a lyric offering to his dame who he hopes will receive it favorably and whose love he hopes to obtain:

> Et certes, je le doi bien faire,
> Quant tu me donnes tel espoir
> Qu'adès mieus recevoir espoir,
> Et que ma douce dame chiere
> De bon cuer et a lie chiere
> Verra ce dit qu'ai mis en rime,
> Comment qu'assez nicement rime.
> Et cils espoirs qui en moy maint

Qu'encor ma chiere dame m'aint
Mon cuer si doucement resjoie
Qu'en grant santé et en grant joie
Li change mal, u tu me dis
Que pris en gré sera mes dis.
Or doint Dieus qu'en bon gré le pregne,
Et qu'en li servant ne mesprengne.
(vv. 4284–98)

[And I should certainly do so when you give me such hope that I hope always for better things and that my sweet, dear lady with good heart and cheerful countenance will see this poem (dit) which I have rhymed although I rhyme rather foolishly. And this constant hope of mine that my dear lady still loves me gladdens my heart so sweetly that it changes suffering into great joy and gaiety, when you tell me that my poem (dit) will be well received. God grant that she receive it favorably and that I not offend by serving her.]

Thus at the very end of the dit, all that the first-person narrator possesses qua lover is hope; he is in the same situation he was in at the beginning and middle of the dit. But if his status as lover has not changed, this is not the case with regard to his status as poet: the dit has been written and this fact is repeatedly emphasized in the Epilogue while the poet-narrator's love seems to be reduced to an increasingly literary hope of being loved, with which he proclaims himself satisfied.[29] It is significant that, while references to the dit and to Amour are in the present indicative or the *passé composé*, references to the dame and the personal love experience associated with her are in the subjunctive or the future. In sharp contrast to the vagueness (reflected in the very tense structure of the Epilogue) of the narrator's final situation as a lover is the fact that the poète's service to Amour has produced the *Remede*. As was the case with the clerkly element of the narrator's identity, the courtly love poet element, as it appears in the Epilogue, overlaps to a large degree with the figure of the poète. This final expansion of the narrator figure also serves to distance him from the first-person account of his love experience that has formed the basis for the dit's story line. This love experience thus takes on a final literary, rather than experiential, cast. At the same time it is implicitly presented as, above all, poetic subject matter.

The implicit primacy of the relationship poète/text that emerges from the Epilogue serves to authorize a reading of the *Remede* as a poetic *liber exemplorum:* for the series of lyric poems embedded in, and integrated into, the narrative functions as an exemplary collection of formes fixes. There is one superlative example of each of the major lyric forms of the fourteenth century — which were to become fixed after Machaut for at least three generations, and which are presented here as models to be imitated.[30] It is in this sense that the *Remede* is to be read as an implicit ars poetica. And it is only in the context of such a reading that the full significance of the didactic orientation of the Prologue becomes evident. Further, an important correspondence emerges between the level of plot and the didactic level of the dit: just as the narrator-protagonist fails as lover but succeeds as poet, so the *Remede* fails as an ars amandi but succeeds as an ars poetica.

The *Remede's* character as an ars poetica involves the most elaborate and authoritative self-presentation of the poète in his text, as well as the most radical differentiation of the poète from the first-person narrator-protagonist, whose identity he subsumes. It is thus highly significant that this crucially important aspect of the dit results from a visibly literary activity (even "experience") on the part of the poète: the self-conscious transformation of an Old French literary tradition, extending back to the early thirteenth century — that of the narrative work with intercalated lyrics.[31]

The poète's service to Amour (even within the context of the narration of a first-person love experience) thus appears primarily as poetic service, a multifaceted literary activity which can incorporate a wide variety of experential perspectives into a greatly expanded lyric identity. The structure and character of the *Remede* function to present this poète figure himself as exemplary, to present Machaut as an exemplum poetae, a model to be imitated. The authority that implicitly guarantees this presentation is in the broadest sense lyric based. It resides nowhere else than in the identity of the poète himself.[32]

Le Dit de l'alerion

In the *Alerion* the poet-narrator again appears as lover-protagonist, but several radical transformations of this construct have been effected. First, the two major components of the narrator figure's complex identity (each associated with a different type of discourse, a different "register") appear to be almost completely independent of each other, held together only by a common je. The dit progresses by means of a series of shifts between these two components, consistently calling attention to the process of shifting. Second, the love experience that is recounted is entirely metaphoric. The poem, in effect, is an extended metaphor in which a man's love for a woman is compared to — indeed, described in terms of — his devotion to a series of four hunting birds. The net result is an emphasis on metaphor as a structuring principle and a valorization of metaphoric discourse (here, synonymous with "poetic discourse") as such.

The first of the two major components of the narrator's identity is established in the Prologue (vv. 1–117). Adopting an authoritative stance and a general perspective, the poet-narrator, exclusively employing commented tenses, discourses on a series of clerkly, didactic topics. He begins by setting forth four principles of behavior necessary for the good life, then goes on to affirm in a good Aristotelian fashion that "chascune chose a III temps . . . commencement, moien et fin" (vv. 19, 26) [everything has three phases . . . beginning, middle, and end] and that "qui vuet bonne ouevre avancier, / Trop tost ne puet encommancier, / Pour ce que temps adès s'en court" (vv. 33–35) [He who wants to carry out a good work cannot begin too early, because time is running out]. He concludes the Prologue (in vv. 49–117) by stating that one's behavior as a child is indicative of what one will become in later life.

The first narrative segment (vv. 118–1510) begins with a transition: the authoritative narrator of the Prologue proposes to take himself as a particular example of the general precepts that he has just set forth by recounting a narrative in which he figures as protagonist (i.e., a narrative deriving from his own experience and thus invested with a lyric-based authority): "Desormais dirai de mon estre, / Comment en juenesse jouay / Et quele enfance desnouay" (vv. 118–20) [From now on I will recount my own case: how I played when I was young and what kind of childhood I had].

The first episode of the narrative proper (vv. 121–97) may

be summarized as follows. When he was a child, the narrator-protagonist loved little birds. As he grew older he became increasingly attracted to hunting birds, especially the "esprivier" (v. 135). At the prompting of Nature and Amour, he sought out knowledgeable bird trainers in order to learn about falconry, but discreetly concealed the intensity of his desire and interest. He continued this process of education until he had acquired substantial knowledge of his subject.

At this point, the narrator, resuming the stance and diction of the Prologue, compares the episode he has just recounted with an aspect of the love experience (vv. 201–72). Speaking from a general perspective as a kind of vernacular auctor — an authority on love — the narrator presents the protagonist's behavior with regard to the esprivier as an exemplary model for the *vrais amis* [true lover] to follow with regard to his beloved: he should acquire *science* by frequenting other amants, but should discreetly conceal his true intentions.

By this point in the dit the two major components of the narrator figure's identity have been established. On the one hand, he is the narrator-protagonist in a first-person account of his experience with four hunting birds in sequence: an esprivier, an *alerion*, an *aigle*, and a *gerfaut*. This account constitutes the story line of the dit and is told from a personal perspective (i.e., it is presented as lyric-based). On the other hand, he is the authoritative poet-narrator who (from the temporal perspective of the time of writing) repeatedly intervenes in the narrative in order to compare it to various aspects of the love experience.

For the purposes of the present analysis, the term "register" will be used to designate the contrasting sets of diction, stance, perspective, etc., associated respectively with the poet-narrator and the narrator-protagonist. The "amatory register" involves a clerkly, didactic, first-person voice adopting an auctor stance in order to discourse on (most often) the love experience in general. This discourse makes extensive use of the vocabulary and constructs of fin'amors as code, especially in the generic context of vernacular artes amandi. It is associated with the tenses of Weinrich's commented world and situated in the present of the time of writing. The "falconry register" involves a first-person voice adopting a narrative stance and personal perspective in order to recount a story situated in the past time of the narrative. It is associated with the tenses of Weinrich's narrated world and makes extensive use of the vocabulary and constructs of twelfth- and thirteenth-century manuals of falconry considered as genre.[33] These two registers are linked by means of an elaborate metaphoric system which may be seen as one of the *Alerion*'s key structuring elements. Throughout the dit, narrative episodes in the falconry register alternate with passages of commentary/comparison in the amatory register.[34] The transitions between the two repeatedly and explicitly call attention to themselves as such. At the same time, however, as the *Alerion*'s two registers function in opposition to one another, a program of interpenetration begins quite early in the dit.

The sequence recounting the narrator's hunt for an esprivier is thus set in a plaisance — a *locus amoenus*. One morning the narrator falls asleep under a bush in the course of keeping watch and is awakened by dew falling on his face. He gets to his feet to see that the branches have been shaken by a "gentils espriviers ramages" (v. 533) [noble wild sparrow hawk] and is struck by the raptor's beauty. Both the conventionalized narrative situation (the *coup de foudre* of fin'amors) and the vocabulary ("l'enamay de droite amour," [v. 549] [I truly fell in love with her]) involve an obvious utilization of an amatory code in the context of the falconry narrative. This process continues as the narrator calls on Amour for help, describing himself as the "amis" (v. 558) of the bird. Realizing that he must postpone the gratification of his desire, the narrator observes the direction in which the esprivier flies off and decides to return to the hunt the following day.

At this point, the poet-narrator intervenes in the story to compare the narrative episode that has just been recounted to an aspect of the love experience (vv. 645–722): "Einsi est il d'aucun, s'il aimme / Et que loiaus amis se claimme" (vv. 645–46) [Thus it is with anyone who loves and calls himself a true lover]. A kind of implicit glossing takes place as the *douce dame* is compared to the esprivier in the bush, who shakes down "la douce rousée / Des dous biens dont elle est ornée" (vv. 655–56) [the sweet dew of the fine qualities which adorn her]. In effect, the same story line is "retold" in a different register (general, abstract, amatory), with the initial simile ("einsi," v. 645) serving to link the two. Again, the perspective of an ars amandi is adopted, as the behavior ("experience") of the narrator-protagonist in the context of the falconry story is taken to be exemplary for an aspiring lover who is instructed to be "humbles, amiables et cois" (v. 667) [humble, obliging, and discreet]. Another narrative episode now follows (vv. 723–92) in which the narrator-protagonist leaves the plaisance and spends the day obtaining a trap ("prise," v. 749), which he baits with an *oiseaus.* Early the next morning he returns to the garden and sets his trap, having chased away all the other birds.

A passage of commentary/comparison (vv. 793–862) follows immediately as stance and diction are shifted, and the first-person narrative voice speaks authoritatively in the didactic mode of the ars amandi, from a general perspective: "Einsi deveroit amans faire" (v. 793) [Thus a lover should behave]. There is a detailed working out of a system of correspondences, an elaborate analogy between the falconry narrative and the love experience. The *prise* of the lover is "de maniere, / Tant en bel samblant comme en chiere" (vv. 795–96) [of pleasant and cheerful manner]. The *oysel* with which the trap is baited is "dous amoureuse regart" (v. 803) [sweet, loving glance] or "bel et courtoisement parler" (v. 808) [beautiful and courteous speech]. The birds that must be chased away are "toutes paroles volages" (v. 829) [all fickle words] which might prevent the dame from being caught ("prise," v. 842).

We have here a reversal of the process found in the preceding narrative episode, as the vocabulary and constructs of the falconry code are now utilized in an amatory context. In fact, a bivalent vocabulary, involving both the sets of falconry words and love words used in both contexts, is functional for this dit, by means of the root comparison between falconry and love. It is the process of this comparison that is thereby emphasized (a process originating in the activity of the poète). For this semantic interpenetration does not bring the two registers of the dit — the two elements of the extended metaphor — any closer together. Rather, it serves to highlight the fact that they are being compared, and thus the primary importance of metaphoric discourse as such.

At the same time, the je that serves to link the authoritative voice of the ars amandi (and his general perspective) with the protagonist of the falconry narrative (and his personal perspective) appears more than ever as a fictional construct, emanating from and contained by the je of the poète, whose "experience" is not a personal love experience, but involves precisely the employment of metaphoric (i.e., "poetic") discourse in the service of Amour. A highly (and self-consciously) literary expansion of the lyric je is here effected. The "lyric experience" of the poète in the *Alerion* is implicitly presented as the process of creating and composing the dit itself. As such it may be seen as involving the interaction between the two contrasting components of the je of the narrator figure (and between the two poetic registers associated with them).

The differentiation and tension between the two components of the narrator figure's identity may be seen in the explicit shift from commentary back to narrative that concludes the commentary passage under discussion:

> Plus n'en di; qui vuet, si l'entende,
> Car dès ore est temps que je tende
> A l'esprivier ou j'entendi,
> Quant la prise pour li tendi.
> (vv. 859–62)

[I won't say any more about it; let him who wishes to understand it do so. Now it is time for me to turn to the sparrow hawk that I awaited when I had set the trap for her.]

The je of line 859 (using the present indicative) is the authoritative, didactic voice of the metaphoric ars amandi who has just (vv. 847–58) given general, almost proverbial, advice to lovers in the abstract. The je of lines 861–62 (using the preterite) is the first-person protagonist of the falconry narrative. The "je" of line 860 (using the present subjunctive) may perhaps be seen as overlapping with that of the poète, in which the other two are "contained" without loss of their distinctiveness. For this "je" is concerned with (indeed, shown in the act of) the composition of the *Alerion* qua structured poetic artifact.[35] The temporality of this line is very emphatically the present of the time of writing. More important still, the self-conscious presentation of the poète in the process of composing, of structuring, the *Alerion* is made to function as a structural marker, dividing one (commentary) unit of the dit from another (narrative) unit.

The ensuing narrative episode (vv. 863–1150) involves the most extensive exploitation so far of the linguistic and behavioral conventions of fin'amors as literary code in the context of the falconry narrative. While waiting with his trap in the garden for the return of the esprivier, the narrator-protagonist undergoes the symptoms of Ovidian love sickness (vv. 881 ff.). When the raptor finally alights on the tree, the narrator describes his reaction by means of amatory terminology, explaining how "tant amoureusement l'amoie" (v. 919) [I loved her intensely]. Yet, the context of the falconry narrative is consistently maintained. The esprivier begins to look for the bird with which the trap is baited, attracted by its chirping, and at last enters the trap and is caught (v. 995). The delighted narrator-protagonist now emerges from his hiding place, takes his captive home and begins the process of training her.[36] The esprivier quickly learns how to hunt properly (vv. 113 ff.) from her devoted trainer, as demonstrated by the fact that no matter how far she flies off after her prey, she always returns to her master.

At this point, the narrative is again interrupted by a passage of commentary/comparison (vv. 1151–96). The authoritative first-person voice of the poet-narrator explains that a dame who is well loved and who loves well, when she goes off into society but always returns to her amant "lors puet l'esprivier ressambler" (v. 1167) [then she can be likened to the sparrow hawk]. Again metaphor (i.e., the comparison between dame and esprivier and the full working out of this comparison) serves to link two distinct poetic systems: the falconry narrative and the amatory discourse, each associated with a different component of the narrator figure's identity, and the interaction of which, "contained" by the larger je of the poète and the larger poetic system of the *Alerion* as a whole, constitutes the dynamic structure of the dit.

In the narrative episode which follows (vv. 1197–275), the first-person protagonist recounts how, after a period of perfect happiness and satisfaction with the esprivier, the raptor molts, becomes "parvertis" (v. 1258), and abandons her grief-stricken master.

At this point the first-person voice shifts from the personal perspective (and narrated tenses) back to the general perspective (and

commented tenses): "Nompourquant se vueil j'encor dire / De l'esprivier la verité / Selonc sa noble qualité" (vv. 1276–78) [Never-
theless I still want to tell the truth about the sparrow hawk's no-
bility]. From the story (*histoire*) of his own particular esprivier,
the narrator shifts to a discourse (*discours*) on the qualities of the
esprivier in general. A clerkly stance, diction, and authority replace the lyric stance, diction, and authority of the preceding episode. Once again the transition itself (and the concomitant expansion of the je) is highlighted, for this is done in such a way as to
stress the present time of writing and the "present" activity of composing a poem, i.e., the identity of the narrative je as poet-author.
The (lyric) grief resulting from the loss of the esprivier (which has
already been implicitly presented as metaphoric) is thus undermined from the outset. A clerkly exposition follows (vv. 1285–
340),[37] in which we are told how the esprivier catches and holds
all night in her claws a small bird in order to warm her feet.

The narrator next proceeds to interpret this clerkly digression,
transposing it into the amatory register by means of an extended
comparison:

> Or vëons comment ce seroit
> Qu'une dame ressambleroit
> L'esprivier qui l'oiselet prent
> Et vers le vespre le sourprent,
> Pour les piez tenir en chaleur.
> (vv. 1349–53)

[Now let us see how the sparrow hawk resembles a lady, when towards
evening she captures a little bird in order to keep her feet warm (during
the night).]

Each element of the learned anecdote on the habits of the esprivier
is made to correspond to an element of the love experience. A
detailed system of analogy is then developed, growing out of the
root comparison in which the lover's heart is likened to the captive bird and the dame holding this love offering in secret is likened to the esprivier warming her feet at night. All of this is presented by the authoritative first-person voice of the poet-narrator,
speaking in the general perspective and didactic mode of an ars

amandi. At the end of the commentary/composition passage (vv. 1349–449), there is an explicit transition as the je of the poet-narrator is retransformed into the je of the narrator-protagonist:

> Mais orendroit plus n'en diray,
> Car a mon propos revenray,
> Pour ramentevoir derechief
> Un petitet de mon meschief,
> Dont j'eus moult le cuer esperdu,
> Quant j'eus mon esprevier perdu,
> Le quel la mue le m'osta.
>   (vv. 1443–49)

[But now I will say no more about it, for I shall return to my subject in order to recall anew a little of my misfortune, which greatly troubled my heart, when I lost my sparrow hawk due to molting.]

As had been the case with previous passages of a similar nature, the transition calls attention to itself as such and thereby functions as a structural marker. An implicit emphasis is thus placed on the dit qua poetic structure. The distinction between the two major components of the identity of the narrator figure (a lyrico-narrative je and a clerkly, didactic je) is insisted upon at the same time as both are implicitly shown to be contained by the larger je of the poète/author figure.[38]

In the narrative episode that follows (vv. 1453–510), the narrator-protagonist, profoundly melancholy over the loss of the esprivier, turns to Amour for help and advice. His brief complainte involves consistent use of the linguistic and situational conventions of fin'amors in the narrative context of the falconry story. The word "esprivier" thus appears (v. 1483) where one would expect the word *dame*:

> Amours, par ton art doucement
> Me feïs l'esprivier amer,
> Dont j'ay orendroit moult d'amer,
> Amer qu'on appelle amertume,
> Par quoy mes cuers en amer tume.
> Tume? mès y est ja tumés

> Et malement amertumés,
> Qu'il morra de dueil entumis,
> Se briefment ne le destumis.
> Si te pri que tu le destournes
> A tel fin que tu le retournes
> Des dolours ou il est tournez,
> Car il est forment bestournez.
> (vv. 1482-94)

[Love, by your sweet art you made me love the sparrow hawk, from whom I now have much grief, grief which is bitter, and thus my heart falls into bitterness/love. Falls? But it has already fallen there and is extremely grief-stricken, so that it will die of sorrow if you do not quickly free it. Thus I beg you to turn (my heart) around so that it returns from the suffering into which it has fallen, for it is badly shaken up.]

This constant intermingling of vocabularies and constructs works to give both to fin'amors as code and to the first-person falconry narrative an increasingly literary dimension. The two different registers of the dit have in effect become metaphors for each other, mutually confirming and reinforcing each other's literariness (and the literariness of the entire construct). At the same time the skillful use of annominatio that characterizes the complainte serves to call attention to the poète figure as author, distanced from what is presented as the experience of the first-person narrator-protagonist.

Within the context of the falconry narrative, Amour replies to the narrator-protagonist's request for help with rather uncourtly advice: having lost his esprivier, he should go find another raptor to remedy his sadness.[39] The first narrative segment (vv. 118–1510) is thus brought to a close in a way which further undermines courtly love as code, at the same time as it prepares the way for the second narrative segment by bringing the narrator-protagonist back to the point at which he had started, ready to undergo the same experience again. This preparation is necessary because, as will be seen, the story line of the *Alerion* involves a fourfold repetition of the basic pattern established in the first segment (desire–possession–loss), which thus serves as a kind of narrative model for the rest of the dit. Within this overall structure of repetition,[40] however, several important kinds of variation and progression may be seen to take place. Further, the repetition itself will be exploited poetically.

The second narrative segment (vv. 1511–3028) continues the basic pattern of alternation between the two registers established in the first. An increasing complexity results, however, from the fact that the narrator figure takes on an increasingly artificial cast, is increasingly differentiated from the poète.

The segment opens with a narrative episode (vv. 1511–632) in which the narrator-protagonist recounts how, seeking to follow the advice of Amour, he begins to frequent an elegant circle of hunting bird enthusiasts. His grief is soon forgotten and by listening and observing he learns many new things concerning the art of falconry. One day in the course of a discussion on the relative nobility of different raptores, he hears the highest praise being given to an alerion (vv. 1568 ff.). There follows a brief discourse on the extreme difficulty involved in obtaining this raptor.

At this point (v. 1633) there is a shift in narrative stance. The narrator-protagonist of the falconry story is superseded by the poet-narrator who proposes a consideration of the respective merits of a desired object won with difficulty versus one achieved with ease. A kind of scholastic debate in miniature ensues in which it is demonstrated that a desired object easily won ought not to be abandoned. Two hypothetical examples — an alerion and a dame — are adduced to reinforce this point, and the poet-narrator concludes his long digression (vv. 1633–968) with the general advice that lovers should accept good fortune when it comes. Thus we have a subversion of the conventional courtly doctrine of the necessity of prolonged love service, a subversion emanating from the authoritative voice of the poet-narrator speaking in a didactic mode.

The narrative episode that follows (vv. 1979 ff.) recounts how the narrator-protagonist, after having learned all about alerions by means of devoted study with experts, sees one for the first time (vv. 2001–3) and repeatedly returns to the spot where the raptor is kept. He is well received by the bird keepers but, since the alerion cannot be obtained by purchase, he must refrain from asking to buy it and is afraid to request that it be given to him. Given the conditions of his situation, the narrator-protagonist resolves not to bid or ask for the "alerion que j'amoie" (v. 2065) [allerion that I loved] but to be content simply with looking at it. With respect to the ultimate fulfillment of his desires, he resolves to trust himself to the power and good offices of Amour. At this point the poet-narrator intervenes to support the decision of the narrator-protagonist by means of a clerkly *exemplum.* First (vv. 2087–304) we have a narrative account of how Guillaume Longue Espée obtained the marvelous horse of St. Louis (which no amount of gold could have bought) by meriting the king's love.[41] Next, we have the interpretation/moral of the story (vv. 2273–304) introduced in a way which once again emphasizes the presence of the poet-narrator and distances him from his subject matter, at the same time emphasizing the structural organization of the dit: "Ci vueil de Guillaume finer / Et la cause determiner / Pour quoy a parler de lui pris" (vv. 2273–75) [Here I want to finish with Guillaume's story and explain why I began to speak about him]. In his gloss, the poet-narrator argues that Amour rather than Fortune was responsible for Guillaume's success and that Amour's gifts are better than Fortune's.

After the completion of this digression, there is a shift back to the falconry register as a narrative episode follows (vv. 2305–400). Having decided to trust Amour, the narrator-protagonist gains the favor of the bird keepers and is allowed free access to the alerion. He attempts to conceal his true desires "pour paour de ceaus courrecier" (v. 2341)[42] [for fear of angering (the keepers)], but the keepers perceive his "samblans amoureus" (v. 2369) [amorous appearance] and decide to give him the alerion in spite of the objections of one of their number ("li menres de tous" [v. 2387] [the least of all]) who is reduced to silence after being summarily struck down by a dame.

A passage of commentary in the amatory register follows immediately (vv. 2401–70) with an explicit comparison serving as transition: "Autel puet on d'un amant dire" (v. 2401) [One can say the same of a lover]. The narrator-protagonist's experience with the alerion is like that of a devoted lover who spends time in his beloved's presence without requesting her love. The preceding episode of the falconry narrative is now, in effect, retold in the amatory register in general terms. The bird keepers are analogous to "la gent qui dames gardent" (v. 2419) [the people who guard ladies] who are Amour, Raison, and the troop of personification characters who serve them (Grace, Pais, Honneur, etc.). When Amour calls his followers together, they advise him that the amant has proved his loyalty and should be granted mercy. An objection is made by Dongier "li despiteus" (v. 2435) [the spiteful], but he is silenced and driven off by Douce Plaisance.

There ensues (vv. 2471–525) a narrative episode that utilizes to a particularly high degree the vocabulary and constructs of the amatory register. The narrator-protagonist speaks of having attained the object of his desires "par l'amoureuse voie" (v. 2480) [in accord with the ways of Love], through the good offices of Amour and Plaisance. It seems as if the preceding passage in the amatory register were now being conflated with a summary retelling of the narrative episode that recounted the winning of the alerion. The narrator-protagonist goes on to describe both his joy in possessing the raptor and his sense that, having been given a gift by Amour, he must show himself worthy of it.

At this point there is an explicit shift back to the authoritative, clerkly, didactic stance:

> Plus ne di de celle matiere;
> Car je me vueil de la maniere
> Des alerions aviser
> Pour les parties deviser.
> (vv. 2527–30)

[I will say no more about this matter, for I want to turn my attention to the allerion in order to describe her characteristics.]

The description that follows (vv. 2531–58) is of the alerion in general (rather than the particular one who figures in the narrative episodes). Certain distinguishing features are emphasized: the alerion flies very high; other birds are afraid of her; she is characterized by two razor-sharp feathers (called "pelles" [v. 2554]).

Another shift occurs at this point (v. 2559) as the poet-narrator announces the beginning of a comparison between the preceding description of the alerion and certain aspects of the love experience: "Or arrestons ci un petit / Pour penre amoureus appetit / En un po de comparison" (vv. 2559–61) [Now let us stop here for a little while in order to depict the amorous inclination through a bit of comparison]. A variation, an elaboration, of the basic pattern of the dit is made here since the comparison is not, strictly speaking, between the love experience and the falconry narrative, but between the love experience in general and the description of the alerion in general. What results from this variation is, on the one hand, a reduction in the importance of the "lyric experience" of the dit (i.e., a first-person falconry narrative) and, on the other hand, an increased emphasis on the process of comparison, of metaphoric diction as such, which emerges as the fundamental structuring element for the dit as a whole. The comparison first (vv. 2565–642) presents the case of an amant who so esteems his dame that she rises, in his imagination, into the highest reaches of honor and nobility. The dame's elevation in her lover's mind is analogous to the extremely high flight for which the alerion is noted. The lover's Volenté and Desir are like "dui oisel moult hardis" (v. 2685) [two very bold birds] who fly after the dame/alerion, whereas the various other aspects of his love are like more timid, low-flying birds who await the descent of the alerion which is compared to the *merci* granted by the dame.

The transition from this elaborate comparison (in the amatory register) back to the falconry narrative explicitly presents itself as a transition:

> J'ay ci assez, ce m'est avis,
> Fait de l'alerion devis,
> Comparé aus honneurs de dame
> Et d'amant qui sans nul diffame
> Vorroit amoureusement vivre.
> Se vorray parler de mon vivre
> Et de l'alerion briefment,
> Qui me fu donnez liement.
> (vv. 2733–40)

[In my opinion, I have by now sufficiently described the allerion and compared her to the honors of the lady and the lover who would like to blamelessly live the amorous life. And so I would like to speak briefly about my life and about the allerion who was gayly given to me.

Again, this transition passage stresses the difference between the je of the poet-narrator (vv. 2733–37 and the "vorray" in v. 2738) and the je of the narrator-protagonist ("mon" in v. 2738 and vv. 2739–40). At the same time the adverb "briefment" (v. 2739) signals an important development that takes place as the dit progresses: an increasing reduction of the size and importance of the falconry narrative linked to an increasing emphasis placed on the process of comparing, on metaphoric discourse.

The ensuing narrative episode (vv. 2738–84) is in fact rather brief, recounting how the narrator-protagonist joyously carried away the alerion that was given to him and how happy he was with the perfections of his beloved raptor, whose elegant and efficient hunting is described in some detail.

In the commentary that follows (vv. 2785–820) the behavior of the alerion is compared to that of a *dame jolie* who enjoys herself in festive company. Amour makes sure that her amant/ *proie* is honorable and chases from her those who speak dishonorably, the *oisel* of *foles pensées*.

There follows (vv. 2821–924) an important digression in the amatory register: an elaborate explanation of the pelles of the alerion (first described in vv. 2553–55) in terms of the fin'amors code. This "explanation" involves a most elaborately self-conscious presentation of metaphor (or metaphoric discourse) as such and as process associated with the activity of the poète:

> J'ay ci tenu mains parlemens
> Qui sont, ce m'est vis, paremens
> De quoy l'alerion paroie,
> Quant a dame l'acomparoie.
> Mieus ne le porroie parer
> Que lui a dame comparer.
> Or ne l'ay pas dou tout paré,
> Quant je ne l'ay pas comparé,
> Selonc ce que Raison me baille,
> Des pelles . . .
>
> (vv. 2821–30)

[I have here held many discussions which are, in my opinion, ornaments with which I adorned the allerion when I compared her to a lady. I could not adorn (the allerion) better than to compare her to a lady. But I have not yet completely adorned her since I have not treated her tail feathers as reason instructs me. . . .]

The repeated linking of "parer" and "comparer" in the rhyme position (vv. 2823–28) stresses the semantic content of this key passage: figurative language (simile, metaphor, i.e., comparison) is being employed to decorate the alerion.[43]

An elaborately structured set of digressions is used to treat, to decorate and explain (the association of these two terms is significant) the pelles. First, a symbolic equivalence is established: the pelle on the right "signefie / Scens, honnesté et courtoisie, / De la senestre le contraire" (vv. 2835–37) [signifies judgment, honesty, and courtesy; the one on the left signifies the opposite]. Second, there is a further explanation by means of narrative elaboration on the right/left opposition in an amatory context: loyal lovers enter the court of Amour on the right, false lovers on the left (vv. 2843–59). Third, this narrative situation in miniature is expanded by means of a speech of Amour directed towards hypothetical false lovers (vv. 2860–904): they will be punished even if they obtain their objective since they can have only superficial pleasure rather than true enjoyment, whereas the *amant loial* will attain either real fulfillment or the satisfaction of Esperence. Fourth, the poet-narrator intervenes (vv. 2904–24) in a didactic mode to comment on his own gloss: the way in which Amour renders just payment to true as well as false lovers will be clear to the reader who understands "ceste comparison faite, / Qui de l'alerion est traite, / Des peles qui tranchamment taillent" (vv. 2909–11) [this comparison which deals with the allerion's feathers, which cut sharply].

The transition from this extended commentary/comparison back to the falconry narrative evinces once again a high degree of textual self-consciousness. On the one hand, the identity of the poète as author of the dit and the primacy of the relationship poet/text are both emphasized. On the other hand, the distinction between the je of the poet-narrator and the je of the narrator-protagonist (and between the two registers associated with each) is stressed even as the shift takes place from one to the other. At the same time there is an implicit presentation of the dit as above all a verbal, a poetic structure greater than and containing both lyrico-narrative experience and clerkly, didactic sapience, which are thus presented as fictions, as *literary* constructs functioning within the context of the dit of the poète:

> De ces peles ay assez dit,
> Si que, pour abregier mon dit,
> Je m'en puis bien dès or mais taire
> Et a la besongne retraire
> De mon fait especiaument,
> Tout pour mettre legierement
> Mon procès a conclusion,
> Sans trop longue division.
>> (vv. 2925–32)

[I have said enough about these tail feathers so that I can henceforth be silent concerning them in order to shorten my poem. I can thus return to the task of my own particular case in order to bring my subject quickly to a close, without too much elaboration.]

The ensuing narrative episode (vv. 2933–3028) first recounts the period of happiness that the narrator-protagonist spent with his alerion. This period ends abruptly with the loss of the raptor, for which no explanation is given (v. 2957). Amour provides elaborate, non-courtly advice to the bereaved narrator-protagonist, telling him that he should use the knowledge gained from his earlier experience with the esprivier and boldly attempt to obtain a new raptor without worrying about possible failure or unworthiness:

> Se tu aucune chose pers,
> Soiez avisiez et apers
> Que tu puisses par bien ouvrer
> A point ta perte recouvrer
> Ou chose qui ta perte vaille.
>> (vv. 2999–3003)

[If you lose something, be attentive and clever so that you can, by working well, quickly recover your loss or something of equal value.]

The end of the second narrative segment thus repeats and elaborates the end of the first narrative segment. And the undermining of fin'amors as code is reinforced by means of this pattern of repetition.

The third narrative segment (vv. 3029–821) is not only shorter than the preceding two, but its purely narrative episodes are significantly reduced in size and importance. As part of the process of progressive reduction of the lyrico-narrative element, the extensive descriptions of the aigle to be found in this segment almost always involve the raptor considered in general (by the clerkly didactic je) rather than the particular aigle who figures in the first-person account of the narrator-protagonist. Indeed, this general description accounts for almost two-thirds of the entire segment. Thus, even though the basic pattern of alternation between the two registers established at the beginning of the dit continues to function in this segment, both registers, as a result of a series of artful modifications, are increasingly presented as fictional constructs.

The aigle segment opens with a narrative episode (vv. 3029–94) in which the narrator-protagonist takes the advice of Amour, leaves his solitude, and begins to frequent the company of noble falconers. (It should be noted that the process of getting over his grief at the loss of a beloved raptor becomes easier and easier for the narrator.) Almost immediately he sees "une aigle souffissant, / Roy des oiseaus, noble et puissant" (vv. 3043–44) [a splendid eagle – the noble and powerful king of birds].

Amour encourages the narrator-protagonist, as if a dame were the object of his affections – which is, of course, the point. The narrator approaches the falconers and is well received; in fact, almost as soon as he sees the raptor he obtains possession of it (v. 3070). Not only are the details of obtaining possession vague, but there is an explicit refusal on the part of the narrator-protagonist to be more precise (vv. 3071–94), which has the effect of rendering the episode more "generalized," more literary.

The next section (vv. 3095–148) involves a description of the aigle, which with the exception of the first line is entirely in commented tenses and concerns eagles in general, rather than the particular aigle of the preceding narrative episode. The poet-narrator presents himself as the clerkly praiser/describer of "l'aigle." The description proper begins with line 3121, introduced in such a way as to associate it exclusively with the voice of the poet-narrator: "Si diray dès or mais m'entente / De l'aigle; car moult m'atalente" (vv. 3119-20) [I will now explain my purpose with regard to the eagle, for I very much want to]. A shift to the general perspective of the clerkly, didactic je (note the commented tenses associated with the first-person pronoun) has been effected. The power and uniqueness of the eagle's eyes are singled out for special consideration, her most striking feature being her ability to look directly into the sun.

This last point leads to a brief digression (vv. 3149-238) in which the clerkly, didactic discourse and general perspective of the poet-narrator become more fully evident. First we have a consideration of how love is like the sun. A metaphoric equivalence is then established: as only the eagle can look at the sun, only purified hearts can look directly at the rays of Bonne Amour.

This brief digression serves as a preparation for one of the most important of all the poet-narrator's interventions. The authoritative, clerkly je here seems to have been expanded to the point where it overlaps with that of the poète:

> Et Bonne Amour m'a commandé
> D'especial, nom pas mandé,
> Qu'a loisir ma pensée avise
> Sus la grace et sus la franchise
> De l'aigle, qui est haute chose,
> Et que si a point me dispose,
> Pour la chose estre mieus parée,
> Que dame a li soit comparée.
> Dont, se je le fais volentiers,
> J'ay droit, car c'est li drois sentiers
> Par lequel viennent a honneur
> Tant li grant comme li meneur.
>   (vv. 3239-50)

[And Good Love has not requested but has directly ordered me to instruct myself fully concerning the grace and nobility of the eagle — an exalted subject — and to prepare a comparison between the eagle and a lady, to better adorn the subject. Thus, if I do this willingly, I am right. For this is the true path by which all people both great and small achieve honor.]

The construct employed here is highly significant. The establishment and "working out" of the complex, extended metaphor that is the *Alerion* is presented as constituting the poète's service to the God of Love, since Amour has commanded him to compare the aigle to the dame. By implication this comparison is made synonymous with poetic activity, both as discourse (i.e., as figurative language) and as process (i.e., as poetic composition over time). It is in this sense that the poète may be seen as containing both the je of the narrator-protagonist and the je of the poet-narrator, as well as the different registers associated with each. For it is by means of the poète's utilization of metaphor both as discourse and structuring principle that these two registers function dialectically within the context of the *Alerion* as a whole. Both lyrico-narrative "experience" (i.e., the falconry narrative) and clerkly, didactic sapience (in large part reminiscent of the ars amandi as genre) seem to have become subordinate in importance to the fact and the functioning of metaphoric discourse as such.

The specific comparison of dame to aigle at this particular point in the dit (vv. 3253–368) takes as its basis the conceit that a lady loyally committed to love in both speech and behavior may be described as dressed in the plumage of an eagle. The raptor's wings correspond to "loiauté"; his tail, to good reputation; his body to modesty and moderation. At this point the poet-narrator intervenes to emphasize both the rhetorical organization of his comparison and the transformative power of poetic language:

> Or ay le plumage et le corps,
> Eles et queue en mes recors
> De l'aigle a dame comparé,
> Et l'estat de l'aigle paré,
> De l'estat de dame ensement,
> On ne puet plus bel parement.
>
> (vv. 3303–8)

[I have now in my narrative compared the eagle's plumage, body, wings, and tail to a lady. And I have thus adorned the status of the eagle and lady alike: there is no more beautiful ornament.]

The comparison now continues on a different basis (vv. 3309 ff.) as the dame is presented as analogous to an eagle who flies into the high air of "bonté" where the sun of Amour shines. The dame's eyes, likened to her "entendemens" and "volentés," can look directly into this sun.

The poet-narrator ends his comparison for the time being in order to speak of another characteristic of the aigle, which is presented as further proof of his nobility: other raptores naturally fear the eagle and are punished if they act against nature by attacking him (vv. 3369–97). A clerkly exemplum (vv. 3398–530) is now recounted in order to demonstrate this point: the story of a king of France who decapitates one of his own hunting birds, after having observed that bird kill an eagle.[44] The poet-narrator then proceeds to gloss (vv. 3531–78) his exemplum in a way which calls attention to his own presence, above all, and to the rhetorical structure of his discourse. A series of analogies are established, not systematically equivalent to the various other sets of analogies from the amatory register linked with the aigle at other points in the text.[45] The eagle is here linked to "honneur." His flight, to the "trés douce vie / D'amours et d'amant et d'amie" (vv. 3535–36) [very agreeable life of Love, the lover, and the beloved]. The attacking bird is equated with the "mesdisans" who wish to remove honor from love. The severed head of the bird represents slanderous speech ("parlers de detraction"), defeated by "bons parlers."

The entire sequence devoted to the aigle in general (vv. 3096–656), in which clerkly description has alternated with clerkly gloss, comes to a close by means of a transition passage that employs as structural marker the poet-narrator's self-presentation as being in the process of composing the dit, whose rhetorical organization and status as fictional artifact are thus simultaneously emphasized: "Si vueil ceste division / Amener a conclusion, / Pour au droit procès revenir" (vv. 3657–59) [Thus I want to conclude this section in order to return to my proper subject].

The shift back to the falconry narrative once again stresses the opposition between poet-narrator and narrator-protagonist at the same time as the latter (the "je" of vv. 3664–65) seems to assume reduced proportions vis-à-vis the former (the "je" of vv. 3661–63):

> Je di que l'aigle de puissance,
> Que j'ay a dame de vaillance
> Comparé en mainte maniere,
> Me fu gaie, douce et maniere,
> Tant comme je la possessay.
> (vv. 3661–65)

[I say that the powerful eagle, which I have compared in many ways to a valiant lady, was joyous, docile, and adroit for as long as I possessed her.]

The abbreviated narrative episodes that follow (vv. 3666 ff.) treat in turn the period of contentment the narrator-protagonist spent with his aigle, then the loss of the raptor — which is recounted without explanation or detail (v. 3779 recalling the abbreviated description of how the aigle was first acquired) and appears to function as a purely formal narrative element.

It is significant that the narrator-protagonist has by this point in the dit largely internalized the non-courtly teachings of Amour in connection with his two previous losses (i.e., the esprivier and the alerion, both of whom are explicitly recalled in vv. 3735–36). A progression is thus established. The narrator-protagonist has learned from his earlier experiences, and the lesson he recites to himself subverts fin'amors as code: having lost a raptor he loves, the best remedy for merencolie is to look for a new raptor as quickly as possible. This lesson is immediately illustrated (and validated) as the narrator-protagonist successfully overcomes his grief at the loss of the aigle by praying to Amour for help which is quickly forthcoming: "Tant priay Amours a celée / Que li aigle fu oubliée" (vv. 3813–14) [I secretly prayed so much to Love that the eagle was forgotten]. A second progression, also subversive with respect to the code of fin'amors, is thus established within the context of the narrative line as the protagonist's love grief becomes increasingly easy to remedy. The memory of the aigle (i.e., the aigle/dame as poetic subject matter) remains (vv. 3815–18), but regret for, and preoccupation with, the raptor on the level of narrative (i.e., the aigle/dame as love experience) cease to function almost immediately. The narrator-protagonist, more a literary construct than ever, is thus ready, at the very end of the third narrative segment of the *Alerion*, to begin the cycle again: "Dont je fui liez, jolis et gais" (v. 3821) [Thus I was happy, joyous, and gay].

The fourth narrative segment (vv. 3822–4248) is the shortest of all, the most abbreviated version in the dit of the basic model established in the esprivier segment. Again, the narrative progresses by means of a pattern of alternation between the falconry and amatory registers with the metaphoric process that serves to link them receiving ever-increasing emphasis. Several particular features characterize this segment and function collectively to further the undercutting of the lyrico-narrative "experience" of the narrator-protagonist and of fin'amors as code,[46] while at the same time reinforcing the systematic valorization of metaphoric discourse (as the activity of the poète, his service to Amour). First, there is a more intricate interweaving of the two registers, which has the effect of emphasizing the metaphoric character of both. Second, a program of variations on the model plot pattern operates to effect a new sort of undermining of the falconry narrative. Third, the element of repetition (this is, after all, the fourth time) informs our reading of this segment in a particularly important way.

The segment opens with a narrative episode (vv. 3822–910) which recounts how the narrator-protagonist returns to the bird keepers with the express intention of finding a new raptor. He notices a gerfaut to whom "m'amour offri" (v. 3860) [I offered my love] but (in a parody of the amant couart topic) he is too shy to do more than look at the bird longingly. The keepers notice his evident affection and are willing to give him the raptor, but one of their number insists that the narrator-protagonist make an explicit request. The narrator consoles himself by thinking of a love situation in which there is a difficulty parallel to his own.

The passage of comparison/commentary in the amatory register that follows (vv. 3911–66) is thus integrated into the narrative line by being presented as a meditation of the protagonist. It involves the hypothetical case of an amant who, though his love is returned, does not dare make an explicit request of his dame. His glances and sighs are not sufficient and merci is delayed until "Amours donne le hardement / Dou demander fiablement" (vv. 3961–62) [Love gives (him) the boldness to make a sincere request].

The ensuing narrative episode (vv. 3967–4084) grows directly out of this passage of amatory analogy, which, presented as a meditation of the narrator-protagonist, provides him with sufficient courage to request the gerfaut. The metaphoric equivalence of narrator-protagonist and courtly lover is explicitly worked into the narrative progression as the narrator-protagonist describes himself "comme uns amis / Qui tout son cuer en dame a mis" (vv. 3979–80) [as a lover who has given his entire heart to his lady]. He courts the raptor (or rather the keepers, for again they function as the "spokesmen" for the beloved raptor, in a construct reminiscent of Bel Accueil/Rose in Guillaume de Lorris; see p. 74, n. 42 above) like a lover courting a dame. After making his request "umblement" and with "chiere debonnaire," he obtains the object of his desire: "Li gerfaus fu miens ligement" (v. 4001) [The gerfalcon was loyally mine]. The rhapsodic expression of his joy coupled with praise of the gerfaut (vv. 4003–18) involves extensive annominatio on "joÿ" and "loër," which may be seen in this context as a sign of the poète. Both the joy and the praise appear (literally) as structured language (i.e., as poetic production) and simultaneously as lyrico-narrative "experience."

The narrator-protagonist had counted on spending the rest of his life happily with his gerfaut, but the raptor, after initial good behavior, begins to act strangely, showing "signes . . . orguilleus" (v. 4075) [signs of pride] and returning to her master *trop envis* [very reluctantly] after catching prey, in striking contrast to the behavioral pattern of the raptores that hunted in the three preceding segments. Not knowing what to do, the narrator-protagonist waits hopefully for some improvement in the gerfaut, and the simile he employs to describe his condition (within the context of the falconry narrative) serves as the transition into a sequence (vv. 4087–184) in the amatory register:

Mais j'atendoie bonnement
Adès de lui l'amendement,
Aussi comme uns vrais amans fait
Qui aimme de fin cuer parfait
Sa dame, et a adès amé.

(vv. 4085–9)

[But I sincerely and constantly expected her to improve, just as a true lover does who loves and has always loved his lady with a pure and perfect heart.]

By means of a subtle interweaving of the two registers that have functioned in opposition throughout most of the dit, a hypothetical love story, recounted in the third person by means of commented tenses, grows out of a simile situated in the first-person falconry narrative. The protagonist of this miniature narration (vv. 4087–178) is the generalized *vrais amans* whose dame, after having shown him favor, becomes harsh and unreceptive. He comes to realize that she is "de volenté muable, / De cuer volage et nouveliere" (vv. 4118–19) [of changeable will, of fickle and inconstant heart] and therefore incapable of behaving honorably. In effect what has occurred here is a proleptic account in the amatory register of the narrative episode that is to follow in the falconry register. This complex narrative construct (in which the two registers are interwoven) functions to place particular emphasis on the metaphoric discourse (cf. the initial simile of v. 4087) from which it is generated. At the same time this metaphoric discourse is implicitly presented as emanating from the poète, the author figure for the dit as a whole. It is thus particularly fitting that a self-consciously authorial voice (overlapping, to be sure, with that of the poet-narrator) provides the transition back to the falconry register:

C'est assez quant a present dit
Selonc la fourme de mon dit,
Voire s'on l'a bien entendu,
Pour la fin a quoy j'ay tendu.

> Se vueil au propos revenir
> Qui bien en fera souvenir.
> (vv. 4179–84)

[In accord with my poem's form, enough has now been said for the purpose I had in mind, provided that (my reader) has been properly attentive. Thus I want to return to the subject that will be well remembered.]

The narrative segment that follows (vv. 4185–248) recounts how the gerfaut was lost. During a hunting expedition, the narrator-protagonist sends his raptor after a suitable prey which the gerfaut abandons in order to pursue "Un oisel lait, vil et puant, / Dont li gentil oisel n'ont cure" (vv. 4220–21) [an ugly, vile, foul bird which noble raptores avoid]. When the raptor does not respond to the narrator-protagonist's calls, he abandons it: "Aussi comme amans qui s'amie / Ne porroit traire de folie" (vv. 4237–38) [Just as a lover who cannot turn his beloved away from folly].

The particular details of the gerfaut's escape (all of which are new variations on the model plot pattern) combined with the fact that this is the fourth raptor lost by the narrator-protagonist, give to this final episode of the fourth narrative segment a somewhat comic air that functions to undercut still further the lyrico-narrative "experience" ostensibly recounted in the falconry register. At the same time the two registers of the *Alerion* have become, by this point in the poem, very closely interwoven. It is in the fifth (and final) narrative segment that the final conflation of these two registers takes place.

The fifth narrative segment (vv. 4249–784) serves to conclude the dit on several different levels. On the level of plot, the basic pattern of desire–satisfaction–loss established in the esprivier segment and repeated four times is finally broken. On the level of formal structure, the two registers which have functioned in opposition throughout the dit seem finally to fuse. Similarly, the two major components of the identity of the narrator figure (each associated with a different register) are finally conflated. At the same time both are shown to be contained by the global poète figure, whose identity resides in the metaphoric discourse that both structures and explains the dit as a whole.

For the purposes of the present analysis, the final segment may be seen as involving, first, an extended sequence of falconry narrative (vv. 4249–648); and second, an elaborate amatory comparison (vv. 4649–764), which in fact serves to effect a conflation of the two registers.

The narrative sequence opens as the narrator-protagonist enters a "molt gracieus vergier" (v. 4265) [a very elegant garden] where he prays to Amour to deliver him from the grief occasioned by the loss of the gerfaut. Amour answers this prayer by sending Raison who, in a brief speech (vv. 4356–402) advises the narrator-protagonist not to blame himself for the meffait of his raptor, but to banish it from his memory and rejoice in the happy exercise of his natural faculties.[47] Raison then goes on (in a second speech, vv. 4410–36) to warn him against the dangers of merencolie and to emphasize the necessity of (non-courtly) self-help: "Aide toy; je t'aideray. / Honnis toy; je te honniray" (vv. 4433–34) [Help yourself and I will help you; disgrace yourself and I will disgrace you]. The narrator-protagonist takes Raison's advice to heart and immediately his grief is changed to joy, and he is able to perceive the beauties of the vergier to which he had previously been insensitive. As the narrator-protagonist sits happily in this *drois paradis*, a flock of contentious birds falls into his lap, then flies off leaving behind a *verdiere*. Since this bird had been the favorite prey of his alerion, he is reminded of his former raptor. Shortly thereafter, an alerion (v. 4582) descends from the sky and alights on the narrator's fist. He verifies its identity by means of a pearl that he had earlier tied to its foot and is overjoyed to discover that his own alerion has returned to him. After praising the raptor as his loyal "biaus trés dous amis" (v. 4613) [good, sweet love], the narrator-protagonist resolves to maintain lifelong fidelity to his alerion.

At this point (v. 4649) there is an intervention by the poet-narrator (whose voice seems to overlap with that of the poète) in which the shift, by means of metaphor ("comparison," v. 4651) to the amatory register is explicitly effected:

> Or puis je moult bien sus ces dis
> Qui ci devant ont esté dis

> Faire un po de comparison
> A mon pooir sans mesprison.
> Pour certein, le cas le desire,
> Et d'autre part mes cuers y tire.
>
> (vv. 4649–55)

[Now I would like to make a comparison to the best of my ability, without any mistakes, based on the words that have been spoken above. It is certain that the subject requires it and in addition my heart is fixed on it.]

The "je" of lines 4649 and 4655 who presents himself as a maker of poetic comparisons, of metaphoric discourse, appears as the poète-author, containing both the first-person narrator and the first-person protagonist.

The extended metaphor in the amatory register begins with the description (vv. 4655–74, in the present tense) of the general case of "uns amans et une amie" [a lover and a beloved] who love each other loyally but are forced to part. It is fitting that they rely on Amour in order to bear their grief and find Esperence.

The metaphor continues by positing (vv. 4675–84, in the future tense) hypothetical "aventures diverses" for the separated amans which end unhappily: "il trouvera maint defaut, / Si comme je fis ou gerfaut" (vv. 4683–84) [he will find many flaws, as I did in the gerfalcon]. We have here a kind of doubling of the initial metaphoric construct: "il" (the generalized, third-person protagonist of the amatory comparison) begins to fuse with "je" (the particularized, first-person protagonist for the falconry narrative). This process of fusion is elaborated in the following sequence:

> Lors ne sara il quel part traire
> Fors vers Amours la debonnaire,
> La ou Raisons l'entroduira
> Et doucement le conduira
> Ou trés dous vergier amoureus
> Qui est plaisans et savoureus.
>
> (vv. 4685–90)

[Then he will not know where to turn except to noble Love. Reason will prepare him and lead him into the sweet amorous grove, which is pleasant and delicious.]

What began as a comparison of two disparate elements has become circular as the reader is led back to the vergier from which he started. At this point il is not simply like je: the two have, in some sense, been conflated, as have the two registers of falconry narrative and amatory commentary/comparison. We have here a "retelling" of the final episode of the falconry narrative — transposed into the amatory register by means of metaphor. It is metaphoric discourse as such (associated with the figure of the poète) that is thus emphasized and valorized.

The final fusion of the *Alerion*'s two registers is effected in the second description of the vergier (vv. 4691–764), in which each element is assigned a new significance as a symbol of part of the love experience, beginning with the vergier as a whole: "Cils vergiers dont je ci raconte, / Par quoy je ne faille a mon compte, / C'est Amours especiaument" (vv. 4691–93) [This garden which I am describing here, in order not to fail at my task, is Love]. The authoritative first-person voice of the poet-narrator (coinciding with that of the poète) proceeds to work out this elaborate metaphor in a very systematic fashion. The hedges surrounding the plaisance are good works and good deeds; the fragrant herbs, "douces pensées" (v. 4701) [sweet thoughts]; the trees, "toutes bonnes vertus" (v. 4705) [all good virtues]; the flock of birds that falls into the lover's lap are grief and joy fighting with each other; the verdiere, the "bonne renomée" [good reputation] of the beloved; and finally, the alerion "puet estre sa douce dame" (v. 4723) [can be his sweet lady]. The terms of the two registers are now used interchangeably as "la dame" (v. 4731) descends from the sky of humility following "la verdiere" (v. 4732). Amour rejoices to see the lovers reunited and the amans discovers that his "trés douce amie" (v. 4741) [very sweet beloved] has not changed but has maintained her fidelity and loyalty, represented by the pearl (v. 4757). With this last detail, the poet-narrator has completed the retelling of the vergier episode in amatory terms and the fusion of the two registers: "Plus n'en di, car qui bien l'entent, / Il voit bien a quoy mes cuers tent" (vv. 4763–64) [I will not say any more about it, for he who understands it well sees what my heart intends].

A final sequence (vv. 4765–84) seems to fuse the two major components of the narrator figure's identity. First, the narrator-protagonist employing narrated tenses states that he regained possession of the alerion and intended to keep it forever (vv. 4765–73). Next, the poet-narrator employing commented tenses states that he still possesses the alerion (at the present time of writing) and that their mutual affection will never cease: "Si que je l'aimme et ameray / Tous les jours que je viveray" (vv. 4783–84) [For I love her and will love her as long as I live].

In the brief Epilogue (vv. 4785–814) we have the first-person voice of the poète speaking of the *Alerion* and of his own identity in a way which presupposes and exploits both the conflations of register and first-person voices effected in the vergier segment and the fact that the dit is self-consciously coming to its conclusion.

First (vv. 4785–800), addressing a potentially universal audience ("Tous et toutes," v. 4787), he presents himself as an example to be imitated in love: "Amez, si comme j'ay amé" (v. 4789) [Love as I have loved]. Those who imitate him will be praised by all who have knowledge of Bonne Amour.

There follows the anagram signature of him "qui a fait ceste rime toute" (v. 4802) [who has written this entire poem] and a concluding commentary: "Par ce verrez tout clerement / Se cils est clers ou damoiseaus / Qui fist ce 'Dit des quatre oiseaus'" (vv. 4812–14) [Through this you will clearly see whether he who wrote the Poem of the Four Birds was a clerk or a gentleman]. It is the three components of the identity of the poète figure that are here enumerated and implicitly fused. The opposition "clers"/"damoiseaus" (of which the opposition poet-narrator/narrator-protagonist is a permutation) is by this point no longer functional (except as a rhetorical strategy operating within the context of a poetic work). The identity of the poète as global author figure has been shown to contain both, as a result of the working out of the *Alerion* itself. It is thus most fitting that the dit should conclude by naming itself, for the last line contains the original title of the work.

A comparison of the *Alerion* with the two earlier dits employing the same narrative configuration reveals a series of suggestive reversals and progressions. First, the vergier as locus amoenus that had served as the thematic and structural center in the *Vergier* and the *Remede* is transferred to the end of the *Alerion*. Second, the advice given by Raison in the *Alerion*'s vergier leads to amorous satisfaction for Amant, in contradistinction to the ultimate "ineffectiveness" of Amour in the *Vergier* and Esperence in the *Remede*. This apparent progression, however, results from the *Alerion*'s treatment of both vergier and love experience as extended metaphors. Machaut seems to suggest that only a *metaphoric* amorous success is possible within the configuration of poet-narrator as lover-protagonist. In this context, the *Voir-Dit* involves a final stage in Machaut's progressively more elaborate exploitation of this narrative configuration. Any resolution suggested by the end of the *Alerion* seems implicitly to be undermined by the *Voir-Dit*, which systematically employs the most overtly non-metaphoric, the most "realistic" discourse of any of the dits amoureux.

III. Poet-Narrator as Lover-Protagonist: *Le Voir-Dit*

Introduction

Le Livre du voir-dit may be viewed as a kind of culmination — the fullest development possible for the narrative stance of poet-narrator as lover-protagonist. We have what appears to be an almost complete fusion of lover, protagonist, narrator, and poet.[1] It is as if a troubadour were to write his own *vida*.[2] Further, there is a progressive reduction of temporal distance between the time of writing and the time of the narrative, until the story is told almost as it happens. This is done with a high degree of literary self-consciousness: one of the principal themes of the *Voir-Dit* is the story of the writing and construction of the book itself, the first time in Machaut's oeuvre that this takes place *explicitly*. The composition of poetry and the craft of writing (including the making of the codex and the business of patronage) here become thematized and linked to the portrayal of love as experience and as poetic inspiration.

The present analysis will focus (as did the preceding chapter) on the complex identity of the first-person narrator figure, as it is progressively revealed in the course of (indeed, by means of) the unfolding narrative. This will involve, first of all, a consideration of the three major components of this identity — lover, clerc, and professional poet — and the way in which they are alternately conflated and differentiated. Second, the relationship between the pseudo-autobiographical first-person narrator[3] and Machaut the

94

poète will be investigated in detail. This will necessarily involve a consideration of the complex and problematic issue of the self-avowed "truth" of the work.[4] Finally, a detailed analysis will be undertaken of the *Voir-Dit*'s narrative structure[5] and its relation to the narrator's identity.

In order to situate this analysis, a few preliminary remarks on the organization of the *Voir-Dit* as a whole are necessary. The work recounts the love affair and literary relationship of Guillaume and Toute-Belle. It may be seen as falling into two broadly distinguishable parts. The first (pp. 2–163) deals with the beginning of the "affair" and the lovers' experience together. The narrative structure of Part 1 is basically *linear:* an extended "progression or gradation leading to a climax"[6] or resolution that is not repeated. Courtly diction (as well as the constructs and topics of the grand chant courtois qua literary tradition) predominates. The narrator figure here appears primarily as a poet-lover. The second (and somewhat longer) part of the *Voir-Dit* (pp. 183–370) deals with the lovers' extended separation. Here clerkly diction (as well as typically clerkly attitudes, stances, and bookishness) predominates, and the narrator figure appears primarily as a clerc-poet. The narrative structure of Part 2 is basically *cyclical* and as such functions both to problematize the apparent resolution of Part 1 and to effect a new kind of resolution. A midpoint sequence (pp. 163–83) functions simultaneously as a transition and a link between the poem's two major parts. It is in this sequence that the question of the work's "truthfulness" is treated most explicitly and linked to the identity not only of its narrator-protagonist, but to that of Machaut the poète.

Le Voir-Dit: Part 1

The *Voir-Dit* opens with a brief Prologue (vv. 1–28, pp. 1–2) which serves to orient our reading of the work as a whole with regard both to the identity of the narrator figure and to the thematic treatment of love and poetry. This is accomplished in large part implicitly. Suggestions are made which will be progressively elaborated as the work advances, but they are not fully developed until the very end.

The Prologue begins with a declaration by the poet-narrator

that he wishes to undertake "chose nouvelle" (v. 7), i.e., the *Voir-Dit*, for the greater glory of Amour and his dame, both of whom he serves through his poetic activity. An initial conflation of love service and poetic service is thus suggested which will become one of the dominant motifs of the *Voir-Dit* and one of the keys to the identity of the narrator figure. There follows (vv. 9–18) a brief and highly conventionalized louange of the poet's dame which recalls (and is an amplificatio of) the end of the Prologue of the *Roman de la rose* (vv. 41–44). It is significant, however, that Machaut does not present his poem as a love offering intended to move or please his dame as was the case with the *Rose* (vv. 40–41), but as an implicitly self-sufficient (and self-justifying) poetic artifact for which the love experience serves as subject matter. The sense in which the *Voir-Dit* has been written *pour* Toute-Belle (vv. 5, 8, 20; cf. *Rose*, v. 41) is at this point suggestively ambiguous. The nature and significance of the relation between the dame, the love experience, and the poem will only become clear as the *Voir-Dit* progresses.

The Prologue concludes with a multifaceted self-presentation on the part of the first-person narrative voice: "Or vueil commencier ma matiere, / Pour ma tres-douce dame chiere; / Et diray toute m'aventure" (vv. 19–21) [Thus I want to begin my subject, for my sweet, dear lady; and I will recount my entire adventure]. Line 19 presents the first-person voice as poet-narrator; line 20, as poet-lover; line 21 as poet-protagonist.[7] At the same time a basically lyric authorization (stressed by means of the repetition of the first-person singular possessive adjective) is implicitly established for the narrative to follow: it is presented as derived from, and authorized by, the experience of the narrator-protagonist.

Finally, the perspective (necessarily limited) of the time of the narrative is contrasted with that of the time of writing as the reader is informed at the outset (vv. 25–28) of the happy ending of the "aventure." This contrast serves to point up the distinction between the je-narrator and the je-protagonist that will be exploited periodically throughout the *Voir-Dit*.

Part 1 proper of the *Voir-Dit* (pp. 2–163) may be seen as falling into two major narrative segments. The first of these (pp. 2–

70) treats the initial phase of the relationship between Guillaume and Toute-Belle, which takes place exclusively by means of correspondence.

The opening episode (pp. 2–23) is set entirely in a vergier and recounts how Toute-Belle initiated the correspondence. The initial temporal indication is significant: "Il n'a pas un an que j'estoie / En un lieu où je m'esbatoie" (vv. 29–30) [Less than a year ago I was in an enjoyable place]. Not only does this involve situating the time of writing in close proximity to the time of the narrative at the outset of the poem, but it prepares the way for the two temporalities ultimately to "overlap" since the story line will unfold over a period of nearly three years.[8]

In a striking reversal of courtly convention (which may perhaps also be seen as an inversion of the opening of the *Rose*), the poet-narrator of the *Voir-Dit* who is situated in a standard locus amoenus is old, alone, ill, melancholy, and poetically unproductive. Guillaume's inability to compose poetry is presented as the result of the fact that he is void of love experience (vv. 47–50). This connection between poetic productivity and love seems to involve the use of a standard lyric construct to characterize Guillaume as poet-protagonist, though this characterization is somewhat undercut by Guillaume's non-courtly traits. However, the order in which the two aspects of his unhappy condition are presented (first, his inability to write poetry; second, his lack of love experience) — as well as the kind of link between them — involves an implicit presentation and valorization of the love experience primarily as poetic subject matter. This suggestion will be increasingly elaborated as the poem develops.

Guillaume's solitude is broken by the arrival of an old friend (p. 3) who brings him the joyous news that he is loved by a beautiful young dame who has never seen him but has heard of his achievements as a lyric poet. The actual declaration of love is in the form of a *rondeau*, presented to Guillaume by the messenger-intermediary: "Celle qui onques ne vous vit, / Et qui vous aime loiaument" (p. 7) [She who has never seen you and who loves you faithfully].[9] Guillaume responds by composing on the spot a rondeau (p. 12) which is a reply to Toute-Belle's whose rhyme scheme it duplicates: the first of the *Voir-Dit's* many sets of "paired lyrics."[10] Further attention is thus called to the fact that the correspondence, indeed the entire relationship, between Guillaume and Toute-Belle has been initiated by an exchange of lyric poems.

After a short but indeterminate period of time (P. Paris estimates "un mois, deux mois peut-être,"[11]), Guillaume, again in the vergier, receives a second visit from his dame's messenger (pp. 13–24). His reaction to the messenger's declaration that Toute-Belle loves him involves an echo of the opening rhyme words of the *Rose* in a way which underscores the literariness of the love recounted in the *Voir-Dit*: "Et vi bien que pas n'estoit songe / Le dit de l'autre, ne mensonge" (vv. 383–84, p. 15) [And I clearly saw that the other's (the messenger's) speech was neither dream nor lie]. The messenger then presents Guillaume with a second rondeau from his lady (p. 15) enclosed with her first prose letter to him (Letter 1, p. 15).[12]

This letter serves to emphasize Guillaume's identity as professional poet at the very beginning of his new love relationship. Toute-Belle requests that Guillaume correct her rondeau and write a virelay on the same theme, then goes on to ask him to compose music for these two poems as well as for the two rondeaux previously exchanged. Her letter closes as follows: "Je vous pri, treschiers et bons amis, qu'il vous plaise à moy envoier de vos bons diz notez: car vous ne me povés faire service qui plus me plaise" (p. 16) [I beg you, good and dear friend, to please send me good poems set to music; for you can do me no service that would please me more]. Combined with her declaration of love is not only an expression of her admiration for his poetic stature but a request that he take her on as an apprentice. "Thus Toute-Belle wants Guillaume to be simultaneously her lover, her teacher and her poet (i.e., the poet who celebrates her). There seems to be a suggestion here of the Abelard and Heloïse relationship, but in a very different register."[13] Remy de Gourmont has suggestively referred to Toute-Belle as a Laura who self-consciously "creates herself" by initiating a relationship with the "French Petrarch."[14]

Immediately after Letter 1 comes a prologuelike intervention (pp. 16–18) on the part of the je-narrator, entirely in commented tenses and addressed to the reader. First we have a rhetorical stance that Guillaume as narrator will be seen to adopt periodically throughout the *Voir-Dit*, and that is closely linked to his implicit self-portrayal as a failed lover: the defense against possible criticism. Here it is the inclusion of his love letters in the *Voir-Dit* that he feels called upon to defend:

> Et s'il est nuls qui me repreingne,
> Ou qui mal apaiez se teingne
> De mettre cy nos escriptures,
> Autant les douces que les sures,
> Que l'on doit appeler epistres,
> (C'est leurs drois noms et leurs drois titres,)
> Je respons à tous telement:
> Que c'est au dous commandement
> De ma dame qui le commande.
>
> (vv. 406–14)

[And if anyone reproaches me or is dissatisfied because I have here included our sweet and authentic writings (which should be termed epistles, [since] this is their proper name), I give the following answer to all: it is done at the sweet command of my lady, who has ordered it.]

Second, he explains any repetitions the *Voir-Dit* may contain as elements deriving from the work's authenticity. A kind of circularity has thus been established here. The form of the *Voir-Dit* (intercalated letters, narrative structure, etc.) serves to guarantee its "truthfulness." At the same time, this "truthfulness" justifies, explains the form — in terms of Toute-Belle's desire for completeness and accuracy:

> Car celle pour qui Amours veille,
> Vuet que je mete en ce Voir-Dit
> Tout ce qu'ay pour li fait et dit,
> Et tout ce qu'elle a pour moy fait,
> Sans riens celer qui face au fait.
>
> Le Voir-Dit vueil-je qu'on appelle
> Ce traictié que je fais pour elle,
> Pour ce que jà n'i mentiray.
>
> (vv. 425–32)

[For she over whom Love watches (i.e., Toute-Belle) wants me to put into this True Story all that I have done and said for her, and all that she has done for me, without concealing any relevant thing. I want this treatise that I am making for her to be called the True Story because I will never lie in it.]

The explicit naming of the work and the glossing of this name thus take place, as it were, simultaneously. And the final guarantee for both the name and its gloss resides in the self-authenticating (poetic) discourse employed by the je of lines 430–32, who here seems to overlap with Machaut the poète.

An explicit return to the narrative line (vv. 441–43) serves to introduce Guillaume's letter of reply to Toute-Belle (Letter 2, pp. 18–21) which mingles two major components of his identity: lover and poet. Speaking as lover, Guillaume first deploys courtly rhetoric with expertise to express his joy and devotion, then goes on to articulate his sense of his own unworthiness, his inappropriateness for playing (rather than writing about) the lover's role: "je suis petis, rudes et nices et desapris . . ." (p. 19) [I am small, awkward, foolish, and ignorant]. Desiring but fearing Toute-Belle's presence, he requests that she send him her portrait ("ymage," p. 20). Speaking as courtly love poet, Guillaume expresses his gratitude to Toute-Belle for having reawakened his poetic inspiration, indeed, for having provided him with poetic subject matter: "Car vous m'avez ressuscité et rendu mon sentement que j'avoie tout perdu: et jamais par moi ne fust fais chans ne lais, se vous ne fussiez" (p. 20) [For you have revived me and restored my emotions which I had completely lost: and I never would have composed songs or lays if it had not been for you]. He then goes on to make a vow of lifelong service, in which love experience and poetic production seem to be conflated.

Finally, Guillaume speaks as professional poet: after complimenting the two rondeaux Toute-Belle has sent him, he adds: "mais se j'estoie un jour avec vous, je vous diroie et apenroie ce que je n'apris onques à créature; par quoy vous les feriés mieus" (p. 21) [but if I were to spend one day with you, I would tell you and teach you things that I have never taught to anyone: and you would thereby compose better (lyric poems)]. The stance of lover as teacher of poetry and music, as magister (initiated by Toute-Belle in her first letter), is to remain an important element in Guillaume's identity as the *Voir-Dit* and the relationship with Toute-Belle advance.

The next episode (pp. 23–42) recounts how a two-month interruption in the lovers' correspondence causes a relapse of Guillaume's illness which is then cured for a second time by the arrival of a letter from Toute-Belle.

The episode opens as Guillaume, unable to communicate with his beloved, passes from *merencolier,* through the range of Ovidian love symptons (p. 24), to a new attack of illness which causes him to believe his death is near. Thinking only of Toute-Belle, he writes his *testament* in the form of two ballades (pp. 25–27) and has them sent to her. This scene is significant on several counts. First, it is an example of the way in which an intercalated lyric poem may be said to function narratively within the context of the *Voir-Dit* as a whole. Second, and more important, it serves to differentiate Guillaume the narrator from Machaut the poète. For the first ballade ("Pleurés, dames, pleurés vostre servant" [Weep, ladies, weep for your servant]), which also appears as number 229 in the Chichmaref edition of the *Louange des dames,* is identified by Daniel Poirion as having been composed independently of the *Voir-Dit.*[15] Far from being an isolated case, "over one third of the lyrics supposedly written and exchanged during the course of the love affair are found in manuscripts which do not contain the *Voir-Dit* itself and were drawn up before its completion. Eight of the lyrics appear in *C* and are much earlier than the *Voir-Dit* (including the rondeau with music 'Sans cuer, dolens,' [discouraged, suffering] which Machaut claims to have composed 'en chemin'). . . . Machaut apparently incorporated suitable lyrics from his earlier work, representing them both to his readers and to Peronne as newly composed."[16] The first *testament ballade* thus participates in a program of self-quotation (very likely perceived as such by fourteenth-century readers, especially given that Machaut's lyrics often circulated individually[17]) in evidence throughout the *Voir-Dit,* by means of which the je of Guillaume the courtly lover and lyric poet is contrasted with and contained by the je of Machaut the poète, the author of the oeuvres complètes. Further, the functioning of this program has important implications for the self-proclaimed "truth" of the *Voir-Dit*, which is implicitly presented as poetic rather than historico-biographical.[18]

No sooner has Guillaume completed his testament than a *varlet* arrives at his sickbed, bearing a letter (Letter 3, pp. 27–29) from Toute-Belle. She begins her epistle by affirming her love for Guillaume and her desire to see him, then goes on to allay his fear of being unworthy, explaining why he should not be afraid to present himself to her in person: "je ne vous aimme point pour biauté ne pour plaisance que je véisse onques en vous, ains vous aime pour la bonté et bonne renommé de vous" (p. 27) [I do not love you for your beauty nor for any charm that I have ever seen in you; rather, I love you for your goodness and your good reputation.] Toute-Belle authenticates her feelings by comparing herself to literary heroines (especially Florence in the fourteenth-century romance *Artus de Bretagne*), promising to play to perfection the role of amie when she and Guillaume meet. This forms part of the process of literarization of the love experience recounted in the *Voir-Dit*, a process which becomes increasingly visible as the story advances. Even Guillaume's correspondence is implicitly presented as literary production when Toute-Belle, replying to Guillaume's fear that his letters are too long, says that even if "ce que vous m'escrisiés tenoit autant comme li rommans de la Rose ou de Lancelot, il ne m'en anuieroit mie à lire" (p. 28) [you wrote me (a letter) as long as the Romance of the Rose or the Romance of Lancelot, reading it would not bother me at all].

The arrival of this letter brings Guillaume such *confort* that he is cured of his illness and able to leave his sickbed within two days (p. 31). At this point Guillaume as narrator interrupts his story to compare his dame to a *sainte* who has just effected a *miracle* by the fact that she "deux fois m'a ressuscité" (p. 32) [twice revived me].[19]

The return to the main narrative line (vv. 821 ff.) involves a presentation of the four lyric poems which Guillaume composed ("dictay") in bed during his two-month relapse and which he encloses in his letter of reply to Toute-Belle. The ballade (p. 36) and especially the three chansons balladées (pp. 37–41) which follow employ courtly diction and conventions to express, to crystallize, lyric moments which are fully explicable only in the narrative context of this stage of Guillaume's relationship with Toute-Belle. Guillaume's letter (Letter 4, pp. 41–42) involves a technique that will be frequently exploited in the *Voir-Dit*. A single narrative event (in this case Guillaume's relapse and subsequent cure) is treated (actually retold) in each of the three formal components of the work: narrative verse (i.e., rhyming octosyllabic couplets), lyric verse (i.e., the formes fixes), and epistolary prose. What results is at once a reciprocal (but intratextual) authentification of the narrative event as such and a dynamic interdependence among the three formal components within the poetic economy of the *Voir-Dit* as a whole. The letter recounts (to the beloved) the (pseudo) autobiographical circumstances that have occasioned the lyric poem(s) — thus "explaining" them. The narrative verse sequences recount (to the reader — addressed either as "vous" or by means of a formulaic vocative such as "bonnes gens") the same circumstances in a way which "explains" both letter and lyric — placing both in the context of a continuous (pseudo) autobiographical narration.[20] In both cases we have a self-conscious utilization of first-person ("autobiographic") narrative as a gloss for lyric, but from different perspectives.[21]

Thus Guillaume in Letter 4 recounts to Toute-Belle how her "douces escriptures" [sweet writings] have cured his illness and returned him to life and joy "et ont faict plus grans miracles à ma personne que je ne vi onques faire n'à saint n'à sainte qui soit en paradis" (p. 41) [and have accomplished for me miracles greater than any I have ever seen accomplished by any saint, male or female, in paradise]. His only remaining problem is Desir which is however held in check by the esperance he has of seeing her.[22] This esperance (briefly elaborated upon in the letter) has formed the subject matter of the preceding sequence of lyric poems — as Guillaume points out explicitly with reference to the "ballade" (on p. 36). Similarly, his "piteus estat" (p. 42) [pitiful condition] during his recent illness provided the subject matter for the first ballade of his testament (found on p. 25).

The following episode (pp. 42–70) recounts how the love relationship between Guillaume and Toute-Belle developed and deepened during the course of the spring (of 1363) entirely by means of correspondence. An initial deployment of courtly lyric conventions (pp. 42–43) serves to establish the canonical season of love as the the basic setting for the renewal (and intensification) of the epistolary exchange. Amorous and literary matters are thus programmatically commingled in Letters 5 (pp. 47–49), 6 (pp. 52–55), and 7 (pp. 57–59). On the one hand, Guillaume articulates his inadequacy, his inappropriateness for the role of lover while Toute-Belle reassures and encourages him. On the other hand, Guillaume's status as authoritative poet/composer is repeatedly emphasized by both correspondents.

The single "external" intrusion into the epistolary progression of the love affair involves the elaboration of a standard courtly lyric motif in Guillaume's first-person narrative: that of the *losengiers*. Guillaume is told that Toute-Belle doubts his love but does not communicate her doubts and displeasure to him.[23] Profoundly upset, he immediately writes Letter 8 (pp. 60–61) in which, after an elaborate and impeccably courtly affirmation of his love and fidelity, he adduces as the guarantee of the truth of his words the fact that from the beginning of their relationship, his love for Toute-Belle has generated all his poetic works: "toutes mes choses ont été faites de vostre sentement et pour vous especiaulment . . . car elles sont toutes de ceste matiere" (p. 61) [All my works have resulted from your love and have been composed especially for you . . . for they are all on this subject]. The lyric construct in which only love experience can appear as poetic subject matter is thus shown to be bivalent: the existence of the poetry authenticates the sincerity, the "truth" of the love, and vice versa. It is significant that the most explicit statement of this lyric process of reciprocal authorization involves Guillaume citing Machaut as *auctor* (though without identifying the citation): "je ne fis onques puis riens qui ne fust pour vous, car je ne say ne ne vueil faire de sentement d'autrui fors seulement dou mien et du vostre, pour ce que: Qui de sentement ne fait,— son dit et son chant contrefait" (p. 61) [Since then (i.e., the beginning of this relationship), everything I have produced is for you, for I do not know how, nor do I desire to make (poetry) out of the feelings of others, but only out of mine and yours, because: He who does not work according to his feelings counterfeits both his poetry and his music]. The self-quotation comes from the *Remede:* "Car qui de sentement ne fait, / Son ouevre et son chant contrefait" (vv. 407–8). It is thus the identity of Machaut the poète, author of the oeuvres complètes, that contains and authorizes that of Guillaume the narrator-protagonist of the *Voir-Dit*. The letter concludes with a restatement of Guillaume's identity as a lyric poet: his poetic production is generated by his love experience with Toute-Belle, who by withdrawing her love and trust can render Guillaume poetically impotent: "si tost comme je le saray, jamais par moi ne seront fais dis, loenges, ne lais, ne chans" (p. 61) [as soon as I should become aware of it, I would never (again) compose poetry, praises, lays, or music]. This self-presentation as a conventional lyric poet (whose song must coincide with his love experience only) serves to heighten the distinction between this lyric poet and Guillaume de Machaut the poète initially evoked in this letter by the process of self-quotation discussed above. In addition, the implicit presence of the poète figure here (as elsewhere in the *Voir-Dit*, especially in Part 1) works to undercut Guillaume's identity as lyric poet — to present him as a fictional construct almost from the beginning of the work. Indeed, one may speak of a progressive expansion of Guillaume's identity in this regard. As the *Voir-Dit* advances, Guillaume comes to *contain* the lyric stance that had defined the poet component of his identity at the beginning of the work; he seems increasingly to overlap with the figure of Machaut the poète (though the two can never become coequal).[24]

After Guillaume has tearfully completed his letter a messenger arrives bringing Toute-Belle's long-awaited ymage (p. 61) and a brief accompanying letter (Letter 9, p. 62), in which she reaffirms her trust in his love. Guillaume retires to his *chambre,* where, overjoyed, he unwraps the ymage and on seeing his dame's features for the first time names her Toute-Belle (v. 1363, p. 63).[25] The ymage quickly assumes the status of an icon as Guillaume goes through a miniature ceremony in which he combines feudal and religious vocabularies, swearing that he will always love, honor, and serve it faithfully.[26] Next, Guillaume hangs the ymage above his bed "com vrais serf et loiaus amis" (v. 1403, p. 64) [as a true servant and loyal lover]; he decorates it richly[27] and, comparing it to Venus, explains how it consoles and comforts him.

At this point (vv. 1455 ff.) Guillaume conceives the idea of taking advantage of a *pelerinage* he had earlier vowed to undertake in order to visit Toute-Belle (whose manoir is only two leagues from the pilgrimage place). A significant instance of textual self-consciousness is woven into the declaration of this intention as Guillaume (implicitly conflating love service with poetic service, as well as the je-protagonist with the je-narrator) refers to his beloved as she "Qui me fait parler et vivre, / Et faire pour s'amour ce livre" (vv. 1466–67, p. 66) [who makes me speak and live and write this book (i.e., the *Voir-Dit*) for love of her]. Before setting out on his journey Guillaume sends Toute-Belle elaborate thanks for the ymage (Letter 10, pp. 67–70), explaining that he regards the portrait as proof of her love in the face of his self-doubts about his role of amant. Even as he affirms his new amorous self-confidence, however, a consistent pattern of comic undercutting is evident: "Et comment que je sache certainement que plusieurs vous ont dit que je suis lais, rudes et mal gracieus, par Dieu, com petis que je soie, j'ay bien vaillant un cuer d'ami" (p. 68) [And although I know for certain that several people have told you that I am ugly, awkward, and graceless, by God, I have, little as I am, the valiant heart of a lover]. Guillaume, the clerc-poet turned courtly lover, proceeds to compare himself to a *chevalier*, who "ne doit avoir autre mestier n'autre science que armes, dames et conscience" (p. 68) [should have no profession or skill other than arms, ladies, and conscience]. The comic incongruity of this comparison becomes evident when Guillaume shows that he is thinking of literary chevaliers, swearing that he will serve Toute-Belle "comme Lancelos ne Tristans servirent onques leurs dames" (p. 68) [better than Lancelot or Tristan ever served their ladies]. Guillaume next announces that he will visit Toute-Belle at Pentecost, in the same breath excusing the delay with his fear of armed brigands ("une grant compaigne") who have made traveling very dangerous. Again his identity as courtly lover with chivalric pretensions seems to be undercut even as it is being established.

The same is not true for Guillaume's identity as poet, however, for here he consistently appears as successful. In exchange for Toute-Belle's ymage, Guillaume sends as his love token a copy of the *Fonteinne amoureuse*:[28] "Je vous envoie mon livre[29] de *Morpheus*, que on appelle la *Fonteinne amoureuse*, où j'ay fait un chant à vostre commandement" (p. 69) [I am sending you my book, *Morpheus*, which is called the *Amorous Fountain*, in which I have composed a song in accord with your command]. Guillaume's identity as professional writer, concerned with the business of patronage and the physical production of manuscripts containing his own works, is explicitly linked to his stance, his self-presentation as conventional lyric poet, within the context of the story line of the *Voir-Dit*. A significant expansion of the identity of the narrator-protagonist is thus effected. He explains to Toute-Belle that he would have brought an edition of his complete works, "mon livre . . . où toutes les choses sont que je fis onques: mais il est en plus de .XX. pieces; car je l'ay fait faire pour aucun de mes seigneures; si que je le fais noter, et pour ce il convient que il soit par pieces" (p. 69) [my book . . . in which are all the works I have ever written: but it is in more than twenty (separate) sections; for I have had (a copy) made for some of my lords, to which I am having music added and therefore (the book) is divided up).[30] Guillaume then goes on to promise Toute-Belle a redaction of his oeuvres complètes as soon as possible: "Et quand il sera notés, je le vous porteray ou envoieray, s'il plaist à Dieu" (p. 69) [And when the music is added, I will take it or send it to you, God willing]. At this point the identity of Guillaume the poet-narrator seems to overlap with that of Machaut the poète.

The second major narrative segment (pp. 70–163) treats the second phase of the relationship between Guillaume and Toute-Belle: the lovers together.

Throughout this segment Guillaume's inadequacy as a courtly lover will become increasingly evident. This portrayal is emphasized by a series of interventions on the part of Guillaume the narrator which attempt unconvincingly to justify the amorous conduct of Guillaume the protagonist, but consistently succeed in justifying the *Voir-Dit* as poetic artifact. In addition, the role of courtly lover as such is undercut in two important ways: first, an impression of comic exaggeration is created by the use of the amant couart topic (a lyric convention) as a behavioral model for Guillaume the protagonist in a sustained narrative context; second, fin'amors as code is systematically undermined on a number of levels. Guillaume's inadequacy as a lover seems to be contrasted with his consistent success as a poet. He is always able to make poetry out of his love experience — which seems increasingly to be presented qua poetic subject matter. Indeed, Guillaume's love experience seems to undergo a visible process of literarization as it is recounted (i.e., on the level of plot). The distinction between the narrator-protagonist's stance as conventional lyric poet and his "larger" identity as professional writer (here overlapping with the figure of Machaut the poète) only serves to make his poetic success (both the intercalated lyrics and the *Voir-Dit* as a whole) more striking.

The opening episode (pp. 70–120) deals with Guillaume's first visit to Toute-Belle and is framed by his novena. It begins as Guillaume journeys to the town where he had vowed to make his pilgrimage[31] and, as he enters the church, makes a second vow (conflating religious and amorous constructs) to write one new love poem for Toute-Belle every day of the novena. Toute-Belle replies to each one of Guillaume's poems, and a long exchange, a series of five paired lyrics, ensues.[32]

It is at this point (p. 75) that Guillaume receives a letter from Toute-Belle telling him to interrupt his novena and come to her immediately. It is interesting that Guillaume explicitly declines to include this letter in the text because it is too long, i.e., for compositional reasons:

> Je ne met pas icy sa lettre,
> Que ce seroit trop long à mettre
> De si petittes lettrelles,
> Jàsoit ce qu'elles soient belles.
> (vv. 1669–72)

[I am not including her letter here, because (the work) would be too long if such insignificant, though beautiful, letters were included in it.]

The story of the love experience of the je-protagonist is thus interrupted at a critical moment by the je-narrator in the process of compiling the *Voir-Dit*, the literary treatment of this love experience whose status as literary subject matter is thus emphasized. At the same time this self-conscious display of selectivity by Guillaume the poet-narrator provides an implicit guarantee for the independent existence of the letters, for the "truth" of the *Voir-Dit* as a whole.

Obedient to his dame's wishes, Guillaume sets out at once but suffers intensely from Ovidian love symptoms (p. 75). He is encouraged, somewhat humorously, by his *secretaire*, who tells Guillaume "qu'elle ne me morderoit pas" (v. 1665) [that she (Toute-Belle) would not bite (him)]. The playful undercutting of Guillaume's identity as courtly lover thus continues even as a new display of poetic virtuosity is about to unfold, for on the way to Toute-Belle's residence two more exchanges of paired lyrics take place. First there are two rondeaux (p. 76) with identical rhyme schemes and answering themes: "I obey your summons" and "Amis, come to me." Next, there are two virelais (pp. 77–78) whose rhymes correspond (though Toute-Belle's poem is shorter by two stanzas) as do their themes: "Though I have never seen you, yet I love you who have twice resuscitated me" and "I fell in love with you from having heard of your reputation." In effect, this concentration of lyric, strategically placed just before the lovers' first meeting serves as a recapitulation both of their immediate narrative situation and of the entire "love affair" from its inception.

After a final moment of hesitation during which he considers sending a substitute in his place, Guillaume arrives at last before his beloved (v. 1772, p. 79). Her beauty is described by means of the standard terminology of courtly rhetoric and she is thus initially presented as a kind of literary convention:

> . . . je vi sa contenence,
> Sa maniere, son bel acueil,
> Son dous vis et son riant oeil,
> Et sa coulour blanche et vermeille,
> Et son gent corps qui à merveille
> Estoit lons et droit et traitis,
> Envoisiés, cointes et faitis.
>
> (vv. 1773–79)

[I saw her countenance, her behavior, her warm welcome, her sweet face and her laughing eyes, her red and white complexion, and her noble body which was marvelously tall and straight and pleasing, gay, elegant, and well made].

After greeting Guillaume as her "dous ami" (v. 1782), Toute-Belle welcomes him with courteous words and takes him by the hand. Guillaume (whose behavior is regulated by the amant couart topic, i.e., who appears as a stock courtly literary character) is so overwhelmed by this treatment that he cannot speak, and Toute-Belle, aware of her lover's discomfiture, leads him away from her servants and followers into a vergier (p. 80), a conventional locus amoenus. The entire sequence of the lovers' first meeting thus appears as a self-conscious interweaving of standard literary topics from the courtly tradition.

As soon as the lovers are alone Toute-Belle (in a reversal of courtly convention) immediately takes the initiative and declares her love for Guillaume upon whom she bestows "tout mon cuer et m'onneur" (v. 1811) [all my heart and honor]. This is consistent with Toute-Belle's behavior throughout the *Voir-Dit* and functions (especially in this narrative segment) to undermine fin'amors as code.

Guillaume begins to tremble and is only able to reply "Tresbelle, vous estes ma dame, / Et je suis vos amis, par m'ame" (vv. 1840–41) [Most beautiful one, you are my lady and I am your lover, by my soul] before he is overwhelmed by tears. After Toute-Belle has comforted him, Guillaume humbly kisses her hand and departs in silence (v. 1864, p. 82). The lovers' first meeting is over.[33]

At this point (v. 1873) there is a sequence of intervention/commentary from the perspective of Guillaume the narrator (pp. 82–85), in which, after stating that Toute-Belle's age is between fifteen and twenty (v. 1912), he proceeds to defend his lady against any charges of being overly bold, then goes on to defend himself against possible charges of indiscretion:

> Ce n'est pas trop grant villenie,
> S'en ce livre riens mettre n'ose
> Qu'ainsi comme il est, et sans glose.
> Car contre son commandement
> Feroie du faire autrement:

Et, puisqu'il li plaist, il m'agrée,
S'obéiray à sa pensée.
(vv. 1937–43)

[It is not a low, base act for me to dare, in this book, to tell things as they
are, without gloss. For to do otherwise would be to go against her orders:
and because it pleases her, it pleases me; thus I will obey her thought.]

The strategic importance of this intervention (punctuating, as
it were, the narrative account of the lovers' first meeting) is twofold. On the one hand, it involves and emphasizes the intermingling of the love experience of Guillaume the protagonist — in the
past time of the narrative — and the making of the *Voir-Dit* — in
the present time of writing. On the other hand, it establishes a
configuration of reciprocal authentification between love experience (the matière) and poetic artifact (the *livre*): the "truth" of
one guarantees the "truth" of the other, and vice versa. This of
course functions as part of a larger program (see pp. 98–99 above)
in which the organization, style, and composition of the *Voir-Dit*
are presented as derived from, and authorized by, Toute-Belle's
"command," hence as guarantees for the authenticity of the poem's
subject matter. The self-proclaimed truth of the *Voir-Dit* would
then reside in the operation of a dialectic between its form and
its content — in the "working out" of the poem in its totality.

A return to the narrative line takes place on page 85 (vv. 1944 ff.)
as Guillaume returns to his *hostel*, and a debate ensues (pp. 85–
91) between Honte and Espoir with regard to the protagonist's
conduct during his first interview with Toute-Belle. Espoir ends
her final speech by predicting that Toute-Belle will soon send for
Guillaume and this prediction is almost immediately fulfilled as
Guillaume's secretaire brings him word that his dame wishes to
see him (vv. 2117 ff.). This effortless linking of personification
characters with "realistic" characters is extremely important for
an understanding of the "truthfulness" of the *Voir-Dit* and will
be much more extensively developed in the course of the work's
midpoint sequence.

Guillaume fearfully obeys Toute-Belle's summons, and the second meeting between the two lovers (pp. 91–97) begins as he re-

enters the vergier and becomes speechless when he attempts to greet her. Unable to cure his muteness by her words, Toute-Belle begins to sing a lyric poem ("Amis, amés de cuer d'amie" [p. 92] [Lover, loved by a lover's heart] to Guillaume who replies immediately with a rondeau ("Douce dame, je vous voy," p. 92) [Sweet lady, I see you] that he composes on the spot, expressing the Honte and Paour he feels in her presence. The rondeau then is generated by this moment in his narrative situation, his love experience. Toute-Belle replies in turn with a rondeau of her own ("Tres-dous amis, quant je vous voy" [p. 93] [Sweetest friend, when I see you]), which duplicates the rhyme scheme of Guillaume's rondeau and answers its theme. The lover and his dame thus in effect communicate by means of lyric poems at the moment of this second meeting (i.e., as part of the progression of the story line of the *Voir-Dit*). The love experience is poeticized as it happens, with an added emphasis given to the process (and to poetic discourse as such) by the fact that a highly stylized set of paired lyrics is used. This may be seen as signaling the implicit presence of Machaut the poète and it is thus the transformation of the love experience into lyric poetry that has been made into one of the principal themes of the *Voir-Dit*.

At this point (vv. 2223 ff.) the two lovers sit down side by side and Guillaume, eager to kiss his beloved, is tormented by Desir. In the shade of a cherry tree they have a long conversation: "Là, maintes paroles déismes / Que je ne vueil pas raconter, / Car trop long seroit à conter" (vv. 2254–56, p. 96) [There we spoke many a word that I do not want to recount, for it would be too long to tell (it all)]. The first-person lover-protagonist of line 2254 (situated in the time of the narrative) is effectively contrasted with the first-person poet-narrator of lines 2255–56 (situated in the time of writing). The latter is again (see pp. 107–8 above) characterized by an attitude of artistic selectivity that at once enhances his identity as compiler of the *Voir-Dit* as a whole (almost overlapping with Machaut the poète) and works to authenticate the subject matter.

When Toute-Belle falls asleep in Guillaume's lap, it is his secretaire who playfully manipulates him into kissing his dame for the first time.[34] Guillaume's behavior throughout this second meeting seems once again to contrast his success as a poet with his inadequacy as a lover.

Guillaume remains near Toute-Belle for eight full days, meeting her every day in the vergier. During what appears to be the last of these meetings a long exchange takes place between the lovers (pp. 98–107) when Toute-Belle, perceiving that Guillaume is pensive, asks what is troubling him. His long reply expresses the unhappy dilemma imposed on a lover by the code of fin'amors, according to which a true "amans" cannot openly express his love or request the favors of his dame but must manifest his feelings indirectly, hoping his lady will grant her love by *franchise:* "Car demander est villonnie, / Et loange est courtoisie" (vv. 2441–42) [For it is base to request and courteous to praise]. The fact that Guillaume verbalizes this dilemma to Toute-Belle undoes the very code he complains of. Finally, Guillaume concludes his speech by exhorting Toute-Belle not to proclaim her love for him in public. Toute-Belle responds to Guillaume's grievances in a way most calculated to encourage her timid and hesitating amant: she makes an explicit statement of her love for Guillaume and offers her "tresor" to him unreservedly. Once again it is Toute-Belle who has taken the initiative in the development of the love affair in what amounts to an inversion of the amant couart topic and a further subversion of the code of fin'amors as expressed by Guillaume. Toute-Belle concludes her speech by agreeing to stop calling him "amy" in public, but she explicitly affirms her desire that this relationship be made known.[35]

The time has now come for Guillaume to complete his novena, and he sets out on his journey back to the church (p. 108). As he travels he composes and sends to Toute-Belle a rondeau expressing his sadness at leaving her: "Sans cuer, dolens, de vous departiray" (p. 108) [Discouraged and sorrowing, I will leave you].[36] She responds with an answering rondeau: "Sans cuer de moy pas ne vous partirez" (p. 108) [You will not leave without my heart]. This pair of narratively "motivated" lyrics thus ends the first visit, balancing the pair on page 76, with which it had begun.

Guillaume soon arrives at his place of pilgrimage where he remains for nine days (pp. 108–20). During this time Toute-Belle comes to visit him briefly with a company of ladies. The two lovers hear Mass together and during the *Agnus Dei* Toute-Belle bestows a kiss[37] on her amant: "Doucement me donna la pais / Entre deux pilers du moustier" (vv. 2666–67, p. 110) [She sweetly gave me the kiss of peace between two pillars of the church]. Toute-Belle's departure, however, plunges Guillaume into an intense melancholy which motivates the exchange of two sets of letters (Letters 11–14, pp. 112–15, 118–20) as the novena draws to a close.

The next episode (pp. 120–39) opens with Guillaume's second visit to Toute-Belle and concludes with his visit to his patron, the duke of Normandy.

The episode begins as Guillaume, his novena completed, returns to Toute-Belle's residence. Her warm welcome dissipates his melancholy and restores him to a state of perfect contentment. At this point the story line is interrupted by a long passage of commentary (vv. 2947–3026, pp. 125–28) from the perspective of Guillaume the narrator. He begins by stating that the gifts of love constitute an inexhaustible treasure that is not diminished by being distributed, then he goes on to affirm the necessity of loving "tel dame . . . / Qui puet garir les maus d'amer" (vv. 2955–56) [a woman who can cure the sufferings of love]. There follows a condemnation, from a general perspective, of false and dishonorable lovers which leads to a "personal" declaration by Guillaume (vv. 3016 ff., still speaking qua poet-narrator) of his scrupulously honorable intentions and his desire to serve women without requesting or expecting any reward:

> Endroit de moy, je vueil tels estre
> Qu'elles seront de moi chieries,
> Sans penser maus ne tricheries;
> Et tous mes jours les serviray
> Et leur loenge adés diray.
> Et feray chose qui leur plaise
> A mon pooir, cui qu'il desplaise,
> Sans salaire et sans guerredon.
> Ne jà n'en quier requerre don,
> En l'onneur de la gracieuse
> Que j'aim de pensée amoureuse.
> (vv. 3016–26)

[For my part, I want to cherish them (ladies), without wicked thoughts or deceitfulness; and I will always serve them and speak their praises. And to the best of my ability, I will do things that please them, no matter who else is displeased by this, without salary or reward. In honor of the gracious lady whom I love with amorous thoughts, I never want to demand payment (for my service).]

We have here a presentation in which poetic service is both equated with love service and valorized as a self-sufficient endeavor detached from the success or failure of a particular love experience. This presentation resembles what Douglas Kelly calls the "sublimation of courtly love,"[38] but it exists here in a context where the primary concern is with poetic production rather than with amorous doctrine for its own sake.

An explicit return to the story line (which of course recounts the love experience of Guillaume the protagonist) is justified in terms of the wishes of Guillaume's lady, and thus the *Voir-Dit* appears as a particular case of the general precept given above, by which love service is conflated with poetic service:

Or vous diray ce qui m'avint,
Et à quel chief cest amour vint;
Car ma douce dame le vuet;
Quant il lui plaist, faire l'estuet.
(vv. 3033–36)

[Now I will tell you what happened to me and what became of this love; for my sweet lady desires this; what pleases her must be done.]

After spending three days with Toute-Belle, Guillaume sets off to visit one of his most illustrious patrons, Charles, duke of Normandy, and dauphin of France, who receives him with great honor. His two-week stay at Charles's court (pp. 131–39) may, however, be seen as a period in which Guillaume's identity as a professional writer impinges on his identity as lover. To reassure himself of Toute-Belle's affection and to give vent to his doubts and amorous suffering, Guillaume sends her Letter 17 (pp. 133–34) in which, as so often in the *Voir-Dit*, the different aspects of the narrator-protagonist's identity are visible as such. First, Guillaume speaks as lover, sadly telling Toute-Belle how much he looks forward to their next meeting and requesting her to make the necessary arrangements and receive him lovingly. Second, Guillaume speaks as poet, complaining that his lyric production has been impaired by the demands of court life: "Je ne vous envoie rien de Rondelet, car il ha tant de gent à ceste court, et de noise, et tant m'i annoie que je y puis po faire de nouvel" (p. 134) [I am not sending you any rondeaux because there are so many people at court here and so much bustle and I am so harassed that I am able to do very little new work]. Nevertheless he does mention that he is working on the *Voir-Dit*: "Toutesvoies, je fais adès en vostre livre ce que je puis" (p. 134) [However, I am constantly working on your book as much as I can]. This is the first time the process of the making of the *Voir-Dit* has been mentioned in one of the letters — i.e., situated within the time of the narrative itself. This is of great significance since from this point on, the story of the love experience becomes at the same time the story of the book (i.e, the *Voir-Dit*). The full implications of this construct will be worked out only in Part 2 of the poem, where the initial *décalage* established here between time of writing and time of the narrative becomes progressively smaller, and the actual making of the *Voir-Dit* becomes one of the poem's major themes.

Toute-Belle replies almost immediately with Letter 18 (p. 135) in which she assures Guillaume that she will act in accord with his wishes in every respect. The circumstances in which Guillaume the protagonist receives the letter are exploited by Guillaume the narrator to make what amounts to a profession of political faith in the present tense in which the narrator seems to be speaking with the voice of Machaut the poète:

> Je reçus ceste lettre cy
> Droit en la ville de Crecy.
> Là fu le duc de Normendie,
> Mon droit Signeur, quoy que nuls die.
> Car fais suis de sa nourriture,
> Et suis sa droite créature.[39]
>
> (vv. 3151–56)

[I received this letter while in the town of Crécy. The duke of Normandy was there — he is my true lord, no matter what anyone says. For he raised me and I am his devoted servant.]

Toute-Belle's letter cures Guillaume of his "maladie amoureuse" (v. 3161) and brings him to a state of complete happiness ("plaisance pure," v. 3168). In this condition the lover-protagonist meditates on his dame's beauty and goodness, reaching a "conclusion" (v. 3175) that takes the form of a clerkly *sententia:*

> . . . on doit prisier les choses belles,
> Seulement plus pour le bien d'elles,
> Qu'on ne fait pour nulle autre chose
> Qui soit, dehors ou ens, enclose.
>
> (vv. 3177–80)

[Beautiful things should be valued for their inherent good, much more than for any other external or internal feature.]

Guillaume the narrator now intervenes (using the present of the time of writing) to comment on the sententia of Guillaume the protagonist by adducing a series of illustrative examples that serve to demonstrate the validity of the statement (pp. 137–39). Speaking from a general perspective and in a clerkly mode, Guillaume considers in turn a *destrier,* a chevalier, and a dame, concluding as follows:

> Pour ce, di veritablement
> Que li sage communement
> Aiment les gens pour leur bonté,
> Assez plus que pour leur biauté.
> Car grant biauté est une grace
> Des menres que nature face.
>
> (vv. 3221–26)

[Thus I truly say that wise men generally value people for their goodness much more than for their beauty. For great beauty is one of Nature's least important gifts.]

This impersonal, clerkly precept is immediately used by Guillaume the protagonist to defend this love of Toute-Belle against possible critics (the clerkly side of Guillaume's identity in Part 1 of the *Voir-Dit* consistently being subordinated to his identity as poet-lover):

> Dont se je l'aim et belle et bonne,
> (Et chascuns bons ce nom li donne,)
> On ne me doit mie reprendre,
> Se de fin cuer l'aim sans mesprendre.
> (vv. 3227–30)

[Thus if I love Toute-Belle who is both beautiful and good (and everyone agrees on her goodness), I should not be reproached, if I love purely, with a true heart.]

What we have here then is a defense of the very premise on which the *Voir-Dit* as a whole rests — that Toute-Belle is worthy of being loved and that Guillaume's love service is both honorable and praiseworthy. There are, however, two "levels" to this defense. On the one hand, there is an (unconvincing) justification of Guillaume — a non-aristocratic clerc — playing the (for him) inappropriate role of courtly lover in an affair that will end in failure (as Part 2 of the *Voir-Dit* recounts). On the other hand, the equation of love service with poetic service enables Guillaume qua poet (convincingly) to present the affair as a success: "Et j'en acquier et los et pris, / Si je l'aim, ser et loe et pris" (vv. 3230–31) [If I love, serve, praise, and value her, I acquire renown and esteem]. The return to the story line (vv. 3247 ff.) emphasizes the dependence of the professional writer on his patron and thus the limitations imposed by Guillaume's "complete" identity on his role as lover. Excited by Toute-Belle's letter, Guillaume wishes to return to her at once, but "Monseigneur me fist attendre / Contre mon gré .III. jours ou quatre" (vv. 3254–55, p. 139) [My lord made me wait three or four days against my will]. It is only at the duke's pleasure ("par *son* gré," v. 3257, emphasis added) that Guillaume (richly rewarded, it should be noted) is finally permitted to depart.

The final episode (pp. 140–63) of the second major narrative segment recounts Guillaume's third visit to Toute-Belle and ends with the lovers' final farewell. It opens as the newly reunited lovers set out together on a pilgrimage journey, accompanied by Toute-Belle's sister and her cousin, Guillemette. The party quickly reaches

Saint-Denis, the goal of their pilgrimage, where they visit the Lendit
Fair and accomplish their pilgrims' vows.[40] Next, they proceed
to an inn at the town of La Chapelle ("à quelques kilomètres de
Paris"[41]) where, after they dine, Toute-Belle expresses an intense
desire to sleep. Since there are no beds at the inn this poses a
problem which is quickly resolved in a mildly comic and strikingly non-courtly fashion. A drunken and accommodating *ser-
gent d'armes*, having overheard Toute-Belle's wish, offers to lead
the party to the nearby house of "un villain" who has a spare bedroom which he puts at the disposal of strangers. This offer is enthusiastically accepted, the four travelers are taken to the house,
and Toute-Belle's sister immediately goes to sleep on one of the
two beds. Toute-Belle invites Guillaume to lie between herself and
Guillemette on the other, and when the timid lover attempts to
refuse, his dame takes him by the hand and forces him to join
her. Toute-Belle then falls asleep while Guillaume lies next to her
in the darkened room not daring to move until at last she awakens
and commands him to embrace her:

> "Amis, estes-vous cy?
> Acolés-moy séurement."
> Et je le fis couardement,
> . . . S'estoie com cils qui se baigne
> En flun de paradis terrestre.[42]
>   (vv. 3484–86, 3492–93)

["Are you there, beloved? Embrace me boldly." And I did it timidly. . . .
and it was like bathing in the river of the Earthly Paradise.]

Once again it is Toute-Belle who has taken the initiative in advancing the "experiential" aspect of the love affair.

The final stage (pp. 149–51) of the pilgrimage journey begins
as Guillaume and his companions are awakened by the singing
of a group of friends who lead them off to an elegant supper party
followed by poetry and music which continue late into the night
until finally the ladies are conducted back to their houses (presumably in Paris).[43]

During the seven days immediately following, Guillaume remains near Toute-Belle's residence (in or near Paris) and his happi-

ness is complete. When the time for his departure finally arrives (vv. 3646 ff.) he goes "moult humblement" [very humbly] to take his leave of Toute-Belle who, moved by his visible grief, bids him to come to her early the following morning so she can say goodbye to him in private "et non pas cy, devant la gent" (v. 3666) [and not here in front of people].

The account of this final early morning meeting [44] between the lovers (pp. 154–63) begins as Guillaume, in obedience to Toute-Belle's "commandement," arrives at dawn (in a variation on the *aubade* situation) and awakens his dame by opening her window. As he softly calls to her, Toute-Belle "par sa grant courtoisie" (v. 3689) [through her great courtesy] turns to reveal her naked body to him then calms his fears by assuring him that no one will interrupt them. Guillaume is struck by his dame's beauty which is described in a brief and highly conventionalized *blason* reminiscent of the courtly rhetoric of the *Voir-Dit*'s first description of Toute-Belle (see pp. 108–9 above). There is thus a literarization of Toute-Belle as love object precisely at the moment of greatest intensity of the "personal" love experience:

> . . . je vi sa couleur vermeille,
> Et sa biauté qui n'a pareille,
> Son dous vis, sa riant bouchette,
> Douce plaisant et vermillette,
> Et sa gorge polie et tendre.
> (vv. 3704–8)

[I saw her rosy coloring and her unparalleled beauty, her sweet face, her laughing little mouth — deliciously sweet and red — and her smooth, soft breasts.]

Guillaume now falls to his knees and addresses a prayer to Venus in the form of a lyric poem (vv. 3712–59, pp. 155–57), asking for her help as one who has always served her loyally. Venus immediately answers Guillaume's prayer, descends into the bedroom and conceals the lovers in a fragrant cloud.[45] The results of Venus's visit are described as follows:

> Et là fist miracles ouvertes,
> Si clerement et si appertes

Que de joie fui raemplis,
Et mes desirs fu acomplis:
Si bien que plus ne demandoie
Ne riens plus je ne desiroie.
                    (vv. 3770–75)

[(Venus) enacted visible miracles there, so clearly and openly that I was filled with joy and my desire was realized so well that I neither requested nor desired anything more.]

Before the goddess departs Guillaume composes a celebratory virelai ("Onques si bonne journée" [pp. 159–60] [Never such a good day]) in which he sings of how Venus has completely satisfied him — enriching him with Soufissance and Plaisance, decapitating his enemy Dangier, but not injuring Honneur.[46] Even at the high point of Guillaume's experience as lover it is his identity as poet that is stressed. The love experience is, as it were, transformed into poetry before the reader's eyes and, as throughout the *Voir-Dit*, it is this process of transformation that is thematized and valorized.

After Venus departs (v. 3842), the lovers are amazed ("esbahis" and "estahis," repeated twice as paired rhyme words, once in the masculine, once in the feminine, vv. 3845–48). In two complementary speeches first Guillaume (vv. 3851–66), then Toute-Belle (vv. 3867–78) bear witness to the miraculous event that has just occurred; they guarantee its "truthfulness" within the context of the *Voir-Dit*. Each of the lovers affirms having seen all that has transpired, an indication of the fundamentally poetic (as opposed to historico-biographic) "truth" of the *Voir-Dit*'s matière.

Their common "experience" with Venus seems to serve as the ultimate proof of their love, and they proceed to exchange stylized vows of eternal fidelity sealed by a ceremonial embrace which is reflected in and, as it were, confirmed by verbal patterning — the annominatio of vv. 3883–86:

Adont la belle m'acola,
Et mis son bras à mon col ha,
Et je de .II. bras l'acolay,
Et mis son autre à mon col ay.

[Then the beautiful lady embraced me and put her arm around my neck and I embraced her with both arms and put her other arm around my neck.]

The final stage of this elaborate farewell involves an exchange of love tokens (the third since the beginning of the affair). First Toute-Belle presents Guillaume with the golden "clef de mon tresor" (v. 3891) [key to my treasure] or "m'onneur" (v. 3895) [my honor], of which she proclaims her lover lord ("seigneur," v. 3892).[47] Guillaume gives his beloved a ring and then takes his leave (v. 3903, p. 162). The lovers' final meeting — and the high point of their love affair — is over. Guillaume and Toute-Belle will not see each other again in the course of the *Voir-Dit*. The linear progression of the narrative structure in Part 1 has reached its culmination.

The episode closes with a final intervention on the part of Guillaume the narrator addressed to possible critics (and employing commented tenses exclusively). Toute-Belle's express command is once again invoked by Guillaume simultaneously as a guarantee of the "truth" of what he has told and as a justification for his manner of telling it. This construct is further exploited to demonstrate that there is by definition nothing dishonorable either in the events of the story or in Guillaume's act of poetic narration:

> Et se j'ay dit ou trop ou pau,
> Pas ne mespren; car, par saint Pau,
> Ma dame vuelt qu'ainsi le face,
> Sus peine de perdre sa grace.
> Et bien vuet que chascuns le sache,
> Puis qu'il n'i ha vice ne tache:
> Et se le contraire y héust
> Elle bien taire s'en scéust,
> Et au celer bien li aidaisse;
> Car par ma foy bien le celaisse.
> (vv. 3909–18)

[And if I have said either too much or too little, I have not done wrong; for, by Saint Pau, my lady wants me to do just this, under pain of losing her favor. And she wants everyone to know this, because it involves neither vice or fault: and if the contrary were true, she would certainly know how to be quiet about it and I would certainly help her to conceal it, for by my faith, I would conceal it well.]

The last couplet of the intervention is a particularly significant example of textual self-consciousness: "Jà vous ay ceste chose ditte, / Mais ne m'en chaut se c'est reditte" (vv. 3919–20) [I have already told you all this, but I do not care if it is repetitious]. Not only is the entire preceding intervention/commentary thus presented (by virtue of its being repetitious) as existing within the context of the literary artifact that is the *Voir-Dit*, but this repetitiousness itself functions to guarantee the "truth" of the poem's matière, in accord with the *Voir-Dit's* explicit program of self-authentification (see especially vv. 422–29 and pp. 98–99, 110–11 above).

Le Voir-Dit: Midpoint Sequence

The midpoint sequence of the *Voir-Dit* (pp. 163–83; f. 256^r–260^v in MS *A* where the *Voir-Dit* begins on f. 221^r and ends on 306^r) functions simultaneously as a transition between the poem's two major parts and as a means of linking them together. It is in this sequence that the question of the *Voir-Dit's* "truthfulness" is treated most elaborately. As we shall see, this treatment is closely linked to the complex relationship between Guillaume the narrator and Machaut the poète.

The midpoint sequence begins as Guillaume, having parted from Toute-Belle, starts his journey home, full of confidence and unafraid of the historically real brigands[48] liable to be encountered on the trip from Paris to Reims. At this point (vv. 3961 ff.) he has an aventure: a noble dame (with a "belle et bonne compagnie") [handsome and noble entourage] appears before him, accosts him by name, declares that he is her prisoner, and accuses him of having wronged her: "vous m'avez griefment meffait" (v. 3987, p. 168) [you have grievously wronged me].

A scene of extraordinary (and playful) textual self-consciousness now ensues, for the dame who has captured Guillaume is Esperence and her troop is composed of four other personification characters: Mesure, Attemprance, Bon-avis, and Confort-d'ami. Referring to earlier sections of the *Voir-Dit* (i.e., the narrative segments in which esperence qua emotional state has played a role),[49] Lady

Esperence reminds Guillaume that she has consistently helped him against his enemies Honte and Desir. Her complaint is addressed simultaneously to Guillaume the protagonist (situated in the past time of the narrative) and to Guillaume the narrator (situated in the present time of writing): "tu n'as encor de moy dit / Rien d'especial en ton dit, / Ne rendu graces ne loenge" (vv. 4015–17) [You have not yet said anything special about me in your poem, (the *Voir-Dit* itself) nor have you given (me) thanks and praise.]

Guillaume readily admits that he is in the wrong and thanks Esperence for all her past favors. When Bon-avis suggests that Guillaume be made to pay an *amende*, Confort-d'ami proposes that this payment be in the form of a lyric poem:

> Ma dame, je los vraiement,
> Que vous le mettés à renson,
> Et qu'il en paie une chanson,
> Rondel, balade ou virelay.
> (vv. 4056–59)

[My lady, I advise you to hold him for ransom and to have him pay it with a song, a rondeau, a ballade, or a virelay.]

Esperance accepts this proposal, choosing the most difficult of the formes fixes:

> . . . "Je vueil un lay
> Apellé: le 'Lay d'Esperance'
> Et par ce li feray quittance:
> Si se partira franchement
> Sans plus avoir d'empeschement."
> (vv. 4060–64)

[I want a lay entitled: the Lay of Hope—for this I will absolve him and he will leave freely, without hindrance.]

After Guillaume agrees to this arrangement he is released (v. 4074, p. 170) and continues on his journey. A brief "realistic" episode is now effortlessly linked to the encounter with personification characters: Guillaume's small party sights a band of highwaymen ("pilleurs") from whom it flees, reaching Reims safely at last (v. 4093, p. 171).

As soon as Guillaume is secure in his *chambrette* his fear of the pilleurs vanishes (somewhat comically), and he immediately sets to work on his poetic ransom:

> Si qu'ainsi mon lay commensay.
> Quant il fu fais, je le tramis
> Si com je l'avoie promis;
> Et tout ainsi comme dit ay
> Vers Esperance m'acquitay.
> (vv. 4101–5, p. 171)

[Thus I began my lay, and when it was finished I sent it off, just as I had promised; and so I acquitted myself vis-à-vis Hope exactly as I have said.]

The "Lay d'Esperance" (pp. 172–80) which follows is a tour de force on the part of Machaut the poète and the only example of this form in the entire *Voir-Dit*. The lay begins by linking Guillaume's love experience with his poetic productivity in a manner reminiscent of the opening scenes of the *Voir-Dit*. The first six stanzas recount the birth of love in terms of courtly conventions: Desir and Esperance are the two *darts* shot from the dame's eyes into the heart of the poet-lover, who desires nothing except to serve his beloved. The final six stanzas celebrate the triumph of Espoir over Desir, a triumph which enables the poet-lover to achieve a state of perfect and self-sufficient contentment, since his love (and love service) do not depend on his lady's favors.

The first-person love experience that forms the matière of the "Lay d'Esperance" thus seems to epitomize what Douglas Kelly terms Machaut's "sublimation" of fin'amors, in that Desire is replaced by Hope and merci becomes a "secondary consideration."[50] However, the sublimation of the first-person poet-narrator of the lay contrasts markedly with the love experience of the first-person poet-narrator of the *Voir-Dit* as a whole, who has requested his lady's favors, received merci, and continues to be subject to Desir. This contrast functions to differentiate Guillaume the poet-narrator from Machaut the poète and to present the lay as the product of the latter. What results is an increased emphasis on Guillaume's status as a literary construct (one permutation of the expanded lyric je of Machaut the poète) and on the presentation of the love experience as primarily poetic subject matter.

As soon as the lay is finished, Guillaume has it and its musical accompaniment sent to Toute-Belle, enclosed with Letter 21 (pp. 180–82). This letter is of special importance because it retells the story of Guillaume's capture by Esperence in narrative prose (in part, a gloss on and "explanation" of the lay). This is done in great detail with substantial quotations in the letter from the direct speeches of the various characters involved in the preceding narrative verse section of the capture episode, including the speeches of Guillaume himself. It concludes with an elaborate restatement of the lyric-poem-as-amende construct in a textually self-conscious context which stresses the *Voir-Dit* qua literary artifact as the poetic system in which both the intercalated lyric and the narrative episode function: "de ce que en ce livre ne avoie riens fait d'especial chose qui feist à conter pour li, je féisse un lay appellé Lay d'Esperance" (p. 182) [(It was decided that) I compose a lay entitled the Lay of Hope, because I had not included in this book (*Voir-Dit*) any piece devoted especially to her (Esperence)]. Guillaume ends his letter by presenting the enclosed lyric poem to Toute-Belle: "n'ay mestier d'Esperance se n'est pour vous" (p. 182) [I have no need of Hope but for you].

Toute-Belle replies promptly with Letter 22 (pp. 182–83) in which she expresses her relief and joy that Guillaume has returned home safely in spite of the dangers and "aventures" (p. 182) that he experienced in the course of his journey. Thus she does not seem to regard the troop of pilleurs and the troop of Esperance as being qualitatively different.

The entire midpoint sequence has significant implications for the self-avowed "truthfulness" of the *Voir-Dit* as a whole — implications which are given a special emphasis by the fact that the sequence is situated near the structurally significant midpoint of the work.

First, the story of Guillaume's capture by Esperence — the most striking personification character episode of the *Voir-Dit* — is effortlessly integrated into the poem's "truthful" discourse. This is accomplished in several different ways. To begin with, the first time the capture episode is told (in narrative verse) it is linked to the historically real archpriest Arnaud de Cervoles, and exactly the same tone is used to speak of the "real" bandit(s) and the "fictional" personification characters. Further, the capture episode is retold in the narrative prose of Guillaume's letter, which serves to confirm its status as a "true" narrative event. (This effect is reinforced by Toute-Belle's similar treatment of the capture episode in her letter of response.) Finally, the "Lay d'Esperance" is presented as, in part, an authentification of the "truth" of the capture episode. By implication, then, the Esperence episode is as "true" as Guillaume's narrow escape from the historically real archpriest and his pilleurs, or as true as the "realistic" narration of his love affair with Toute-Belle. This implied equivalence of veracity makes perfect sense if one understands the "truth" of the *Voir-Dit* to be the "poetic truthfulness" of a literary artifact.

Second, the entire capture episode calls attention to the presence of Machaut the poète, thus emphasizing the *Voir-Dit*'s status as one among many of his poetic creations. This is effected by implicit references to certain of Machaut's earlier dits whose constructs are here reworked. On the one hand, there is the *Remede,* in which Esperence had helped the first-person poet-narrator in a love situation (and had also revealed her identity at the midpoint). There is also the *Jugement dou roy de Navarre,* in which the first-person poet-narrator was captured by a female personification character who accused him of having committed a meffait, and in which his amende involved the composition of a lay.[51]

The "truthfulness" of the *Voir-Dit* thus resides not in its historico-biographic accuracy, but in its existence as poetic artifact.

Le Voir-Dit: Part 2

Part 2 of the *Voir-Dit* (pp. 183–370) may be seen as falling into two major narrative segments which treat, in turn, the two cycles of contentment-estrangement-reconciliation in the lovers' relationship once their long-term separation has begun. Both this cyclical structure as such and the construct of reconciliation *in absentia* work programmatically to undermine the "experiential component" of the love affair. At the same time, the book progressively replaces (and displaces) experiential amorous fulfillment as the

goal of, and justification for, Guillaume's love service: throughout Part 2 the making of the *Voir-Dit* itself is explicitly and elaborately thematized. A corresponding shift occurs in the self-
presentation of the narrator-protagonist. Guillaume's increasingly
visible failure as a courtly lover is linked to a progressive expansion of the clerkly side of his identity: what is an impediment
to Guillaume the lover is a necessity to Guillaume the writer.

On the one hand, therefore, Part 2 problematizes the apparently successful resolution of Guillaume's love experience effected
in Part 1. The tensions and contradictions inherent in the earlier
depiction of the professional clerk-poet as *fin'amant* are here explicitly treated as such.[52] On the other hand, however, Part 2 effects a new and more valid resolution on what are, in effect, the
only terms possible: those deriving from Machaut's global identity as poète.

In this context, the cyclical narrative structure of Part 2 takes
on special importance, for it replaces and "corrects" the linear structure (linked to the *gradus amoris*) of Part 1. The necessity for
a detailed analysis of narrative patterning in Part 2 is underscored
by the tendency of earlier critics to ignore or deny this aspect
of the work.[53]

The progressive redefinition of Guillaume's status as lover begins almost at once in the first major narrative segment (pp. 183–
280) of Part 2. The initial episode (pp. 183–212), which covers
the period (summer, 1363; see note 8 above) of regular correspondence between the lovers following Guillaume's return to Reims,
opens as he finds himself once again tormented by Desir who de-
feats Esperance (v. 4399). Thus the victory of Esperence celebrated
in Guillaume's lay is not permanent, but, rather, the love experience of the *Voir-Dit*'s protagonist is shown to involve a kind
of continual Desir/Esperence dialectic. What is significant is that
Guillaume the protagonist can successfully make poetry out of
any stage, any aspect of this love experience. This is illustrated
in the passage under consideration by the fact that the suffering
Guillaume experiences as a result of Desir immediately leads him
to compose a complainte: a letter in verse (Letter 23, pp. 184–85)
which is an example of technical virtuosity insistently calling at-

tention to itself as patterned language: fifty lines with the same rhyme, with every other line being the refrain: "Mon cuer, ma suer, ma douce amour" [My heart, my sister, my sweet love].

Guillaume's next letter (Letter 25, pp. 189–92) opens the extensive discussion of the making of the *Voir-Dit* that characterizes this entire episode. It is significant that this discussion begins by focusing on Guillaume's identity as professional poet, intensely concerned with the business of patronage. He first explains to Toute-Belle that the story of their love is known to "pluseurs grans signeurs" [several great lords] who have requested and received from Guillaume several of the *Voir-Dit's* lyric pieces: "pluseurs de vos choses et de miennes" [several of your pieces and mine]. Next he recounts that he showed Toute-Belle's ymage to his patrons' messengers by way of guaranteeing the "verité" of the narrative content of the *Voir-Dit*, which he also communicated to his noble clients. It is only at this point that Guillaume announces that he is hard at work on the book we are in the process of reading: "me suis remis à faire vostre livre, enquel vous serés loée et honnourée de mon petit pooir"[54] (p. 191) [I have once again set to work on your book in which you will be praised and honored to the best of my small ability]. This is only the second explicit mention of the composition of the *Voir-Dit* and once again (see Letter 17 and pp. 114–15 above) it is the context of the work's extradiegetic courtly audience that seems to be the determining factor. The thematization of the making of the *Voir-Dit* introduced in Part 2 by the present passage is thus from the outset linked to a programmatic inscription of the work's readers. On the one hand, this incorporation into the unfolding story line of an extratextual public knowledge of the *Voir-Dit's* matière functions as an authentification device. On the other hand, the status of the *Voir-Dit* (and the love affair it "recounts") as literary artifact, necessarily intended for a specific audience, is foregrounded.

In her reply (Letter 26, pp. 193–95), Toute-Belle gives emphatic expression to her pleasure at the fact that the story of their love has become public knowledge: "car je vueil bien que Dieu et tout le monde sache que je vous aime" (p. 193) [for I want God and man to know that I love you]. This reaction is linked to her sense of the importance of the *Voir-Dit* itself: "ay grant joie de ce que vous estes remis à faire nostre livre, car j'ay plus chier que vous le faciés que autre chose" (p. 194) [I am overjoyed that you have once again set to work on our book, for I would rather have you do that than anything else].

Guillaume's response to Toute-Belle's letter involves the most elaborate manifestation of the clerkly component of his identity in the *Voir-Dit* up to this point and marks the beginning of a pattern that will continue throughout Part 2, where Guillaume is increasingly portrayed as a clerc-poet. Having read carefully Letter 26, Guillaume thinks of his dame and is led to a learned comparison: "Et certes quant bien l' ymagine, / Je la compere à la roÿne / Qu'on appelloit Semiramis" (vv. 4567–69) [And truly, when I think of (Toute-Belle) I compare her to the queen called Semiramis]. An example of clerkly sapience in the service of love (a lyricization of clerkliness) now follows as the comparison of Toute-Belle to Semiramis is elaborately worked out (pp. 196–201) in two parts. First (vv. 4575–638, pp. 196–98), an exemplum — the Semiramis narrative — is recounted, after a bookish authority is adduced in good clerkly fashion: "Valerius Maximus conte / Et se dit ainsi en son conte" (vv. 4573–74) [Valerius Maximus recounts it, and in his account he tells it in the following way]. Next (vv. 4639–726, pp. 198–201), this Semiramis narrative is treated as the model for a miniature retelling of Guillaume's love experience in terms of personification characters, introduced by the comparison between Semiramis and Toute-Belle: a rebellion is led by Desir and Merencolie who extinguish the lantern of Espoir; Toute-Belle, like Semiramis, acts immediately on hearing the news (i.e., on receiving Guillaume's letter), puts down the rebellion, and reinstates Esperence.

Letter 27 (pp. 201–4) announces a new phase in the story of the composition of the *Voir-Dit* — the composition itself thus assuming a more dominant thematic role. Speaking qua professional poet, Guillaume explains how "Vostres livres se fait et est bien avanciés; car j'en fais tous les jours .c. vers" (p. 202) [Work continues on your book and it is already well advanced because I compose one hundred lines per day]. A compositional difficulty has arisen, however: "j'ay trop à faire à querir les lettres qui respondent les unes aus autres. Si vous pri qu'en toutes les lettres que vous m'envoierés d'ores-en-avant, il y ait date" (pp. 202–3) [It is too much for me to discover which letters correspond to which. From now on, therefore, please date all the letters that you send me]. This statement/request seems to imply that any disorder in the arrangement of the letters[55] functions (along with repetitions in the text, supposed indiscretions, etc.) to authenticate the "truth" of the *Voir-Dit*'s subject matter and thus as part of the work's program of self-authentification (cf. note 8, above). In addition, it seems to imply that the initial décalage between the time of writing and the time of the narrative has been largely overcome. The love experience is henceforth to be transmitted into poetry — into the Book — almost as it takes place.[56] Guillaume's letter is dated August 8 (presumably 1363).[57]

Toute-Belle promptly responds by sending her amant the "love relics" he had requested in an earlier letter: a rosary and a clasp that she has worn. Her accompanying letter (Letter 28, pp. 206–8) is dated "le diemenche devant la mi-aoust" [the Sunday before mid-August].

Having received "reliques" (v. 4817) from his "dieu terrein" (v. 4820), Guillaume now proceeds to "adore" (v. 4818) them — wearing them close to his heart and deriving great pleasure and strength from them. This experience (involving once again the use of religious terminology in a secular amorous context) leads Guillaume to make a second extended clerkly comparison, structured in essentially the same format as the Semiramis sequence. First we have a clerkly narration (vv. 4837–57): the story of how Hebe, the goddess of youth, rejuvenated the aged Iolaus.[58] Next (vv. 4858–77), this clerkly bookishness is lyricized — made into a metaphor for Guillaume's personal love experience: Toute-Belle has made him young again.

Given the dynamics of the love experience in Part 2, this apparent high point is necessarily followed by the episode (pp. 211–60) recounting the first break in the lovers' correspondence and their subsequent estrangement. Over two months elapse, during which Guillaume hears nothing from his dame and finally, tormented by Desir (v. 4911), falls prey to a deep melancholy and begins to doubt that he is still loved. Obsessed by the thought that Toute-Belle's feelings toward him have changed, Guillaume falls asleep and has a dream (vv. 4934–5467, pp. 213–32). This is the first in a series of two long dreams in Part 2 of the *Voir-Dit* and involves a considerable expansion of Guillaume's identity both as clerc and as poet. In addition, it develops the presence of Machaut the poète in a subtle and complex way. The dream begins as Guillaume sees Toute-Belle's ymage turn its face away from him and dress in green (signifying a change of heart).[59] Greatly upset by this incident, Guillaume (the protagonist of his own dream) flees the unfavorable ymage[60] and arrives at "une place" (v. 4963) where a noble company is playing the game entitled "le Roi qui ne ment" (v. 4979) [the king who does not lie], in which questions are put to a player called the king (here, Charles, duke of Normandy and dauphin — the same patron visited earlier by Guillaume in "real life"; see pp. 114–17 above) who must answer them truthfully. After waiting his turn Guillaume is allowed to participate, and the rest of the dream is taken up by his exchange with the king.

First comes Guillaume's long "question" (pp. 215–24): a direct speech in which he alternates general political advice with a request for help in his "personal" love affair. In effect, what we have in this speech is Machaut the poète visibly shifting from one stance (that of authoritative adviser, as used in the *Confort d'ami*) to another (that of the lover-protagonist of the *Voir-Dit*) — all the while maintaining a first-person context: a set of permutations of the lyric je made possible by Machaut's identity as poète and functioning to signal his presence in the text.

Guillaume begins his direct address to the king with a series of general political precepts delivered in the clerkly style of the *Miroirs des princes* (but with an implicitly lyric authority). A shift then occurs as Guillaume recounts his love problem (his "maus d'amour" [v. 5125]) to the king, explaining that he has not heard from his dame in almost nine weeks, that he has begun to doubt her love, and that her portrait has turned away from him and changed its dress from blue to green. Guillaume then returns to the subject of politics, dealing at length with the disastrous condition of contemporary France devastated by war, taxes, brigands, and plague. Finally, Guillaume shifts again to the "personal" perspective of a courtly lover, contrasting the kingdom's public calamities with his private amorous suffering, which for him is much more important. He concludes by requesting the king's advice.

The king's reply (pp. 224–32) evinces a high degree of playful textual self-consciousness and a refined clerkliness, both of which may be seen as manifestations of Machaut the poète. His initial treatment of Guillaume's amorous difficulties involves a presentation of the entire dream as a fictional construct, a literary convention. First, he tells Guillaume that the changes he has observed in Toute-Belle's ymage are only part of a dream and therefore should not be taken seriously: "Et si m'est avis que tu songes. / On ne doit pas croire les songes" (vv. 5274–75) [It seems to me that you are dreaming. And dreams should not be believed]. We are confronted with a playfully paradoxical configuration: a dream which advises that dreams are not to be believed as an interpretation of, a gloss on, a dream. The king therefore advises the dreamer-protagonist to wake up and reexamine the ymage, asserting that if any change has really occurred, Guillaume would be more surprised and afraid than if he had seen one of the metamorphoses recounted by Ovid (v. 5289). To elaborate this point, the king recounts two examples of metamorphoses ("mutations"): first, the story of Lot's wife, for which Josephus is twice (vv. 5292, 5324) cited as auctor; second, the story of Perseus and the head of Medusa, for which Ovid (v. 5342) is cited as auctor. Next, the king shows that his is a courtly clerkliness (not at all the traditionally misogynistic variety) by reproving Guillaume for his reaction to Toute-Belle's silence and by adducing several possible explanations for this state of affairs. Finally, the king gives a long, learned list of the great inventors and sages of antiquity, then concludes by saying that all these wise men together could not help Guillaume, and that therefore: "Si te convient à ce venir / Que laisses Amours convenir" (vv. 5456–57) [You should leave it at this: let Love take care of things]. The king thus seems to regard the question of Guillaume's amorous success or failure as a matter of no importance, advising him simply to continue to love. This final response to Guillaume's request for advice causes all of the king's courtiers to laugh since, as is usual in the *Voir-Dit*, Guillaume as lover has made himself ridiculous. It is at this point (v. 5467, p. 232) that the dreamer awakens, immediately examines the ymage, and finds that it has not changed. Guillaume's final assessment of his dream places it in a purely literary context by means of a textual reminiscence of the opening lines of the *Rose* (which may be seen as a sign of Machaut the poète): "Car clerement vi que mon songe / N'avoit riens de vray fors mensonge" (vv. 5484–85) [For I clearly saw that my dream contained no truth, but only lies]. Further, this assessment is undermined even as it is made, for only the very first part of the dream (in which the metamorphosed ymage appeared) was a "lie"; the rest (Guillaume's speech and the king's advice) must be viewed as "true" in the context of the *Voir-Dit's* story line. In other words, the dream (which was "false ") contained its own gloss (which was "true").

Almost immediately after Guillaume awakens, a messenger arrives bringing him the long-awaited letter from Toute-Belle (Letter 29, pp. 233–36) which begins with an account of her recent travels that serves as an implicit excuse for her long delay in writing. She goes on to reaffirm her love for Guillaume, instructing him not to be melancholy or to doubt her. Finally, she renews her request that he send her lyric poetry and music as well as the copy of the *Voir-Dit* itself ("vostre livre," p. 235) that he had promised her.

Although pleased by Toute-Belle's message, Guillaume wants her to know that her long silence has made him suffer. He therefore sends her two letters at the same time. The first (Letter 30, pp. 238–39) had been written before the arrival of Toute-Belle's long-awaited epistle and, under the heading "longue demourée fait changier amy" [a long delay makes a lover change] gives full expression to Guillaume's self-doubt, melancholy, and despair. The second letter (Letter 31, pp. 239–42) is Guillaume's reply to the letter (Letter 29) he has just received from Toute-Belle and presents a full account of his behavior over the preceding two months. First he tells how his sadness over Toute-Belle's long silence interfered with the composition of the *Voir-Dit*: "je fui tellement blecié en l'esprit que je laissay de tous poins l'ouvrer en vostre livre" (p. 240) [My spirit was so wounded that I completely abandoned work on your book]. Next he recounts his dream concerning Toute-Belle's ymage, which, since it has just provided extensive (and largely non-amorous) subject matter for the *Voir-Dit*, serves to undercut Guillaume's "lyric" claim of recent poetic sterility. Guillaume then proceeds to describe his present condition qua lover, in which his intense desire to see Toute-Belle is mingled with lingering doubts about her love. Guillaume's current situation qua poet is, by contrast, remarkably positive especially with regard to the *Voir-Dit*: "Je suis si enbesongnez de faire vostre livre que je ne puis à rien entendre. Et sachiez que je en fais autant .III. fois comme tient *Morpheus*. . . . Et en ay plus fait depuis la Magdeleine que je ne cuidoie faire en un an entier" (pp. 241–42) [I am so busy working on your book that I can attend to nothing else. And you should know that it is already three times as long as *Morpheus* (i.e., the *Fonteinne amoureuse*). . . . And I have done more on it since Saint Madelaine's Day than I thought I could do in a full year]. After a brief consideration of the feasibility of sending Toute-Belle a copy of what he has written so far, Guillaume informs her that he is returning various poems and letters (presumably his own) because they have now been incorporated into the text of the *Voir-Dit*: "car tout est mis par ordre dedens vostre livre" (p. 242) [for all is put into order in your book]. The thematization of the making of the *Voir-Dit* thus becomes increasingly elaborate and explicit as the work advances.

Toute-Belle's reaction on receiving Guillaume's two letters (p. 242) continues, on the level of plot, the literarization of the love experience implicit in this thematization of the composition of the *Voir-Dit*. First she manifests conventional Ovidian love symptoms, then she gives expression to her feelings in an elaborate *complainte* ("Dous amis, que t'ay-je meffait?" [vv. 5546–734, pp. 242–48] [Sweet friend, how have I wronged you?] The thematic content of this intercalated lyric is relatively simple: Toute-Belle claims that her love for Guillaume is unchanged and that he makes her suffer by his doubts and unfair accusations. However the *complainte*'s technical complexity[61] as well as its extensive clerkly references[62] emphasizes its status as the product of Machaut the *poète*. This moment of emotional intensity in the love experience of the character Toute-Belle is thus made to appear simultaneously as a moment in the literary experience of the poet-author.

As soon as Guillaume receives Toute-Belle's complainte, he realizes that he has wronged her within the context of courtly convention: "Mesfait ay, si l'amenderay" (v. 5770) [I have wronged her; thus, I will make amends]. As was the case with Esperence, Guillaume's amende once again takes the form of a lyric poem that has a precise narrative function. In his complainte (vv. 5774–906, pp. 252–56) Guillaume, speaking qua lover, requests Toute-Belle's pardon for his meffait and swears himself to her service. At the same time the complainte's status as a poetic artifact independent of its immediate narrative context is emphasized both by its numerous clerkly references to classical and vernacular literature[63] and by its technical virtuosity, which is explicitly noted in the text:

> Vescy la response de fait
> Que j'ay à sa complainte fait.
> Mais nulle rime n'y ay prise
> Qui soit à la sienne comprise;
> Et si n'est mie de tel mettre.
> (vv. 5935–39)

[Here is the actual response I made to her complainte. But I did not use a single rhyme from her poem, nor did I employ the same verse form.]

Guillaume encloses his complainte in a letter to Toute-Belle (Letter 33, pp. 257–59) in which he begins by speaking qua lover: after assuring his dame of his love and devotion he begs her to pardon him declaring: "je me suis cent fois repenti des lettres que je vous envoiay" (p. 258) [I have repented one hundred times for the letters I sent you]. For the remainder of his letter, Guillaume speaks qua professional poet, describing how his time has been entirely occupied by his work on the *Voir-Dit* and by the demands of his patrons: "j'ay esté si enbesongnés de faire vostre livre et suis encores, et aussi des gens du Roy, et de monseigneur le duc de Bar qui a géu en ma maison, que je n'ay peu entendre à autre chose" (p. 259) [I have been, and still am, so busy working on your book and also with the king's men and with my lord the duke of Bar who stayed in my house, that I have been able to attend to nothing else]. Next, he informs Toute-Belle that he will soon be sending her the (necessarily) incomplete manuscript of the *Voir-Dit* and requests that she revise what he has written: "je vous envoieray bien tost et par certain messaige ce qui est fait de vostre livre. . . . et se il y a aucune chose à corrigier, [je vous pry] que vous y faites enseignes. Car il vous a pleu que je y mette tout nostre fait, si ne scay se je y met ou trop ou po" (p. 259) [I will soon send you by a reliable messenger what I have thus far completed of your book. . . . Please indicate if there is anything to correct. For you wanted me to treat our whole story and I do not know whether I have put down too much or too little]. Within the context of the story line, then, the two lovers are portrayed as literary collaborators on the *Voir-Dit* itself. Finally, we have what amounts to a thematization of the codex, as Guillaume explains to Toute-Belle that he wants the *Voir-Dit*, when completed, to form part of the manuscript of his oeuvres complètes. The je of Guillaume the narrator-protagonist and the je of Machaut the poète seem here to be conflated: "Quant vous arez vostre livre, si le gardez chierement, car je n'en ay nulle copie et je seroie courrecié s'il estoit perdu et se il n'estoit ou livre ou je met toutes mes choses" (p. 259) [When you receive your book, be very careful with it, for I have no other copy and I would be angry if it were lost and thus not included in the master copy of my complete works].[64]

In her letter of reply (Letter 34, p. 260) Toute-Belle pardons Guillaume for his meffait and requests that he send her the *Voir-Dit* manuscript by return messenger. The lovers' first period of estrangement has thus ended with a reconciliation, which is directly linked to their mutual involvement with the composition of the Book.

This partial displacement of the love experience by its literary treatment is elaborated in the following episode (pp. 261–80) in which the central activity of the newly reconciled lovers is their collaboration on the *Voir-Dit* during October and November of 1363. The episode opens as Guillaume sends Toute-Belle his copy of the *Voir-Dit*[65] accompanied by Letter 35 (pp. 262–66), which begins an important discussion concerning the process of the composition of the work. First Guillaume, speaking as poet, expresses his desire to complete the *Voir-Dit*, revealing his conception of what the remainder of the work will contain: "le me vueillez renvoier, quant vous l'arez leu, par quoy je le puisse parfaire. . . . Ores vient le fort et les belles et subtives fictions dont je le pense à parfaire, parquoy, vous et li autre le voiez volentiers, et qu'il en soit bon memoire à toujours-mes" (pp. 262–63) [Please send it (the *Voir-Dit*) back to me when you have read it, so that I can finish it. . . . Now the end is approaching as are the beautiful, subtle fictions with which I plan to complete (the work) so that you and others will be pleased with it and it will always be well remembered]. It is significant that Guillaume's use of the word "fictions" to characterize the remaining subject matter of the *Voir-Dit* is followed by an elaborate presentation of the work as "truth." Invoking the name of the as-yet-uncompleted work ("vostre livre avera nom le *Livre dou Voir dit;* si, ne vueil ne ne doy mentir" [p. 263] [Your book will be entitled the Book of the True Story; therefore, I should not, and do not want to, lie in it]), Guillaume requests Toute-Belle's permission to express his amorous suffering (as well as his joy) in order to give a "truthful" portrait of his "sentement." The *Voir-Dit*'s subject matter is thus presented as "fiction" and "truth" simultaneously.[66] This point receives further elaboration as Guillaume goes on to describe his "present" love experience in terms of personification characters deriving from the *Rose* in a visible and explicit process of literarization: Raison has informed Guillaume that Dangier has a key to Toute-Belle's tresor and that Malebouche is ready to sound the alarm if the treasure is opened. The poet-lover's only hope thus lies in Toute-Belle herself, who holds in her hands "ma mort et ma vie, mon deduit et ma joie, ma doleur et ma santé" (p. 265) [my death and my life, my delight and my joy, my suffering and my gaiety].

Guillaume's diegetic naming of the *Voir-Dit*, addressed to Toute-Belle (cf. pp. 98–99 above, for the extradiegetic naming of the work, addressed to the reader) seems to authorize the diegetic naming of Toute-Belle herself: enclosed with Letter 35 (along with the Book) is a rondeau ("Dis et sept, V, XIII, et XV," pp. 266–67) [ten and seven, five, thirteen, and fifteen] in which Toute-Belle's "true" name, Péronne, (see n. 25 above) is encoded.

Toute-Belle's prompt reply (Letter 36, pp. 267–68) begins by acknowledging her receipt of the *Voir-Dit* manuscript, then goes on to grant Guillaume permission to "complaindre de voz doleurs" [complain of your sufferings] provided that he also give expression to his "reconfort et bonne esperance" [comfort and good hope]. Next, Toute-Belle promises to help Guillaume against Dangier and Malebouche, thus carrying his literary characterization of their love experience one step further by suggesting, in a self-conscious transformation of the subtext, that the Rose will herself act to aid Amant. Toute-Belle ends her letter with an explicit indication of how she is actively involved with the composition of the *Voir-Dit*: "Je vous envoie la darreniere lettre que vous m'envoiastes, pour ce que vous le m'aviez mandé; mais je ne vous envoie pas vostre livre pour ce que je ne l'ay encores leu. Mais quant je l'aray leu, je le vous envoieray" (p. 268) [I am sending you the last letter you sent me, because you requested it (for inclusion in the *Voir-Dit*); but I am not sending your book because I have not yet read it. But when I have read it, I will send it to you].

Guillaume is initially pleased by Toute-Belle's letter, but Desir (v. 6023) soon begins to torment him again with the thought that he must find a way to see his beloved. This leads to a brief meditation by Guillaume the narrator on the nature of love:

> Amour et Desir, ce me semble,
> D'une laisse courent ensemble:
> Et quant li desirs amenrit,
> Cuers qui faussement aime en rit,
> Et cuers qui aime loyaument,
> En pleure; car certainement
> L'un ou l'autre convient acroistre,
> Entre les mondains et en cloistre.
> Et de tel piet et de tel dance
> Com li uns va, li autre dance.[67]
>   (vv. 6035–44)

[Love and Desire, it seems to me, are linked together: when desire diminishes, the false heart laughs and the faithful heart cries; for one or the other must certainly increase among the secular and the religious. And as the one goes, so goes the other.]

Next, there is a return to the time of the narrative as Desir causes Guillaume[68] to "complaindre" (v. 6045) in a particularly clerkly manner. A series of six exempla are evoked: lovers who overcame great difficulty to see their beloved. (These are with one exception all literary figures: Pyramus and Thisbe, Leander, Lancelot, Pierre Tousac, Paris and Helen, and the Chastelaine de Vergi.)

However, not only is Guillaume unable to find any help for his own situation in these "examples" (v. 6103), but he ends by drawing a general lesson from them that seems most unfavorable for his future prospects as lover:

> . . . s'à un en voy bien chéoir,
> J'en voy à .XII. meschéoir. . . .
> Car c'est uns grans perils, par m'ame,
> De trop ou po véir sa dame.[69]
> (vv. 6705–6, 2709–10, p. 273)

[If I saw things work out well for one, I saw things work out badly for twelve. . . . For, by my soul, it is very dangerous to see one's lady either too much or too little.]

Guillaume therefore decides to write Toute-Belle in order to ask for her advice on the matter. It is important to note that he encloses with this letter (which represents in a particularly striking manner his ineffectiveness as a lover) a most dramatic demonstration of his success as a poet, in which his identity overlaps with that of Machaut the poète in a particularly explicit way. We have the results of a "poetic contest": a set of two ballades (pp. 274–76) on the same refrain ("Je voy assez puis que je voy ma dame") [I see enough because I see my lady] employing the same meter and rhyme scheme. The rules of the contest are such that the second contestant's reply cannot utilize any of the rhyme words found in the first poem. The initial ballade is by one Thibaut Paien[70] and the second is preceded in manuscript A by the superscription "Response. G. de machaut": the only time Machaut's name appears in the Voir-Dit. It is as if the poète figure temporarily "lends" his powers and virtuosity to Guillaume the lover, for not only does the second ballade appear to win the contest in spite of more difficult technical requirements, but Machaut lays special stress on the excellence of the musical settings he has written for both ballades.[71]

Guillaume's accompanying letter to Toute-Belle (Letter 37, pp. 276–78) continues the thematization of the making of the Voir-Dit, stressing the lovers' collaboration on the work: "je vous pri que vous gardez bien mon livre, et que vous le monstrez à miens

de gens que vous pourrez. Et s'il y a aucune chose qui vous des-
plaise, ou qui vous semble qui ne soit mie bien, si y faites un
signet et je l'osteray et amenderay à mon povoir" (pp. 276–77)
[Please be careful with my book and show it to as few people
as you can. And indicate anything that displeases you or that
you think badly done, and I will remove or revise it as well as
I can]. Toute-Belle responds almost immediately (Letter 38, pp.
279–80) by declaring that she has read the *Voir-Dit* through twice,
is very pleased with it, and at their next meeting "je vous diray
aucune chose dont il amendera" (p. 279) [I will tell you something
to be revised]. This elaborate construct of a poetic work which
describes its own construction continues to function as part of
the *Voir-Dit*'s self-authorization program to guarantee the work's
"truthfulness."

The final major narrative segment (pp. 280–370) treats the second cycle of contentment-estrangement-reconciliation in the lovers' relationship. Throughout this segment Guillaume's failure as
a lover is contrasted with his success as a poet in an increasingly
dramatic fashion. At the same time, the presence of Machaut the
poète becomes more and more visible.

The opening episode (pp. 280–308) recounts how the arrangements for Guillaume's projected journey to Toute-Belle are thwarted
through the intervention of a series of losengiers. It begins at what
appears to be a new high point in the lovers' relationship, initiated, as is usual in the *Voir-Dit*, by Toute-Belle. Having changed
her residence for the express purpose of being able to see Guillaume more easily, Toute-Belle sends her amant Letter 39 (pp.
281–82, dated November 13 [1363]) urging him to visit her as soon
as possible. She claims to have "emprisonné" Dangier and Malebouche, then goes on to give Guillaume detailed instructions on
how to arrange a secret meeting and ends by promising that "à
mon povoir, le tresor sera deffermez avant qu'il soit nulle nouvelle de vostre venue" (pp. 281–82) [to the best of my ability, the
treasure will be opened before there is any news of your coming].
This is her solution to the problem of "amer long" [loving from
afar] articulated by Guillaume in his two preceding letters. There
is, I think, the suggestion that Toute-Belle is prompted to arrange

this second visit as a result of her having just read the account of the first visit in the copy of the *Voir-Dit* that Guillaume had sent to her. This implicit configuration will serve to emphasize the inadequacy of Part 1 as a model for Part 2.

Joyful and excited by Toute-Belle's letter, Guillaume is prepared to set out at once and sends for his absent secretary, the date of whose arrival is explicitly noted: "Ce fu droit ou mois de novembre .XXVIII. jours, bien m'en remembre" (vv. 6874–75, p. 283) [It was well into the month of November — the twenty-eighth, as I well remember]. The latter, however, refuses to accompany his master on the proposed journey even though Toute-Belle had explicitly requested his presence.[72] When Guillaume asks the reason for this unexpected refusal, the secretary replies in a long and clerkly speech (pp. 284–95) carefully organized into four sections: first, the presentation of the argument; next, the illustration of the argument by means of two Ovidian exempla; finally, the conclusion. Both the highly rhetorical structure and the clerkly content of this speech may be seen as signs of the presence of Machaut the poète.

The first section of the speech (pp. 284–86) involves an implicit undercutting of Guillaume's identity as lover, an almost systematic demonstration of his unsuitability for this role, as the secretary enumerates the three ways in which the proposed journey to Toute-Belle would be dangerous for Guillaume. First, the roads are teeming with armed bands and if Guillaume is captured he will die: "Car vous estes un tenres homs" (v. 6940) [For you are a delicate man]. Second, an exceptionally violent windstorm is raging,[73] which along with the normally harsh weather of early winter would be dangerous for a man of Guillaume's age. Finally, Guillaume's bad health makes him unfit to travel. The secretary therefore refuses to undertake a journey that would place Guillaume "en peril de vostre vie" (v. 6981) [in danger of your life].

The second section of the speech (pp. 286–89) involves the expansion of a rhetorical figure by means of an Ovidian narrative. The secretary first reinforces his initial argument by proclaiming that not even Circe could protect Guillaume from the dangers he would encounter by making the proposed journey: "Le vent, le froit et les compaignes" [The wind, the cold, and the brigands].

Next (vv. 7004–61, pp. 287–89), there is an intercalated clerkly narrative to illustrate Circe's power: the story of Picus and Canens.[74]

The third section of the speech (pp. 289–95) employs the same
format as the second and involves an even more elaborate display
of artful clerkliness. The secretary again employs an Ovidian exemplum to reinforce his initial argument, proclaiming that the
giant Polyphemus would treat Guillaume better than "li pilleur
. . . li frois, li vens qui vente" (vv. 7227, 7230, p. 295) [the pillag-
ers . . . the cold (and) the wind that is blowing] that he would
encounter on his journey. A terrifying description of the giant
is followed by a brief account of his love for Galatea and the killing of Acis. Next comes a narrative account of the blinding of
Polyphemus by Ulysses which is followed by a rendition of the
giant's love song to Galatea.[75]

The secretary concludes his speech (p. 295) by advising Guillaume to give up the idea of visiting his beloved and to write her
a letter instead.

Guillaume disapproves of his secretary's advice and a lively
disagreement ensues, which is interrupted by the arrival of "uns
sires" (v. 7266, p. 296) who declares that he also would like to
dissuade Guillaume from making the projected visit to Toute-Belle.
He begins by establishing his clerkly authority in matters of love
with an elaborate description and gloss of the ancients' "image
d'Amour" (v. 7301) [image of Love]. The sires then proceeds to
criticize Toute-Belle's behavior, claiming that she has several "intimate friends" who visit her often, that she indiscreetly shows
Guillaume's letters everywhere, and that she calls Guillaume "amy"
simply from courtoisie, not from love: "Dont ce n'est qu'une
moquerie, / Et po y a qui ne s'en rie" (vv. 7426–27, p. 301) [This is
nothing but a mockery and there are few who do not laugh at it].

Profoundly upset by the speech of the sires (who may be seen
as the first losengier), Guillaume remembers a recent letter from
"uns miens amis" (v. 7470, p. 303) [one of my friends, i.e., the
second losengier] who had advised him to give up his love for
Toute-Belle, stressing its inappropriateness for the clerc-poet. Putting these two testimonies together, Guillaume concludes that there
must be some truth in them but he retains enough composure
to reply to the sires that he needs further confirmation of the other's

statements and that he does not want to act in haste or to show ingratitude, given the great favors Toute-Belle has bestowed on him. Guillaume goes on to present himself in terms of the lyric love poet stance, claiming that if he withdraws his love from Toute-Belle he will become poetically unproductive (vv. 7536–41). In fact, throughout the final major narrative segment, Guillaume's identity as lyric love poet will be systematically undermined by the contrast between his claims of poetic sterility in this capacity and the poetic fact of the continuing composition of the *Voir-Dit*. This process of poetic composition is thus implicitly presented as being derived from Machaut the poète and author figure, with whom Guillaume the poet-narrator (in contradistinction to Guillaume the lover-protagonist) here overlaps to some degree.

A series of three additional losengiers (numbers 3, 4, and 5) now follow in quick succession. The third losengier is described by Guillaume as "uns miens amis especiaus" (v. 7572, p. 306) [a special friend of mine] who informs the poet-lover that he has a rival for Toute-Belle's love who will defeat him. The fourth losengier is none other than the duke of Normandy himself, who greets Guillaume by laughing at him in public, saying: "Amis, vous batez les buissons / Dont autres ont les oisillons"[76] (vv. 7586–87, p. 307) [Friend, you are beating the bushes, but others are catching the birds]. Even as he walks down the street Guillaume is mocked by "chascuns" (v. 7603, p. 307, a kind of anonymous collective losengier, the fifth in the series that approaches Guillaume) because of his relationship with Toute-Belle.

Once again Guillaume has been made to appear ridiculous in the role of courtly lover:

> Ains chascuns me rigoloit,
> Pour ce que ma dame voloit
> Que nos amours fussent chantées
> Par les rues, et flajolées;
> Et que chascuns appercéust
> Qu'elle m'amoit et le scéust.
> (vv. 7606–11, pp. 307–8)

[Thus everyone was making fun of me because my lady wanted our love to be sung and blabbed in the streets; and for everyone to see and know that she loved me.]

The next episode (pp. 308–41) treats the period of estrangement between the lovers that follows Guillaume's exposure to the losengiers. It is characterized by a greatly increased prominence of the clerkly side of Guillaume's identity, which is coordinated with the systematic undercutting of his identity as lover: to the extent that Guillaume believes the reports of the losengiers, the would-be courtly amant is transformed into a non-courtly *jaloux*. This process of transformation may be viewed as an innovative exploitation of certain generic conventions of the grand chant courtois and of courtly romance (where the amant and the jaloux are normally found only in complementary distribution, as it were) effected by Machaut the poète to create yet another self-consciously literary permutation of his expanded lyric je.

The episode opens "droit en mois de novembre" (v. 7616) [well into the month of November] (a non-courtly and non-lyrical season) as Guillaume, profoundly upset by what he has heard about Toute-Belle, decides not only that he will not visit her but that he will not write to her. He even goes so far as to remove Toute-Belle's ymage from the wall and lock it up in a "coffre" (v. 7631, p. 308), before going on to compose a ballade in which he repents of his love. The refrain of this ballade ("Qu'en lieu de bleu, dame, vous vestez vert" [p. 309] [In place of blue, lady, you dress in green]) strategically recalls the lovers' first estrangement in Part 2 where Guillaume's doubts about Toute-Belle (prompted, we remember, not by losengiers, but by a break in the correspondence) were epitomized by his fear that "En lieu de bleu ne vestit vert" (v. 4929, p. 213) [In place of blue (she) dressed in green]. This phrase in the third person and in a sequence of narrated tenses is here, as it were, rewritten in the second person (reinforced by the vocative) and a commented tense. Not only has the speech situation been transformed, but we have shifted from narrative verse to forme fixe. What is here being foregrounded is thus the fact that Guillaume's non-courtly *jalousie* has generated a lyric poem.

Shortly after this "transformed" lyric moment, he receives a letter (Letter 40, pp. 310–12) from Toute-Belle in which she reproaches him for his long silence[77] and accuses him of having ceased to love her, adding that he does so unjustly, since she has always been faithful to him. Next, after declaring that Guillaume has made her suffer greatly, she begs him not to abandon her and not to believe the reports of the losengiers. She concludes her letter with a reaffirmation of her love for Guillaume and a plea that he write to her by return messenger.

After receiving Toute-Belle's letter, Guillaume decides to send her a deceptive reply, explaining his strategy in two direct addresses to the reader (pp. 313, 315). In Letter 41 (pp. 313–15), Guillaume thus conceals both the rumors he has heard about Toute-Belle and his own emotional state, pretending that all is well.[78] After thanking her profusely for having arranged for him to visit her, he promises to come as soon as possible. An exploitation of the contrasting perspectives of narrator/reader and protagonist/ beloved (inherent in the *Voir-Dit's* format of prose letters intercalated in narrative verse, see n. 20, above) thus functions to present the immediate product of Guillaume the protagonist's love experience (i.e., Letter 41) as "false" in itself but "true" in the context of the *Voir-Dit* as a whole. After finishing his deceptively cheerful letter, Guillaume, profoundly melancholy, goes to sleep and has a dream.

This dream (vv. 7719–8160, pp. 315–30, the second in a series of two long dreams in Part 2 of the *Voir-Dit*) involves an elaborate and playful deployment of clerkliness in a way which emphasizes both the presence of Machaut the poète and the *Voir-Dit's* status as literary artifact, as fiction. The dream begins as Toute-Belle's ymage, weeping and sighing, appears before Guillaume and reproaches him for his recent behavior.[79] First, he has unjustly put her (the ymage) into the coffre when she should not be blamed for Toute-Belle's alleged misconduct. Second, Guillaume has unjustly believed the gossip about Toute-Belle and condemned her without allowing her to defend herself. The ymage therefore advises Guillaume to tell Toute-Belle all and to hear her explanation, rather than to listen to the tales ("mensonges et frivoles" [v. 7766] [untrue and frivolous]) of the mesdisans: "c'est grans pechiés de si tost croire, / Et plus grans dou dire" (vv. 7769–70, p. 317) [it is a great sin to believe (slander) so quickly, and a greater one to speak it].

In order to "prove" her point, the ymage proceeds to recount an Ovidian exemplum which constitutes by far the longest section of the dream (pp. 317–28): the story of how the crow became black. The narrative[80] may be summarized briefly as follows. The Corbiaus, originally a beautiful white bird, one day witnessed Coronis, Apollo's beloved amie, in the act of "adultery" and hastened to inform the god. The Corneille attempted to dissuade him from his intention, asserting that "Tous voirs ne sont pas biaus à dire" (v. 7833, p. 319) [All truth is not good to say]. To illustrate still further the argument that "Souvent meschiet de dire voir" (v. 7847, p. 320) [It is often a calamity to speak the truth], the Corneille recounts the (intercalated) story of her own banishment by Pallas (pp. 320–24). The Corbiaus, however, remains unconvinced by this advice and proceeds to tell Apollo the truth about Coronis. No sooner has the enraged god killed his unfaithful amie, than he repents, and, blaming the Corbiaus's gossip ("mauvaise janglerie" [v. 8095]) for his misfortune, he punishes the bird by changing its feathers from white to black. The ymage, who has cited clerkly authority ("mon livre," [v. 8084]) for her Ovidian narrative, ends by presenting it as a lesson for Guillaume: he should not believe the words of Toute-Belle's detractors or he will kill her with grief and then repent—let him remember the example of Apollo. This use of the exemplum has playfully ambiguous, if not deeply ironic, overtones for it implies that the rumors about Toute-Belle (like the Corbiaus's report of Coronis's misbehavior) are true—but still should not be believed. Once again, the "truth" dealt with in the Voir-Dit is shown to be a function of its status as poetic artifact. The ymage concludes by cursing all mesdisans (those "qui amour ainsi deffont / Par faus et par mauvais rappors" [vv. 8138–39, p. 329] [who destroy love with false and wicked stories]) and by demanding to be restored to her former place of honor.

It is at this point (v. 8160, p. 330) that Guillaume awakens, amazed at having "oÿ parler image" (v. 8166, p. 330) [heard a portrait speak]—for the entire dream has in fact been composed of the long direct speech of the ymage. A brief "explanation" follows in which the dream is presented, in retrospect, as a literary construct emanating from Machaut the poète, a kind of variation in miniature of the Fonteinne amoureuse:

> Que di-je? elle ne parla mie,
> Car Morphéus, par grant maistrie,
> Prist de l'image la figure,
> Et à mon lit, de nuit obscure
> Où je songeoie moult forment,
> Vint et me dist, en mon dormant,
> La requeste et la complainte
> De l'image qui estoit painte.
>
> (vv. 8167–74, p. 331)

[What am I saying? She (the portrait) did not speak, for Morpheus, through his great power, took on the appearance of the portrait and came during the dark night to my bed where I was dreaming very soundly. He came while I was sleeping and told me the request and the complaint of the painted portrait.]

As if to make sure we get the point, the link with the earlier work is finally made explicit in a way which presents Machaut as a kind of vernacular auctor: "Qui ne scet qui est Morphéus . . . Lise L'amoureuse fonteine, / Si le sara à po de peine" (vv. 8175, 8177–88, p. 331) [If anyone does not know who Morpheus is . . . let him read the Amorous Fountain and he will know with little trouble].

After this preliminary consideration of the import of his dream, Guillaume takes the ymage out of the coffre and replaces it on the wall (p. 331). However, further contemplation of the story of the Corbiaus in light of his own situation leads him to curse Amour and Fortune for what he views as Toute-Belle's lack of fidelity.[81]

What follows (pp. 333–39) involves the clerkly aspect of Guillaume's identity exploited in a distinctly non-courtly fashion to poeticize his jalousie (thus, a reversal of the process employed by Guillaume qua courtly clerc for the narratives of Semiramis and Hebe, cf. pp. 129–30 above). Once again Guillaume appears to have failed as a lover (adopting the outlook and diction of a clerkly misogynist) but remains successful as a poet. Seeking relief from his love melancholy, Guillaume turns to the books of the auctores Fulgencius and Titus-Lyvius (vv. 8235–36), discovering in the latter an elaborate description of the "image" of Fortune,[82] a summary of which now ensues: the matrons of ancient Rome represented the goddess Fortune as a beautiful woman[83] enclosed by a large circle, with two smaller circles on her right and two more on her left—each of the five circles bearing a Latin inscription.

After pondering this description in light of his doubts about Toute-Belle, Guillaume proceeds to make an elaborate comparison between his dame and Fortune. This comparison (pp. 336–39) involves a series of five "responses" to each of the five inscriptions on Fortune's circles: the general maxims concerning Fortune's character and behavior are applied to the particular case of Guillaume and Toute-Belle. Each of these responses ends with a couplet: "S'il est voirs ce qu'on m'en a dit / Autrement, ne di-je en mon dit" [If what one said to me about it is true—otherwise, I would say nothing of the sort in my poem], as does the conclusion of the comparison:

> Or est ma dame comparée
> A Fortune la forsenée,
> Car bien pevent aler ensemble;
> Pour ce qu'à Fortune ressemble,
> En cas de variableté
> Où il n'a point d'estableté.
> Car vraiement elle se mue
> Si com fait espreviers en mue.
>   (vv. 8381–88, p. 338)

[Thus is my lady compared to mad Fortune, for they well belong together; because she resembles Fortune with regard to variability (having no stability). For, indeed, she transforms herself like a molting sparrow hawk.]

A further non-courtly comparison (seemingly suggested by the mention of the "espreviers" in v. 8388) serves to conclude this episode and to reemphasize Guillaume's failure as lover. He first (pp. 339–40) describes the training techniques employed by a count of his acquaintance to correct the aberrant behavior exhibited by falcons after molting. Guillaume goes on (pp. 340–41) to compare Toute-Belle's behavior to that of the raptor and to propose that he attempt to "correct" his dame by using a method analogous to that of the falconer. This is of course highly reminiscent of the *Alerion* and may, I think, be taken as an implicit intertextual reference to the earlier work, signaling the presence of Machaut (author figure for the oeuvres complètes), whose poetic success would thus be contrasted with Guillaume's amorous failure at this point in the narrative.

The final episode (pp. 341–70) of the *Voir-Dit* treats the resumption of the lovers' correspondence and their final reconciliation.

The episode begins as Guillaume, unable to bear his amorous melancholy any longer, decides to write to Toute-Belle "courtoisement," i.e., without openly reproaching her and mentioning only one of the rumors he has heard concerning her. He thus sends her Letter 42 (pp. 341–42) in which he complains that "vous monstrez à chascun ce que je vous envoie, dont il semble à pluseurs que ce soit une moquerie. . . . Car il semble que ce soit pour vous couvrir, douce amie, et faites semblant d'un autre amer" [you show everyone what I send you, and thus it seems a mockery to several people. . . . For it seems that you do this in order to cover yourself, sweet friend, and you appear to love another]. Guillaume then goes on to speak of the composition of the *Voir-Dit*, claiming that difficulty in love has led to difficulty in writing: "Et certes je ne fis rien en vostre livre puis Pasques, et pour ceste cause; ne ne pense à faire, puisque matiere me faut" (p. 342) [And, indeed, I have done nothing on your book since Easter, and for this reason; nor do I think of doing so, because I am lacking subject matter]. This claim of poetic sterility is, however, almost immediately belied by the fact that Guillaume announces that he is sending Toute-Belle the part of the *Voir-Dit* completed since their last exchange.

Her reply (Letter 43, pp. 344–47) begins by reproaching Guillaume for not having kept his promise to visit her as well as for his lack of faith in her, swearing that her behavior has been honorable and discreet, and that Guillaume should not believe rumors about her since she will remain his "bonne et loial amie, tant come je vivray" (p. 346) [good and loyal lover, as long as I live]. Toute-Belle concludes her letter by addressing Guillaume qua poet. First, she requests that he send her new lyrics, saying that she knows he has composed some since they last corresponded, having seen the ballade "Qu'en lieu de bleu, dame, vous vestez vert" (which was apparently circulating independently). Second, she requests that he send her by return messenger the first part of the *Voir-Dit* (which she had earlier returned to him) so that she can have a copy of it made for herself.

After reading Toute-Belle's letter, Guillaume is strongly inclined to believe in her good faith and is thus favorably disposed towards a personal messenger from his dame who arrives at his house (v. 8553, p. 348) about two weeks later.[84] This messenger is a friend of Guillaume who has become Toute-Belle's confessor, and as such he bears witness to the lady's virtuous conduct as well as to the suffering Guillaume's lack of faith has caused her. He then reproaches Guillaume in a long and clerkly speech (pp. 351–59) which begins with two specific charges, both involving Guillaume's literary production. First, the confessor criticizes him for having written the ballade "Qu'en lieu de bleu, dame, vous vestez vert," which has caused Toute-Belle to suffer unjustly. Second, the confessor reproaches Guillaume for having compared Toute-Belle to Fortune, explicitly discounting the "disclaimer" that Guillaume had built into this comparison with the refrain: "S'il est voirs ce qu'on m'en a dit" [If what one said to me about it is true].

Next, the confessor undertakes Toute-Belle's defense in earnest by means of elaborate literary reversal: he compares Guillaume to Fortune. This comparison is significant for several reasons. First, it emphasizes the *Voir-Dit*'s status as a highly structured literary artifact. Second, it functions as an important part of the program of literarization of Guillaume's love experience in evidence throughout the work. Finally, it calls attention to the presence of Machaut the poète as the author figure for the *Voir-Dit* as a whole, able both to assume a variety of first-person stances (in this case, those of Guillaume the protagonist and Toute-Belle's confessor) and to provide a structured poetic coherence for this variety.

The confessor begins the comparison with a description (vv. 8652–732, pp. 352–58) of how "li Paien figuroient l'ymage de Fortune" [the Pagans represented the image of Fortune] that contrasts sharply with Guillaume's earlier version.[85] Fortune is depicted as a blind woman with two faces (one expressing joy, the other sorrow) in the middle of a turning wheel, located in a great city. The city contains five fountains at which five beautiful virgins sing prayers to Fortune on behalf of her worshipers.

The confessor next proceeds to compare Guillaume and his behavior to Fortune and her fountains (vv. 8736–830, pp. 355–58). First comes a series of parallels between Guillaume's character and the goddess's appearance: Guillaume is like a woman in that his "corages" changes often and is not "estables"; his changeability resembles Fortune's turning wheel; he has a "double visage," simultaneously crying and laughing; he is blind in that he believes whatever people tell him. Next, the confessor undertakes a metaphoric treatment of Guillaume's experience with the mesdisans. The five losengiers[86] are likened to the five virgins, and Guillaume's reaction to their gossip is compared to the signs of the different fountains.[87] The confessor concludes his long speech (pp. 358–59) by advising Guillaume to seek a reconciliation with Toute-Belle, swearing that she loves him faithfully.

Guillaume is completely convinced of Toute-Belle's innocence by the confessor's speech and immediately reenters her "tres-dous servage" (v. 8866, p. 359) [very sweet service].[88] He then asks the confessor to convey a double message to Toute-Belle: his request that she pardon him for having foolishly believed the losengiers and his assurance that he is now and will always be her "loial amy" (v. 8881, p. 360). As a further confirmation of his sentiments, Guillaume writes Toute-Belle a letter, which he asks the confessor to deliver to her in person.

In this letter (Letter 45, pp. 360–63, the last one written by Guillaume in the Voir-Dit), he speaks first as lover, then as poet. He begins by restating (in prose) what he has just recounted in narrative verse: her confessor's intervention has convinced him of Toute-Belle's innocence and of his own meffait; he therefore humbly proposes reconciliation and mutual pardon. Guillaume concludes his letter by announcing the near completion of the Voir-Dit, "giving at the same time an amazingly professional, closely calculated estimate of its length,"[89] which serves to stress the physical aspect of the book's existence: "Et quant à vostre livre, il sera parfait, se Dieus plaist et je puis, dedens .XV. jours. Et le fust pieçà: mais j'ay esté lonc temps que je n'ay riens fait. Et tenra en-

viron .XII. quahiers de .XL. poins. Et quant il sera parfais je le
feray escrire et puis si le vous envoieray" (p. 363) [And as far as
your book is concerned, it will be completed in fifteen days, with
God's help and my own. And it would have been completed a
long time ago; but for quite a while I have not done any work
on it. And (the book) will contain approximately twelve quires
of forty lines (each). And when it is finished I will have it copied
and then I will send it to you]. The thematization of the making
of the *Voir-Dit* thus takes on new importance as the work draws
to a close. Indeed, adroit exploitation of textual self-consciousness
here works to highlight the displacement of experiential amorous
fulfillment by the poetic "fulfillment" of the completed Book. The
approaching conclusion of the *Voir-Dit* as text functions as a closing signal for the *Voir-Dit* as story line.

The confessor leaves Guillaume to return to Toute-Belle "Le pre-
mier jour du moys de Moy" (v. 8978, p. 366) [The first day of
May]. Given the insoluble confusion of chronology in evidence
throughout this episode[90] this date must, I think, be invested with
an essentially *poetic* significance: spring is the canonical season
of love, hence the literarily appropriate time for the final reconciliation between the two lovers (just as November was the literarily appropriate time for their estrangement). The final moments
of the love experience recounted in the *Voir-Dit* are thus endowed
with an extra dimension of literarity.

After arriving before Toute-Belle, the confessor-messenger per-
forms his mission so well that Guillaume states:

> . . . en droite union
> Mist nos .II. cuers, et si les joint
> Que jamais ne seront desjoint,
> Departis, ne desassemblez;
> Car par amours sont assemblez,
> Et par la déesse Venus.
> (vv. 8983–88, p. 366)

[He placed our two hearts in close union and joined them so closely
that they will never be separated, parted, or sundered; for they have been
brought together by love and by the goddess Venus.]

A final letter from Toute-Belle is presented as confirmation of the lovers' reconciliation. She begins the letter (Letter 46, p. 367–69, the last in the *Voir-Dit* and, it is significant to note, undated) by addressing Guillaume qua lover. After reaffirming her constant love and fidelity, she goes on to express the joy she feels now that all "misunderstandings" have been resolved: "Si vivrons en joie et en plaisance, et si aurons parfaite souffisance. Et aussi, nous serons hors des dangiers de Fortune" (p. 367) [We will live in joy and delight and we will have perfect contentment. And we will thus be outside Fortune's power]. Toute-Belle concludes her letter by addressing Guillaume qua poet in a brief discussion of their collaboration on the *Voir-Dit*: "Je ne vous envoie pas vostre livre, pour ce que j'ay trop grant doubte qu'il ne fust perdus. Et aussi, c'est tout mon esbatement et que je y vueil aucunes choses amender, lesquelles je vous diroie volentiers de bouche. Et toutevoie le vous envoieray-je le plus tost que je porray avoir certain message" (p. 369) [I am not sending you your book, because I am very afraid of its being lost (in transit). Furthermore it constitutes my entire delight and I want to have certain passages revised —which I would be very happy to indicate to you in person. However, I will send you (the book) as soon as I can find a reliable messenger]. Enclosed with this letter is a *rondel* ("Cinq, sept, douze, un, nuef, onze et vint" [pp. 369–70] [five, seven, twelve, one, nine, eleven, and twenty]), the last intercalated lyric of the *Voir-Dit* in which Guillaume's name is encoded.

The two lovers are thus reconciled at the end of the *Voir-Dit*[91] but in such a way as to present their entire relationship as an elaborate poetic construct. The cyclical structure of Part 2 has a cumulative effect: the completion of the second cycle of contentment–estrangement–reconciliation involves the implicit suggestion of a potentially open-ended repetition, in which a meeting between the two lovers will *never* take place. The possibility of a physical relationship, indeed of a love experience as direct experience, seems not only to have receded out of reach but to have become a matter of secondary importance. What remains, becoming by contrast increasingly tangible, is the poetic expression of the love experience: the *Livre dou voir-dit* itself. The elaborate annominatio with which the final episode of the *Voir-Dit* concludes (and which is largely omitted from the P. Paris edition) serves to give a final and definitive confirmation to the *Voir-Dit*'s status as verbal arti-fact, emanating not from the love experience of Guillaume the narrator-protagonist, but from the poetic experience of Machaut the poète:

> Ainsi fusmes nous racordé,
> Com je vous ay ci recordé [,]
> > vv. 9012–13 (p. 370)
>
> Par tresamiable concorde.
> Grant joie ay quant je m'en recorde,
> Et grant bien est dou recorder,
> Quant on voit gens bien acorder,
> Et plus grant bien de mettre acort
> Entre gens ou il a descort,
> Et pour ce, encor recorderay
> Briefment ce qu'a recorder ay:
> Comment Toute-Belle encorda
> Mon cuer, quant a moy s'acorda.
> Et le trehy a sa cordelle
> Par le noble et gentil corps d'elle
> En une chanson recordant
> D'une vois belle et accordant
> Et si doucement acordée
> Qu'estre ne porroit descordée.
> > f. 305ᵛ (MS *A*)

[Thus we were reconciled in loving harmony, as I have recounted here. I am very joyful when I recall this. It is a very good thing to report that people are reconciled and an even better thing to reconcile people who are estranged. Therefore, I will again recount briefly what I have to say: how Toute-Belle tied up my heart when she was reconciled with me. She won it over through her noble, graceful body, singing a song with a beautiful, harmonious voice, so sweetly tuned that it could not be refused.]

The brief Epilogue of the *Voir-Dit* (vv. 9014–37, pp. 370–71) in-volves a summary reaffirmation of the implicit self-presentation of the work found in its concluding episode. The je of Guillaume the narrator-protagonist has been expanded to the point where it seems to correspond with that of Machaut the poète, speaking now in his own voice as he introduces the anagram signature that functions as a closing signal:

> Or est raison que je vous die
> Le nom de ma dame jolie,
> Et le mien qui a fait ce dit
> Que l'en appelle le *Voir-Dit*.
>   (vv. 9014–17, p. 370)

[Now it is fitting that I tell you the name of my beautiful lady and my own (name) — I who have made this poem called the True Story.]

The final declaration of eternal love service to Toute-Belle (with which the poem closes — its very last words being the "poetic" name: Toute-Belle) is thus to be understood as a continuing and self-sufficient poetic service. For the organization of the *Voir-Dit* has consistently presented Guillaume as a successful poet despite his having been an unsuccessful lover[92] (as a Jean de Meun rather than as a Guillaume de Lorris). The relationship with Toute-Belle fails as a love relationship but succeeds consistently as poetic inspiration — both in the sense of "generating" the lyric poems that are embedded in the narrative (presented as deriving from Guillaume's love of Toute-Belle) and in the sense of producing the *Voir-Dit* as a whole. In the final analysis the love experience is valorized, it seems, primarily as a generator of poetry, as poetic inspiration, even as matière. At the same time love is shown to be immortalized only because it has been treated in poetry.

IV. Poet-Narrator as Witness-Participant

Introduction

The narrative stance employed in the *Jugement dou roy de Behaingne*, the *Dit dou lyon,* and the *Fonteinne amoureuse*[1] involves the poet-narrator functioning as witness-participant, no longer the protagonist in the story he recounts. In effect, what we have in these three dits is the poet-narrator singing the love experience of someone else, but in a first-person context — the whole being conceived of always as part of the poète's service to Amour. This narrative stance may be seen as at once a result and an illustration of the transformation (and expansion) of the lyrico-narrative je made possible by Machaut's concept of poetic identity. A progressive development, an increasingly elaborate exploitation of this narrative configuration — of this possibility for first-person narration of a lyric matière — is revealed by a detailed consideration of the three dits in question.

As in the preceding chapters, two central and interrelated features provide the focus for the present analysis: first, the narrator figure — his identity and function in each individual dit as well as the way in which he is related to the global poète figure of the oeuvres complètes; second, the narrative structure, or organization, of the dits in so far as it may be considered both as deriving from the identity of the narrator figure and as serving to define that identity.

Le Jugement dou roy de Behaingne

The *Behaingne* begins without a formal prologue, plunging immediately into the narrative proper. There is no preliminary establishment of the identity of the narrator figure who in the first, introductory, section of the work (vv. 1–55) begins to recount what appears to be a story about himself. First we have an evocation of the lyric setting of a spring morning on which the (as-yet-unnamed) narrator tells how "cointement m'acesmay / Com cils qui trés parfaitement amay / D'amour seüre" (vv. 10–12) [I dressed myself elegantly, like one who loved purely, with an unfailing love]. The first-person narrative voice of the *Behaingne* is thus at the outset "contained" in his narration.[2] In addition, this voice is marked both implicitly (by its use of conventional lyric diction and topoi) and explicitly (vv. 11–12) as that of a lover.

As the story line advances, resonances of the opening of the dream narrative of the *Roman de la rose* abound. The narrator of the *Behaingne* is captivated by the birdsongs he hears:

> Et cil oisel,
> Pour la douceur dou joli temps nouvel,
> Si liement et de si grant revel
> Chantoient tuit que j'alay a l'appel
> De leur dous chant.
> (vv. 20–24)

[Because of the sweetness of the lovely, new season, all those birds were singing so happily and so joyously that I followed the call of their sweet song.] (Cf. the *Rose*, vv. 67–83, 94–102, esp. vv. 94–97.)

He follows one particularly beautiful song and is led to a plaisance where he sits down (v. 32), enraptured by

> le trés dous son de son joli chanter.
> Si me plut tant en oïr deliter
> Son dous chanter, que jamais raconter
> Ne le porroie.
> (vv. 37–40)

[the sweet sound of his lovely singing. The delight of hearing his sweet singing pleased me more than I could ever describe.] (Cf. the *Rose*, vv. 640–80.)

The fact that the veritable symphony of singing birds in the ver-gier of Deduit has here been reduced to the song of a single bird serves to highlight a consistent process of *abbreviatio* performed by Machaut on the earlier poem. What results is a kind of reduc-tion of the narrator-protagonist of the *Rose* to the minimal first-person voice of the *Behaingne*, while at the same time an implicit link is established between the two figures.

Thus by this point in Machaut's poem, the reader's expectation (reinforced by the *Rose* references) is that a first-person adventure will follow — indeed, that it is already underway. However, in the sequence that ensues (vv. 41–55) there is a radical shift in perspec-tive. The narrator ceases to function as a character and takes on the role of witness, becoming, as it were, a kind of narrative device. As he listens to the birdsong, he sees a chevalier and a dame ap-proach. Thinking them to be lovers, he discreetly hides himself in a bush (v. 54). From this vantage point the narrator is able to witness everything that transpires, unseen by the protagonists.

The Introduction of the *Behaingne* thus presents the narrator as a character in the story whose unfolding explicitly transforms him (on the level of plot) from active participant into passive witness — a transformation which, as we shall see, can be reversed. This witness perspective, which allows the narrator to recount the love experience of other characters in a first-person context, will continue to operate throughout the first major narrative seg-ment of the *Behaingne* (vv. 57–1184, the debate segment).[3]

The dame and chevalier meet and begin to talk to each other (vv. 57–124). Each has a sad story to tell, neither one concerning the narrator whose love experience is no longer a matter of con-cern to the dit as it unfolds. The dame speaks first, addressing the chevalier ("Sire" [v. 125]), and recounts how her loyal lover has recently died, leaving her broken-hearted (vv. 125–205). At this point there is a brief intervention on the part of the narrator, speaking in his own voice: "Et je qui fui boutez dedens le brueil / Vi qu'a ce mot la dame au dous acueil / Cheï com morte" (vv. 205-7) [And from my position in the bushes, I saw the gracious lady fall down as if dead at the sound of that word]. This seems to be a means of reconfirming the narrator's position as witness, of calling attention to the narrative configuration through which the embedded, secondary narration of the dame is being transmitted to the reader. The dame (a secondary narrator) recounts a story to the chevalier (a secondary addressee) which is overheard by the primary narrator who simultaneously presents it to the reader, the primary addressee. That this intervention on the part of the narrator may indeed be regarded as a means of highlighting the narrative structure as such seems to be confirmed by the fact that it is situated strategically between the embedded secondary narration of the dame and that of the chevalier, and thus serves as a structural indicator.

After he revives her from her faint and assures her that he bears a greater grief (vv. 209-60), the chevalier proceeds to recount to the dame (addressed in the vocative in v. 261) how his beloved has recently left him for another man (vv. 261-880). He describes his amorous experience in some detail and concludes his story by reaffirming that his grief is greater than that of the dame (vv. 861-80).

A debate now ensues between the two interlocutors over which one suffers more because of love (vv. 881-1184). Unable to resolve their dispute they both declare their willingness to submit the matter to judgment if a suitable judge can be found. An impasse (both in their debate and, narratively, in the progress of the story line) is reached as each insists that the other choose the judge.

It is only at this point (vv. 1185 ff.) that the narrator reappears as character: "Et quant je vi qu'il voloient que fais / Fust jugemens de leurs dolereus fais, / Mes cuers en fu de joie tous refais" (vv. 1185-87) [And when I saw that they wanted their sad cases to be judged, my heart was again filled with joy]. His reappearance is motivated narratively, as was his initial transformation into passive witness: he knows of a judge who would be ideal for the dispute he has just overheard.[4] Throughout the second major narrative segment of the *Behaingne* (vv. 1185-442, which can be termed the transition segment) the narrator will function as active participant in the story he recounts. Indeed, his intervention as character is essential for the advancement of the story line.

After a certain hesitation, the narrator decides to approach the disputants (vv. 1188–201). As he nears the couple, the "petit chien" (v. 1204) [little dog] of the dame rushes at the narrator, barking loudly, and bites his cloak (vv. 1202–11). The narrator is delighted as he now has a pretext for approaching the dame:

> . . . en mon cuer forment m'en deportay,
> Pour ce qu'a sa dame le reportay,
>   Pour avoir voie
> Et occoison d'aler ou je voloie.
>
> (vv. 1214–17)

[. . . inwardly I was greatly pleased to carry it (the dog) back to his mistress, in order to have the means and the opportunity to go where I wanted.]

It is especially significant that a playfully subverted literary reference is the means by which the narrator (as witness) is reintegrated (as participant) into the story line of the *Behaingne*. The reference is to the "petit chienet" who serves as intermediary between the lovers in the *Chastelaine de Vergi* (vv. 34 ff.).[5] The adept and playful reworking of this motif stresses the literariness of the narrator figure of the *Behaingne* and the elegant artificiality of the narrative configuration in which he functions. At this structurally significant moment, the text is thus made to call attention to itself as text, as literary object. A distinction is thereby implicitly suggested between the first-person narrator of the *Behaingne* and Machaut the poète, into whom this narrator is subsumed and from whom this intertextual reference may be said to emanate.

The narrator now arrives before the couple (v. 1219) and fully reenters the story line as character, no longer a simple witness but a participant. In a long speech of self-introduction (vv. 1267–330), the narrator integrates his witness role into the story line proper. This involves a process of textual self-authentification, as the narrator begins by retelling (within the context of the advancing plot) the beginning of the dit to the dame and the chevalier (who replace the reader as addressee). The main narrative thread of the *Behaingne* thus becomes, in summary form, a secondary narration embedded in itself. This process of what might be called narrative doubling will be repeated several times in the course of the poem. The narrator first recounts how he had entered the vergier, led on by birdsong; then how he had hidden himself (i.e., how he had become a witness) and overheard the extended conversation between the chevalier and the dame. This first part of the narrator's speech employs narrated tenses exclusively.

In the second part of his speech (vv. 1285–93), the narrator switches to commented tenses as he explains that, realizing the desire of his interlocutors to settle their dispute, he has come to propose a judge. The way in which the narrator as participant functions to advance the plot of the dit could not be more explicit.[6]

The final part of the speech (vv. 1294–1327) is a highly rhetorical encomium (couched in clerkly diction) of the proposed judge: John of Luxemburg, the "roys de Behaingne" (v. 1337).

The dame and the chevalier agree enthusiastically to accept the narrator's offer to lead them to the king:

> Je respondi: "Bien vous say assener
> La ou il est et, s'il vous plaist, mener.
>   Certeins en sui,
> Car vraiement, je mengay yer et bui
> Avec ses gens en chastiau de Durbui.
> Et il y est, ne n'en partira hui;
>   Ne ce n'est mie
> Loing, qu'il n'i a ne lieue ne demie,
> Nom pas de ci le quart d'une huchie."
>   (vv. 1362–70)

[I answered: "I can certainly inform you where he is and lead you there, if you like. I am certain of this because I ate and drank with his courtiers yesterday at the castle of Durbui. He is there and will not be leaving today. It is not far — not even a league or half a league — it's not even out of earshot.]

This is the first point in the dit where the identity of the narrator acquires an explicitly extradiegetic dimension. This expansion of the narrator's identity results from its being made to overlap with that of Machaut the poète who had spent many years in the service of John of Bohemia and who was familiar with Durbui, one of King John's favorite residences.

The chevalier and the dame are eager to accompany the narrator but object that they do not know the way. The narrator replies:

> ". . . Dame, bien le vous vueil aprendre.
>   Venez adès.
> J'iray devant et vous venrez après."
> Si qu'au chemin me mis, d'aler engrès.
>   (vv. 1375–78)

["Lady, I am very willing to teach you (the way). Come right now. I will go ahead and you will come after." And I set out, eager to be off.]

We have here a dramatization of the construct of poet-narrator as intermediary — his most active intervention as participant in the plot sequence on behalf of the lovers, the dame and the chevalier. The narrator leads the protagonists out of the vergier in which all the action up until now has taken place and to Durbui, where all the remaining action will be situated.

With no interval in the text the two lovers, guided by the narrator, arrive at the castle and marvel at its beauty. At this point the narrator intervenes to describe the castle from an extradiegetic perspective (vv. 1385–422). This realistically exact description[7] set in the present tense (i.e., in Weinrich's commented world in contrast to the exclusively narrated tenses that surround this descriptive passage) serves to expand still further the identity of the narrator figure, giving it an important extranarrative dimension and linking it more closely with the figure of Machaut the poète. The description closes as the expanded first-person narrative voice explicitly resumes his role as the narrator of, and participant in, this particular text: "Mais revenir m'estuet a ma matiere" (v. 1423) [But I must return to my subject].

It is as participant that the narrator leads his two charges up to the castle door, which opens (vv. 1424–33). Then, referring to his extradiegetic identity as a kind of authorization, the narrator speaks to the doorman:

> Je qui hurtay et qui fui li premiers
> Et de laiens estre assez coustumiers
>   Parlay einsi:
> "Cils chevaliers et ceste dame aussi
> Viennent parler au roy, s'il est yci."
>   (vv. 1434–38)

[I who was in front knocked. And being rather familiar with the household, I spoke thusly: "This knight and this lady are coming to speak to the king if he is here."]

There is an explicitly double structure for this "je" who speaks, for he is self-identified as simultaneously within and without (contained by and containing) the narrative he recounts. In line 1434 the narrator speaks of himself from an intranarrative perspective ("Je qui hurtay . . ."); in line 1435, from an extranarrative perspective ("Et de laiens estre [= "iere" in MSS *CEKJP*] assez coustumiers"), the two being linked by a coordinating conjunction.

A sustained elaboration of the identity of the narrator figure has thus been effected, a progressive expansion from the minimal first-person voice of the introductory section of the dit.

It is precisely at this point in the work, the beginning of the third major narrative segment (vv. 1443–2051, the judgment segment) that the narrator begins to recede, as it were, back into the text. He reassumes the witness perspective, but in stages and implicitly — without the explicit narrative device (i.e., hiding in a bush in order to be discreet) that had served to introduce the first major narrative segment of the dit.

As the doorman is going off to execute the narrator's request, two of King John's courtiers arrive abruptly to lead the party to the king. These courtiers, Honneur and Courtoisie, are the first personification characters that appear in the poem and they take over the function of the narrator as character, superseding him, as it were. It is as if the unexpressed je of Machaut the poète — the creator of these personifications — had stepped in and taken over from the expressed "je" of the narrator figure, who thus ceases to be an active agent in the advancement of the story line. It is significant that the pronoun "je" ceases from this point on to be employed to designate the narrator as character (though it does appear when he speaks qua narrator in vv. 1459 and 1474); this may be seen as the first stage of the narrator's reassuming the witness perspective. Rather, the first-person plural pronoun is employed to designate the group composed of the narrator, the dame, and the chevalier, a group which is for the moment acted upon rather than acting:

> Mais tout einsi com de *nous* se partoit
>> Pour aler sus,
> Uns chevaliers, biaus et gens et corsus,
> Jolis et gais, en est a *nous* venus;
> Honneur ot nom, et s'en sot plus que nuls.
>> N'il ne vint mie
> Tous seuls a *nous,* eins li fist compaingnie
> Une dame belle, gaie et jolie;
> Si ot a nom la dame Courtoisie.
>> Bien y parut;
> Car aussi tost qu'elle *nous* aperçut,
> *Nous* salua, et puis biau *nous* reçut.
> Si fist Honneur, si com faire le dut.
>> (vv. 1443–55, emphasis added)

[But as he was leaving *us* to go back inside, a knight — handsome, noble, strong, joyous, and gay — came out to *us;* Honor was his name and he knew more about it than anyone. Nor did he come to *us* alone, but rather a beautiful lady — joyous and gay — accompanied him; and the lady was named Courtesy. She certainly seemed so; for as soon as she saw *us,* she greeted *us* and then received *us* well. Honor did the same, as was right to do.]

The second stage of the narrator's retransformation into witness takes place as Honneur and Courtoisie lead the dame and the chevalier into the king's presence (vv. 1456–67). The "nous" has now disappeared and the entire sequence is recounted in the third person. The narrative proceeds with no reference on the part of the narrator to himself as a participant in the events recounted. After a brief encomium, the initial description of the king sitting in state opens with the mention of: ". . . un clerc que nommer ne saroie / Qui li lisoit la bataille de Troie" (vv. 1474–75) [a clerk whose name I do not know, who was reading the Trojan War to (the king)]. There seems to be the suggestion of an ironic self-reference on the part of Machaut the poète. The "je" of the clerkly narrative voice is contrasted with the brief glimpse of an apparently supernumerary clerc figure in the act of serving his patron. Next (vv. 1477–93), the sixteen personification characters who surround and serve the king are named: Hardiesse, Prouesse, Largesse, Richesse, Amour, Biauté, Loiauté, Leësse, Desirs, Pensers, Volonté, Noblesse, Franchise, Honneur, Courtoisie, Juenesse, as well as Raison. This self-consciously literary (and laudatory) presentation of the king again seems to emanate from the poète rather than the narrator, generated by Machaut's relationship to his patron. The king receives the chevalier and the dame courteously and asks the purpose of their visit. In response to the king's inquiry, the chevalier recounts to him the entire story line of the dit up to the present moment (vv. 1509–608). This is the second instance of the process we had earlier termed narrative doubling: a retelling of the narrative in summary form which functions to advance the narrative line while providing a kind of textual self-authentification. A further development of the process occurs here as the chevalier duplicates in miniature the role of the narrator figure for the dit as a whole. The relationship narrator/audience (on the extradiegetic level) is doubled by that of the chevalier/king (on the intradiegetic level). At the same time, the chevalier's narrative role recalls and expands that of the narrator himself in lines 1267–330 (discussed above). The embedded, secondary narration of the chevalier (vv. 1509–608) is of course a first-person account from his perspective. In the course of his narration the chevalier thus refers to the narrator in the third person, as a character in his story: "Sire, et cils clers / Qui me samble gais, jolis et apers, / Fu atapis ou jardin et couvers" (vv. 1584–86) [Sire, this clerk, whom I think to be gay, joyous and open, was hidden under cover in the garden]. Yet within the narrative configuration of the *Behaingne* as a whole, the chevalier as a narrator is himself a third-person character in the narrator's first-person account. The reader is thus confronted with a construct of extreme intricacy which calls attention to its own artifice. The narrator figure appears more than ever as a structural device.

In addition, the chevalier's narration to the king may also be viewed as the third stage of the narrator's retransformation into witness. His increasingly indirect presence is now attested to exclusively by other characters. Yet this attestation provides a kind of built-in confirmation of his witness status. As in the debate segment, the continual presence of the narrator as witness (to the judgment segment) is again carefully established and again functions structurally. A third-person narration whose subject matter is the love experience of characters other than the narrator can thus be presented within the framework of the narrator's first-person account.

As the chevalier continues to speak, he refers to his unfolding narration (in which he himself plays a major role) as a written text:

> Car longuement
> Avoit duré de nous le parlement,
> Et si aviens fait maint arguement,
> Si comme il est escript plus pleinnement
>   Ici dessus.
>   (vv. 1592–96)

[For our conversation had lasted a long time and we had had many arguments; just as it is written very clearly above.]

This witty instance of textual self-referentiality has several important effects. First, it carries the implication that the narrator's act of witnessing is equivalent to the poète's act of writing. The subordinate relationship of narrator to poète is thus emphasized and the primacy of the poet/text relationship is implicitly affirmed. Second, the essentially literary, rather than mimetic, nature of the subject matter of the dit is given special emphasis. This subject matter may thus be seen as constituting the "experience" of the poète as well as (on a structural level) that of the narrator figure.

The chevalier concludes his speech with a request that the king render judgment on his dispute with the dame (vv. 1597–608).

The judgment scene itself (vv. 1609–956) opens as King John agrees to preside but calls for assistance from four of his courtiers. The king first restates the facts of the case (vv. 1625–62, the third instance of narrative doubling in the *Behaingne*), then asks for the advice of Raison, who replies at length (vv. 1665–784), arguing that since "Amour vient de charnel affection" (v. 1709) [Love comes from carnal attraction] the dame will forget her sorrow with the passage of time while the chevalier will constantly be reminded of his. Raison ends her speech with an appeal to written authority, but the text cited is none other than the *Behaingne* itself:

> Et, a mon gré,
> Cils chevaliers en a moult bien parlé —
> *Car en escript l'ay ci dessus trouvé —*
> Et par raison s'entention prouvé,
> Ce m'est avis.
> (vv. 1780–84, emphasis added)

[To my mind, this knight has spoken about it very well — *for I have found it written out above* — and has in my opinion proven his point through reason.]

We have here a particularly intricate (and playful) example of textual self-referentiality. Not only does a character refer to herself as a reader of the text in which she figures, thus calling attention to the poem as written object, as écriture, but in addition this reference involves a doubling of the very process of textual self-referentiality. For it is (most specifically) the chevalier's recent speech to which Raison refers as a written text. And that speech, as we have already observed, had itself referred to the entire dit (in the process of unfolding) as a written text.

After listening to further arguments from Amour, Loiauté, and Juenesse, King John states that the question at issue is not whether the chevalier should continue to love, but whether it is the chevalier or the dame who suffers more from love; he decides in favor of the former (vv. 1923–56).

The final scene of the third major narrative segment of the dit (vv. 1957–2051) opens with the king taking the chevalier and the dame (who have both acknowledged his decision) "loing des autres, si qu'il n'i ot qu'euls trois" (v. 1971) [far from the others, so that there were only the three of them]. The fact that their private conversation is effortlessly integrated into the story line implies that the narrator has by now become a kind of disembodied omniscient witness to the events recounted. King John advises the two disputants not to let themselves die of grief, then calls his *maisnie* and orders them to honor the dame and the chevalier whose request for leave is refused. A sumptuous dinner is served, and the two lovers spend the following eight days as the king's guests, before they finally depart, loaded with rich presents and accompanied by John's courtiers, who then return to Durbui.

The narrator who had, as character, initiated the judgment sequence does not participate in it at all. Rather, he functions (as he had for the dispute in the vergier) simply as a witness to the story he recounts. It is only when the narrative proper is over that he reappears, speaking in the Epilogue (vv. 2052–79), not as character but as the clerk-poet who has composed the entire dit: "Ci fineray / Ma matiere, ne plus n'en rimeray; / Car autre part assez a rimer ay" (vv. 2052–54) [Here I will finish my subject; I will not rhyme it any more; for I have enough other (material) to rhyme elsewhere]. A significant elaboration and expansion of the identity of the narrator figure has thus taken place. The "je" of the Epilogue (employing commented tenses) contains the narration that has just finished in contrast to the "je" of the Introduction who (employing narrated tenses) was contained by the narration as it unfolded. The expression "ma matiere" (v. 2053) places the whole of the preceding story in the context of poetic subject matter. The reference to "autre part" (v. 2054) evokes a poet figure whose identity (and oeuvre) transcend this particular work.

It is only at this point that the poet-narrator names himself, by means of an anagram signature:

> Mais en la fin de ce livret feray
>   Que qui savoir
> Vorra mon nom et mon seurnom de voir,
> Il le porra clerement percevoir
> En darrein ver dou livret et vëoir,
>   Mais qu'il dessamble
> Les premieres set sillabes d'ensamble
> Et les lettres d'autre guise rassamble,
> Si que nulle n'en oublie ne emble.
>   Einsi porra
> Mon nom savoir qui savoir le vorra.
>   (vv. 2055–65)

[At the end of this little book I will arrange it so that whoever wants to know my true full name will be able to discover and see it in the last verse. But he must separate the first seven syllables from the rest and reassemble their letters in a different way, without forgetting or suppressing a single one. In this way he who wants to know my name will be able to know it.]

It is as if the completion of the poetic work were the necessary prerequisite for the full establishment of the identity of the poet-narrator. Yet a reciprocal relationship is involved here. While the completion of the work provides the poet-narrator with his identity, this identity (the name contained in the anagram signature) serves as signal for the closure of the work itself, since the anagram is contained in the very last line which when unscrambled reads: "Guillemin de Machaut."[8] Poetic identity and poetic work thus become mutually self-defining in such a way as to highlight Machaut's verbal dexterity — his poetic craft which the anagram as process seems to emblematize. In this connection it is important to note that the *Behaingne* is the first dit which contains an anagram signature in MSS *CVgAFGMJK*.

The narrator figure of the *Behaingne* has functioned throughout the dit as witness-participant, thus providing a narrative configuration which allows a third-person story (whose subject is the love experience not of the narrator but of the chevalier and the dame) to be recounted in a first-person context. Yet as the narrative advances (indeed, because it advances), this narrator figure, little more than a structural device at the beginning of the work, is "expanded," made to overlap with the figure of Machaut the poète. This process of expansion is evident when the "je" of the Introduction (vv. 1–55) is compared with the "je" of the second major narrative segment (vv. 1185–442). The "je" of the Epilogue (vv. 2052–79) may be seen to complete the process, for at the conclusion of the work Machaut the poète is, as it were, speaking through his narrator figure. Or rather, the two are able to speak simultaneously. The narrator of the *Behaingne* has recounted the love experience of someone else in a first-person context while the composition of the dit as a whole may be seen as part of the poète's service to Amour.

The last section of the Epilogue seems to involve an expansion of this suggestion:

> Et nompourquant ja pour ce ne sera
> > Que je ne soie
> Loiaus amis, jolis et pleins de joie;
> Car se riens plus en ce monde n'avoie
> Fors ce que j'aim ma dame simple et coie
> > Contre son gré,
> Si ay j'assez, qu'Amours m'a honnouré
> Et richement mon mal guerredonné,
> Quant a ma dame einsi mon cuer donné
> > Ay a tous jours.
>
> (vv. 2067–76)

[Nonetheless, I shall never cease to be a loyal lover, gay and joyful; for if I have nothing in this world except loving my modest, elegant lady against her will I have enough, in that Love has honored me and richly rewarded my pain when I thus gave my heart to my lady forever.]

The first-person poet-narrator affirms his identity as a lover (referring back to vv. 11–12 of the Introduction) content, unlike the chevalier, with the condition of loving and nothing more. There is thus a final distancing of the poet-narrator from his protagonist and of the poète from his matière, which is given a literary (rather than an "experiential") cast.

This is in keeping with Machaut's global poetic identity, for whom the love experience is important primarily as poetic subject matter. The closing lines of the *Behaingne* underscore the fact that the narrator's own love experience has not supplied the matière of the dit. Indeed, this love experience (alluded to only in the Introduction and the Epilogue) appears as literary convention which operates to distance the narrator as poet from the narrator as lover.

Le Dit dou lyon

In the *Lyon* the narrator figure is much more extensively developed than in the *Behaingne*, and his own love experience serves as one of the most important means of establishing both his identity and his narrative function. It is not, however, the love experience of the narrator that furnishes the narrative matière of the dit; it is not the story of his love that is told.

The *Lyon* is the first-person account of a marvelous journey, framed temporally and spatially by a seemingly more realistic setting. The seven narrative segments may be seen as successive stages in the narrator's journey. The poem involves a significant generic innovation,[9] combining the structure of a *roman d'aventures* with the subject matter of a love allegory. As we shall see, the identity of the narrator figure, as it is progressively disclosed, provides the key element in Machaut's transformation and combination of these two generic systems.

The first narrative segment (vv. 1–158) opens with a disembodied lyric evocation of the arrival of springtime (vv. 1–30), which may be seen as a kind of implicit prologue. The narrator introduces himself as only one among the multitude of living creatures who rejoice at the coming of the new season: "et j'aussi l'aim" (v. 6) [and I too love it (the springtime)]. His poetic activity thus seems to be emblematized (and marked from the outset as lyric) by the extended description of birdsong as an expression of this rejoicing, which concludes the dit's opening sequence: "Car Nature si leur commande / Que chascuns a chanter entende. . . . / Chascuns de bien chanter se peinne" (vv. 19–20, 30) [For Nature commands each of them (the birds) to concentrate on singing. . . . Each one exerts himself to sing well].

The beginning of the story line itself (vv. 31 ff.) involves the narrator setting a particular moment in the historical past (April 2, 1342) and a particular person (himself as a character in his own narration) into the highly literary, conventional evocation of spring with which the poem had opened. The distinction between the narrator qua narrator (situated temporally in the "present" of the time of writing) and the narrator qua character (situated in the narrated past of the unfolding story line), as well as the relationship between narrator and audience, are thus stressed from the outset:

> En ce dous temps dont je vous cont,
> Dou mois d'avril le jour secont,

> L'an mil trois cens quarante deus,
> Forment estoie sommilleus,
> Si qu'en un lit couchiez estoie,
> Pour ce que mestier en avoie.
>   (vv. 31–36)

[In that sweet season that I am describing to you, on the second day of April, in the year thirteen hundred forty-two, I was sleeping soundly while lying in bed, because I needed (rest).]

What follows may be seen as simultaneously an exploitation and a variation of the narrative framework established at the beginning of the *Roman de la rose*. A variation, because the narrator of the *Lyon* does not proceed to recount a dream—as the *Rose* resonances would lead the reader to expect—but rather an adventure that befell the narrator after he was awakened (by birdsong) the following morning. An exploitation, since a dreamlike aura is bestowed on the narrator's adventure by means of this initial intertextual presence of the *Rose* as (transformed) narrative model.

A catalogue of the various birds whose songs awakened the narrator leads him to a brief digression (vv. 45–70), in which the major components of his identity are, as it were, established for the first time in the poem. A short discourse on the properties of the *calendre* bird displays the narrator's clerkly learning, but this is immediately lyricized as the narrator, identifying himself as a lover, compares the calendre to his dame.[10] The fact that commented tenses exclusively are employed in this initial digression endows the narrator figure with an explicitly extradiegetic dimension almost from the outset of the dit. A pattern is thus established that will be followed in the two later digressions in which the narrator, interrupting his narration from the temporal perspective of the time of writing, meditates on his dame. It is in large measure by means of these digressions—lyric meditations embedded in the narrative progression—that the identity of the narrator is established.

Returning to the story line (vv. 71 ff.) the narrator recounts how he had set out from the "manoir ou je gisoie" (v. 81) [the manor where I was staying] in search of a marvelous vergier. On reaching the river that surrounds the vergier, however, the narrator is temporarily thwarted, unable to effect a crossing until he discovers a magic boat: "Si vi en l'ombre d'un arbril, / Droitement le tiers jour d'avril, / Un batel si bel et si riche" (vv. 139–41) [Then, on April third, I saw a very beautiful and precious boat in the shadow of a tree]. The fact that the discovery of the magic boat is carefully situated in "objective" time seems to stress once again that the events described are not those of a dream-narrative.

Happily anticipating what awaits him at the other side of the river, the narrator enters the boat and his marvelous journey begins in earnest. The terminology used to describe this action is significant: "si pris l'aventure" (v. 158) [thus I took up the adventure]. The expression[11] suggests the beginning of a romance-type narrative sequence and indeed, this suggestion will be constantly exploited by Machaut throughout the *Lyon* in an extended example of generic transformation.

Various romance constructs, deriving by and large from Chrétien de Troyes whose narrative works seem to function collectively as a generic model, will be incorporated into the *Lyon* but radically modified to suit Machaut's own poetic purpose.

The second narrative segment (vv. 159–432) begins as the narrator crosses the river and lands on the island where the vergier lies (vv. 159–74). As he strolls contentedly through the delightful surroundings, he falls into a reverie:

> Si qu'en escoutant le deduit
> Des oisiaus, Amours qui me duit
> A faire son trés dous plaisir
> De fin cuer et de vray desir
> Me fist a ma dame penser.
> (vv. 201–5)

[While I was listening to the joyful birds, Love, who teaches me to do his sweet pleasure with pure heart and true desire, made me think of my lady.]

The extended meditation on his beloved that follows (vv. 207–78) constitutes the second of the digressions which serve to establish the narrator's identity both as poet and as lover, elaborating and strengthening suggestions contained in the first digression. The narrator's identity as exemplary fin'amant is demonstrated by means of standard thematic constructs of courtly love poetry: complete and lifelong devotion to the beloved, portrayed as the source of both all joy and all suffering — a devotion which manifests itself as love service. This love service is implicitly identified with verbal expertise, with poetic service, and the narrator's identity as courtly lover and courtly poet are thus established simultaneously and are mutually defining.

The language of the digression, more densely patterned than that of the surrounding narrative, serves to reinforce the identity of the narrator. A highly rhetorical style extensively exploiting anaphora (esp. vv. 215–28, 229–34) and annominatio (on *voloir*, vv. 243–45; on *servir*, vv. 252–77) and employing the most refined courtly diction is used to express the stylized (and highly literary) emotional condition of the devoted fin'amant. Standard conventions of the Ovidian vernacular tradition, especially paradox (e.g., vv. 223–24, 242) and hyperbole (e.g., vv. 260, 265–66) are handled with great virtuosity. The appearance of this degree of technical poetic expertise — calling attention to itself and thus to the figure of Machaut the poète from whom it emanates — also serves implicitly to differentiate the narrator from the author, a difference that will be exploited as the dit progresses.

The narrator concludes his lyric meditation by setting it back into a narrative framework and describes how it caused him to lose his way:

> Einsi pensoie et repensoie
> Comment ma dame serviroie.
> Si pensai si parfondement
> Qu'ailleurs n'avoie entendement,
> Et si forment y entendi
> Qu'en vergier ma sente perdi.
>   (vv. 279–84)

[Thus I thought repeatedly about how to serve my lady. And I thought so deeply that I was aware of nothing else; and I became so intensely absorbed (in this) that I lost my way in the garden.]

The sudden appearance of a lion (v. 289) startles the narrator out of his meditation, leaving him terrified. Thinking himself lost as the lion approaches him, the narrator nevertheless remembers his beloved and cries out: "Chiere dame, a vous me commant!" (v. 313) [Dear lady, I entrust myself to you]. The lion immediately becomes docile and the narrator thanks "devotement/Ma dame et Amours ensement" (vv. 321–22) [devoutly both my lady and Love]. Not only is this scene pivotal in the narrative progression of the *Lyon* itself, but it recalls and transforms the scene of Yvain's first encounter with the lion in Chrétien's *Chevalier au lion* (vv. 3337–478). Yvain, we remember, won the loyal companionship of his lion by a deed of chivalric *prouesse:* the killing of the serpent. Machaut's narrator tames his lion by means of a verbal feat: the properly courtly articulation of his properly courtly love experience.[12] The implicit comparison between Chrétien's protagonist and Machaut's narrator built into this episode thus both reinforces the narrator's identity as poet-lover (a transformed Yvain) within the context of the *Lyon* and highlights the literary process by which Machaut the poète incorporates and transforms the work of his predecessor.[13]

After a display of gentleness the lion indicates that he wants the narrator to follow him, and the two set off together (v. 353). They pass through a wasteland where the narrator is pricked by thorns (vv. 356–60) and thoroughly frightened by various savage beasts (catalogued in vv. 380–92) before realizing that they are solely concerned with injuring the lion (vv. 407 ff.). They harass him and howl at him in a kind of inversion of the lyric birdsong with which the dit had opened. Visibly pained by all this "li gentils lions" (v. 418) [the noble lion] appears to the narrator to be several times almost on the point of dying, but he continues on his way, leading the narrator after him. This entire sequence employs generic constructs taken from the fourteenth-century love allegory and is especially reminiscent of the *Dit de la panthère* (c. 1300), which features a first-person narrator who dreams that birds carry him off to a marvelous forest in which a wide variety of animals (catalogued in vv. 61–83) are subject to the panther "pour l'amour de sa douce alaine" (v. 111) [for love of her sweet breath], with the exception of the dragon (vv. 116 ff.) who is hostile and envious. (Calin notes that the motif of narrator-lover scratched by thorns is found both in the *Dit de la panthère* and the *Lyon*.[14]) The possible significance of Machaut's exploitation of the *Dit de la panthère* (and the love allegory in general) as a generic model will be discussed below.

The third narrative segment (vv. 433–852) begins as the lion leads the narrator into a plaisance where they arrive before a "plus gente dame" (v. 461) [very noble lady]. At this point there is a shift in perspective, and in the ensuing sequence (vv. 499–708) the narrator, formerly an active participant in the story line, serves as witness to the spectacle of the lion as lover. The narrator establishes his witness status almost at once: "Bien le vi; pour ce le tesmong" (v. 514) [I certainly saw it; thus I bear witness to it]. Next, the lion is presented as lover by means of the vocabulary used to describe his behavior on seeing the dame:

> Et sans attendre, doucement,
> Humblement et courtoisement,
> Devers la dame se treÿ
> Qu'il ama moult et oubeÿ,
> Et devant li s'ageloigna.
>
> (vv. 523–27)

[The lion did not wait, but went softly, humbly, and courteously towards the lady whom he greatly loved and obeyed. Then he kneeled down before her.]

When the dame asks the lion where he has been, it is the narrator who provides verbal expression for the feelings of the mute lover: "Et sambloit qu'il li vosist dire / La grant doleur, le grief martyre / Que les autres bestes li font" (vv. 547–49) [It seemed that he (the lion) wanted to tell her the great suffering, the cruel torment, that the other beasts caused him.] In his articulation of the lion's emotional state (vv. 547–83) the narrator first reiterates how greatly the lion suffers from the persecution of the other beasts, then affirms that only the dame can protect and save him. Authorization for the narrator's role both as witness and as interpreter is built into the narration itself:

Mais li lions, se Dieus me gart,
Pluseurs fois vers moy regarda. . . .
Et me sambloit a son corage
Qu'il me traisist en tesmognage
Pour tesmongnier la verité
De ce que j'ay ci recité.
(vv. 584–85, 87–90)

[But the lion — may God help me — looked at me several times. . . . and it seemed to me that he desired to call me as witness, to testify to the truth of what I have here recounted.]

The hostile beasts now reappear and the narrator describes (vv. 593–703) how the lion suffers intensely whenever the dame looks at them, but becomes immediately happy as soon as his dame's gaze returns to him: "La dame le lion maistrie / Seulement par son dous regart" (vv. 682–83) [The lady controlled the lion solely through her sweet gaze.] The lion's repeated alternation between despair and joy as a result of the gaze of his beloved seems to be a dramatization of the effect of the *regart* of the narrator's dame on him (described in connection with the calendre simile in vv. 58–66 and alluded to again in the second digression, vv. 226–28). A link is thus suggested between the lion as lover and the narrator as lover (as well as between their respective dames), a link that is reinforced by repeated verbal similarities in the descriptions of the amatory experience of the two characters. Close correspondences are evident in several places. To take only one example among many, the lines "en riens son vueil ne desvoloit, / Eins faisoit quant qu'elle voloit" (vv. 629–30) [he did not oppose her will in any way; rather, he did whatever she wanted], which describes the lion, echo the lines "Ne son vueil ne puis desvoloir, / Eins ne vueil fors ce qu'elle vuet" (vv. 244–45) [I cannot oppose her will; rather, I want only what she wants], in which the narrator describes himself. At one point the identical line is used to describe the narrator (v. 243) and the lion (v. 662) with regard to their respective dames: "Et resjoïr a son voloir" [to rejoice in her will].

The similarity between the narrator and the lion as lovers, rather than being explicitly stated, is thus established by means of re-

peated topoi and verbal parallels, deriving from the poète figure
and directed at the reader. The result of this is twofold. First,
the love experience both of the narrator and of the lion takes on
an increasingly literary aspect. By implication, the narrator's ostensibly extratextual dame begins to appear rather as a literary
convention, a generic construct. Second, increasing emphasis is
placed on verbal activity as such, especially the linguistic and rhetorical conventions associated with fin'amors. It is in the context
of this verbal dexterity that qualifies the narrator to speak of the
love experience of the lion that we must view the narrator's identity as poet-lover. For he employs the same set of linguistic and
literary conventions, the same diction, to articulate what is essentially the same love experience but cast in two different yet complementary forms within the context of the dit. Thus the narrator's articulation of the lion's love experience is primarily narrative,
serving to advance the story line. His articulation of his own love
experience is primarily lyric, serving to define his identity. In terms
of narrative configuration, what emerges from the narrator's description (as witness) of the lion's behavior before his dame is
the lion as lover-protagonist who wants the poet-narrator to act
as the interpreter of his love.

At this point (v. 709) the narrator, who has simply described
the previous scene (vv. 499–708) shifts from witness back to participant. He approaches the dame in order to question her concerning "la verité de pluseurs choses / Qui eu vergier furent encloses"
(vv. 711–12) [the truth about several things that were enclosed
in the garden]. On entering into her presence, however, the narrator, struck by her beauty, falls into a trance as he is reminded
of his own dame:

> Lors au resgarder m'oubliay,
> Si que tout mis en oubli ay
> Ce que li devoie requerre;
> Car sa douceur faisoit tel guerre
> Par sa force et par sa rigour
> A moy, que n'os scens ne vigour
> Que la sceüsse arraisonner,
> Ne que peüsse en mot sonner,
> Eins estoie tous estahis

Et aussi com tous esbahis,
Car au goust de ma chiere dame,
Qui a mon cuer, mon corps et m'ame
Conquis par son regart soutil,
Remiroie son corps gentil
Par un gracieus souvenir
Qu'Amours faisoit en moy venir.

(vv. 767-82)

[When I saw her I forgot myself to such an extent that I forgot everything I was to ask her; for her sweetness so overcame me by its power and intensity that I had no faculty or force with which to speak to her, nor was I able to say a word. Rather, I was completely speechless and astonished because Love sent me a gracious memory of the noble form of my dear lady — she who has conquered my heart, my body and my soul through her subtle glance alone.]

This is the last and the shortest of the three digressions which serve to establish the narrator's identity as lover. Again a lyric meditation on his dame is integrated into the narrative progression. On this occasion the dames of the narrator and the lion are, as it were, commingled: the one evokes the memory of (indeed, becomes a mirror image of) the other. A further link between the two dames and their respective lovers is suggested by the reference to the regart motif (vv. 57-59).

The fact that the narrator as lover is twice characterized by trancelike meditation on his beloved (both here and earlier, in vv. 202-78) is, I would suggest, meant to recall the Perceval of the blood drops on the snow scene of the *Conte du Graal* (vv. 4144-602). This would fit into the system of intertextual references to the oeuvre of Chrétien present in the *Lyon*, serving collectively to identify one of the major generic models (i.e., courtly romance or, in Hoepffner's terminology, "le roman d'aventures") that Machaut exploits in the poem. The fact that Perceval's trance is intimately linked to the discovery and revelation of his identity[15] perhaps strengthens the suggestion that the blood drops scene serves as a model for the revelation of the identity of the *Lyon*'s narrator.

The dame immediately perceives the narrator's difficulty and courteously asks him how he has arrived at the plaisance, thus recalling him from his trancelike state. Ashamed at his momentary lapse, the narrator replies to the dame's inquiry by recounting in summary form the day's adventures (vv. 797–807). He then requests that she explain the behavior of the lion, the nature of the vergier, and the power of the magic boat (vv. 808–21). Instead of answering herself, the dame calls upon one of her retainers, an old chevalier, who replies to the last two questions of the narrator in a speech that takes up almost half of the dit (vv. 853–1800).

The chevalier begins by explaining that only true and faithful lovers can enter the vergier, which was arranged in this way by an ancient king, the ancestor of the dame who is the present ruler. The river and the lion bar the way to disloyal lovers and the magic boat will not work for them. Before the king established this arrangement, the vergier had been open and accessible to all, false lovers as well as true. The chevalier goes on to describe in detail the various types of lovers (as well as their respective ladies) in a series of vivid character portraits (vv. 939–1698).

It finally became impossible to distinguish, on the basis of appearance, the true lovers from the false (vv. 1717–24) and "Li preudons de jadis," [The noble man of yore] in order to exclude the latter, had the river and the magic boat constructed (vv. 1725–72), then named the vergier "L'Esprueve de fines amours" (v. 1778) [The Test of pure love]. Hoepffner astutely points out that "le vergier du *Dit* ressemble à celui d'*Erec* (v. 5739 ss); ici une rivière pour interdire l'entrée, là une muraille d'air, et, ce qui ne saurait être une simple coïncidence, les deux vergiers portent un nom: ici la 'Joie de la Court,' là 'l'Esprueve des fines amours.'"[16] The vergier itself thus participates in the system of intertextual references to the oeuvre of Chrétien against which Machaut's dit must be read. The narrator thus seems implicitly to be presented as a transformation of the romance protagonist as such. Not only does his unfolding narrative identity combine transformed elements of Erec, Yvain, and Perceval, but he can even be viewed as a playfully reworked Lancelot in whom vasselage has been entirely superseded by the ability to give elegant stylized articulation to an exemplary (but highly conventional) amorous sentiment.

The chevalier concludes his long speech with a panegyric to the narrator who has demonstrated his impeccable credentials as a loyal lover by the fact that he has successfully penetrated the vergier. The entire discourse of the chevalier (as well as the plot structure of the dit as a whole) thus serves to emphasize and authorize the narrator's identity as lover. In this sense, the narrative structure of the *Lyon* may be viewed as simultaneously deriving from the identity of the narrator figure and serving to define that identity. Implicit in this process, however, is a differentiation between the narrator and Machaut the poète. The impeccably courtly language, sentiment, and behavior that the dit confers upon the narrator are necessarily contrasted with the remarkably varied depiction of love found in the chevalier's speech. His multileveled diction incorporates sermonic invective (vv. 1192–212), clerkly learning (vv. 1315–21), satiric *descriptio* (vv. 1248–70), and a stylized rustic register (vv. 1546–78), as well as the standard courtly speech. And each of these different aspects of the chevalier's richly varied diction is associated with a different literary genre. This extended virtuoso performance, both linguistic and literary, not only vastly enlarges the scope of the dit, but serves to indicate the presence of Machaut's global poetic identity.[17] The valorization of the narrator as lover which is the ostensible function of the chevalier's speech within the context of the story line thus takes on a new dimension. Not that the narrator is undercut by his juxtaposition with the chevalier; far from it. But he is implicitly distanced from his creator, Machaut the poète of whom this particular first-person narration is but one permutation.

Following the speech of the chevalier comes the brief fourth narrative segment (vv. 1801–44, the second part of the sequence involving the narrator and the lion in the plaisance). The narrator, seated next to the dame, observes once again how the hostile beasts cruelly harass the lion who suffers intensely from this persecution until the dame's calming gaze restores him to joy. The narrator asks the dame to explain all these aspects of the lion's behavior: her reply (vv. 1845–977) involves a rhetorical organization that is almost clerkly. First, she discourses on the power and ubiquity of "Envie," found even in "les bestes mues" (vv. 1845–78) [mute animals]. Second, the dame gives a "naturalistic" explanation of the lion's devotion (vv. 1879–916): she has raised him and cared for him from infancy. Third, she explains that Amour moves the lion to obey her and that her preference for him over other, unfamiliar beasts follows logically from their long and intimate relationship (vv. 1917–45). Finally, referring back to her opening general statement, the dame identifies envie of the lion's privileged position as the reason the other beasts are so hostile towards him (vv. 1946–74).

The reply of the dame takes on special significance in the context of the numerous reminiscences of the genre of the love allegory that have been incorporated into the *Lyon* (as discussed above). The "explanation" of emblematic events (stylized dramatizations most often involving precious stones, plants, and/or animals) in this generic context normally involves a systematic and reductive "decoding" in which each component item is assigned a specific equivalent in a different (moral or emotional) register. This is in fact precisely what happens in the *Dit de la panthère* when the God of Love "explains" to the narrator the significance of his vision (vv. 431–684): the panther signifies the beloved, the animal's sweet breath signifies the beloved's wise and reasonable words, the dragon signifies the *envieus*, the thorns signify the mesdisans, etc. The reply of the dame in the *Lyon* may thus be seen as a playful undercutting of this reductive allegorical discourse, a subversion of the expectation created by the earlier generic references and thus a transformation of the love allegory as generic model, for the purposes of Machaut's new poetic work. At the same time this process serves to indicate the presence of Machaut the poète, and to differentiate him from his narrator figure.

In the fifth narrative segment (vv. 1978–2094, the third and last part of the sequence involving the narrator and the lion in the plaisance) the narrator acts literally as the spokesman for the lion, addressing himself to the dame in order to provide verbal expression for the lion's unarticulated love experience:

Pour li humblement vous depri
Que vous entendez son depri;
Car plus volentiers le dëist

> A vous, que dire nel feïst,
> Ce m'est vis, mais parler ne scet.
>
> (vv. 1985–89)

[On his (the lion's) behalf I humbly ask that you (the dame) listen to his plea; for, in my opinion, he would most willingly say it himself — but he does not know how to speak.]

First, the narrator requests, on behalf of the lion, that the dame have a wall built to protect him from the hostile beasts (vv. 1992–2006). Next (vv. 2007–24), the narrator makes a declaration of love to the dame on behalf of the lion:

> Car li est vostres tous entiers,
> Et si fait bien et volentiers
> Tout ce qu'il pense qui vous plaise. . . .
> Car asseürés ne puet estre
> Sans vous, qui estes sa main destre,
> Qui estes toute s'esperence,
> Ses reconfors, sa soustenance.
>
> (vv. 2007–9, 2015–18)

[For he is entirely yours and thus he willingly accomplishes whatever he thinks pleases you. . . . For he has no confidence without you who are his right hand, his entire hope, his comfort, his sustenance.]

The dame replies to the narrator's request by explaining that no wall of any kind is allowed in the vergier, but that the lion can defend himself from the hostile beasts by ignoring them: "Einsi toutes les veinquera / Par souffrir. . ." (vv. 2073–74) [Thus he will defeat them all through patience]. Though his request is denied, the narrator has nonetheless obtained effective advice for the lion.

Having received satisfactory answers to all his questions, the narrator thanks both the dame and the chevalier, then takes his leave after realizing abruptly that he has been in the vergier "presque jour et demi d'esté" (v. 2088) [almost a summer day and a half].

The sixth narrative segment (vv. 2095–135) opens with the narrator leaving the vergier, accompanied by the lion. The effectiveness of the narrator's role as intermediary for the lion is demonstrated by the fact that when the envious beasts begin to harass him again, the lion reacts exactly as the dame had instructed, prompting the narrator to exclaim:

> Et je croy, se Dieus me doint joie,
> Que tout ce qu'a la dame avoie
> Dit de li, que bien l'entendi
> Et tout ce qu'elle respondi.
> (vv. 2107–10)

[And I believe, may God give me joy, that he completely understood everything that the lady had said about him and her entire reply.]

Having vanquished his tormentors, the lion, now "liez" (v. 2120) [happy], leads the narrator to the shore. The narrator enters the magic boat and crosses the river, all the while staring intently at the lion who returns his gaze. As the narrator arrives at the far bank, the lion runs away.

In the seventh (and final) narrative segment (vv. 2136–68) the narrator returns to the manoir from which he had set out. He arrives at dinner time to find

> . . . compaingnie
> Bele, bonne et bien enseingnie
> Qui m'ot perdu jour et demi,
> Sans nulle riens savoir de mi,
> Comment qu'elle m'eüst moult quis.
> Si m'a trop durement enquis
> que c'estoit, et donc je venoie,
> Ne comment einsi me perdoie.
> (vv. 2141–48)

[a fine, handsome, noble company which had spent a day and a half without me and had no information concerning my whereabouts, even though they had made careful inquiries. Thus they eagerly asked what had happened, where I had been and how I had disappeared.]

A spatial and temporal, as well as narrative, frame is thus provided for the marvelous journey that constitutes the central sections of the dit. This journey is now retold to the assembled company at the inn. Many of the listeners are so impressed with the narrator's tale that they vow to attempt to reach the vergier themselves. In assessing these vows, however, the narrator distances himself from his narration, shifting from narrated to commented tenses to describe his ignorance with regard to these matters: "S'il y passerent, plus n'en say" (v. 2157) [I do not know whether they ever got there].

This initial distancing of the narrator from his narration (in vv. 2157–68) serves as a transition from the last narrative segment to the Epilogue (vv. 2169–2204), in which the identity of the narrator figure is significantly elaborated and expanded. This final expansion involves the two major interrelated components of the narrator's identity that have been established in the body of the dit: poet and lover. First, the expanded narrative voice speaks authoritatively as the creator of this particular work. A final distancing of the narrator from his creation thus results from the presentation of the latter as a literary object: "Si feray ma conclusion, / En finant le Dit dou Lyon" (vv. 2169–70) [And so I arrive at my conclusion as I finish The Poem of the Lion]. The act of naming the work, in addition to serving as a particularly literary closing signal, seems to be at once a manifestation and an authentification of the narrator's identity as poet.[18] The poet-narrator goes on to name himself by means of an anagram signature (vv. 2171–80) after declaring explicitly that: "ce livre ay mis en rime" (v. 2173) [I have rhymed this book].

In the final section of the Epilogue (vv. 2181–204), the expanded narrative voice presents itself as that of an amant in the service of his dame. Yet this is done in such a way as to conflate the notions of love service and poetic service. The reader is requested:

> Qu' Amours priez qu'elle me teingne
> Pour sien, et que ma dame deigne
> Mon petit service en gré prendre;
> Car je ne puis a rien entendre,

Fors seulement que si la serve
Que sa bonne grace desserve.
                    (vv. 2183–88)

[to pray that Love take me as her own and that my lady deign to receive
my service favorably; for I can concentrate on nothing except serving
her in such a way as to merit her favor.]

It is the composition of the dit that constitutes the narrator's service both to Amour and to his beloved. And in a final transformation of the romance construct of chivalric service, the completed
poetic artifact, the *Lyon* itself, is presented to the dame as a love
offering. A deed of poetic *prouesse* is, as it were, substituted for
a deed of knightly *prouesse*, and the poet-narrator of the *Lyon*
may thus be seen as yet another permutation of Machaut the *poète*,
though not, of course, identical with him.

The clerkliness that constitutes an essential part of Machaut's
global poetic identity and discourse, while present in the *Lyon*
as a whole, is only peripherally associated with the unfolding identity of the narrator figure, whose almost exclusively courtly diction thus serves to differentiate him from his creator. Yet within
the context of the story line, it is precisely the narrator's verbal
expertise in a courtly register that establishes both his identity
and his narrative function. Not only is the marvelous journey
initiated and successfully completed by the narrator by virtue of
his identity as a perfect courtly poet-lover (his love experience
and its verbal expression seem inseparable), but this journey may
be seen as constituting a kind of narrative expression (and confirmation) of that identity. Further, the narrator's role as participant
in his unfolding narration alternates with his function as witness
to, and interpreter of, the love experience of another character —
the lion, who feels intensely but cannot articulate his feelings.
It is his verbal dexterity, his poetic expertise, that qualify the narrator to serve as a kind of necessary interpreter of another's love
experience. For the lion seems to be an emblem of the lover who
is not a poet, of love as pure experience, bereft of verbal expression. As such it is shown to be not only incomplete but ineffec-
tive. It is only through the verbal mediation of the poet-narrator

that the lion, as lover-protagonist, is able to articulate his love experience and (precisely because of this articulation) to improve his condition as a lover. All of these suggestions are elaborated and made more explicit in the third dit in which the poet-narrator functions as witness-participant, the *Fonteinne amoureuse.*

La Fonteinne amoureuse

The *Fonteinne* begins with a Prologue of sixty lines in which the narrator figure presents himself. The various sides of his composite character, each associated with and derived from a different literary tradition, appear sequentially. The narrator speaks first as a poet-lover who asserts his work is begun "En l'onneur ma dame jolie" (v. 8) [in honor of my beautiful lady] to whom his "vray cuer" (v. 12) [true heart] belongs. Both the attitude expressed and the diction employed in this section of the Prologue (vv. 1–12) recall the first-person voice of the grand chant courtois (cast, however, in a narrative mode). The poetic work to follow is described as "chose. . . / Faite de sentement joli / Et de vray cuer" (vv. 9, 11–12) [a thing . . . made out of joyous affection and a true heart]. The impression (created by means of generic expectation) is that the poet-narrator's own love experience is about to be recounted — and a kind of lyric authorization is suggested. On closer examination, however, the construction of the phrase permits a polysemy which will be exploited as the dit progresses.[19]

In the second section of the Prologue (vv. 13–29) there is a shift in discourse and attitude as the narrator adopts a clerkly, didactic mode in speaking about his work. Readers are instructed to "Laisser le mal, le bien eslire" (v. 16) [Leave the bad and choose the good] in the work they are about to read.

In the third section of the Prologue (vv. 30–54), the narrator speaks as a professional writer, a court poet whose work is commanded by a patron: "Celui pour qui je fais ce livre" (v. 32) [He for whom I undertake this book]. A double anagram is given (vv. 40–41) in which the names of poet and patron are contained.[20] The significance of this anagram is manifold. First, because it commingles (on a graphic level) the identities of the poet-narrator and the lover-protagonist, it may be seen as related to the narrative stance which will be exploited with great skill in the *Fonteinne,* enabling the poet-narrator to sing the love experience of another in a first-person context. Second, the poet is commanded to give this double anagram, to reveal the two names, by "amours fine" (v. 37). What seems to be suggested is that the poetic activity — more specifically, the verbal artfulness — of the professional poet in the service of his patron constitutes service to Amour (a suggestion that is both implied and authorized by the global poetic identity of Machaut the poète established in the Prologue). Third, the anagram serves as a demonstration of the truthfulness of the narrator figure which is thus presented as residing in his linguistic ability: after the key to the anagram is given (vv. 46–51) we find: "Or resgarde que je ne mente! / Car vraiement, se je mentoie, / Confus et honteus en seroie (vv. 52–54) [Now see if I am lying! For if I lied I would truly be abashed and shamed]. What is important is not extratextual verification of the names, but the fact that the anagram "works," i.e., that Machaut's language functions successfully qua poetic discourse. The final guarantee of the poet-narrator's reliability is thus his poetic craft itself. Poetic activity becomes, in an important sense, self-authorizing (and self-sufficient). Subject matter (in general) and the "personal" love experience of the courtly lyric (in particular) necessarily assume a secondary importance.

The final section of the Prologue of the *Fonteinne* (vv. 55–60) underlines the dual nature of the narrator figure. He speaks first as poet — referring to the "events" to be recounted in the poem as "ma matiere" (v. 55); then, as character — referring to those same "events" as an "aventure" (v. 57) that befell him. Our first-person narrator is self-presented as a direct participant in his own narration — which thus forms part of his experience. We have a lyric construct used to authenticate a narrative subject matter in a way reminiscent of the opening of the *Roman de la rose*. In the *Fonteinne*, however, a further development has been effected. Because of the nature of Machaut's poète figure, the love experience articulated by the poet in a lyric framework (i.e., as his own experience) need not (within the context of the story line) be that of the first-person narrator qua character.

To summarize, the Prologue to the *Fonteinne* establishes a composit, multifaceted, first-person narrator figure (as a kind of necessary precondition to the dit's existence) who can speak as lover, as clerc, and as professional court poet, assuming in turn the attitude and diction associated with each. The narrator figure is shown to have an existence outside the context of the narrative proper by the fact that he employs, throughout the Prologue, the tenses of Weinrich's commented world. A certain emphasis thus seems to be placed on the poet-narrator's function as narrator in contradistinction to his function as a character in the narrative. At the same time this distinction itself — a duality inherent in first-person narration — is underlined at the outset of the work. As we shall see, it will be employed throughout as an important informing element. Repeatedly, and with much greater frequency than in the *Behaingne* or the *Lyon*, the narrative will be interrupted by the narrator speaking qua narrator (i.e., using commented tenses, expressing an extradiegetic point of view, etc.).

Further, the narrator figure of the *Fonteinne* presented to us in the Prologue may be seen to be distinguishable from, but contained by, Machaut's global poète figure. This is accomplished in large part by linguistic means — what may be seen as traces of the poète (as distinct from the narrator) embedded in the language of the text. The Prologue begins with a series of elaborate annominationes (vv. 1–12). These verbal pyrotechnics, reminiscent of Rutebeuf,[21] are not simply gratuitous ornamentation. Situated strategically at the very beginning of the *Fonteinne*, they call the reader's attention, from the outset, to the poetic artifact as, above all, patterned language. Further, they may be seen to emanate from a poetic identity different from, larger than, the je who speaks in this particular poem: the global je of the oeuvres complètes — Machaut the poète who contains and speaks through the je of the dit's poet-narrator.[22]

In lines 13–22 the implicit presence of the poète figure becomes intensified. The wordplay that in lines 1–12 had been primarily formal in character now takes on a semantic dimension. The repeated pairing of "lire" [read] with "eslire" [choose] in different forms (future indicative, vv. 13–14; infinitive, vv. 15–16; past participle, vv. 21–22) results in semantic interpenetration, compounded by "eslite"/"delite" (vv. 17–18) and "lit"/"delit" (vv. 19–

20). A commentary on the kind of reading required by this text (active [eslire] and pleasurable [delit]) is thus built into the form of the text itself in a way which not only intensifies the implicit presence of the poète figure but characterizes that figure by means of his superlative poetic craftsmanship. This characterization as well as the differentiation between poète and poet-narrator which is established in the Prologue inform the poem that follows in several important ways, as may be shown through a detailed analysis of its narrative structure.

The first narrative segment (vv. 61–234) opens with the poet-narrator in bed but unable to sleep, alone in the room of a chateau.[23] He hears lamentations coming from the room next door and is profoundly frightened. At this point the narrative is interrupted by a digression (vv. 101–92) in which the narrator (employing commented tenses, i.e., speaking qua narrator) discourses on his own identity and his extradiegetic ("personal") past — elaborating certain suggestions found in the Prologue. The point of departure for this digression is the narrator's self-avowed cowardice ("Car je sui plus couars qu'uns lievres" [v. 92] [For I am more cowardly than a hare]), which is presented as consistent with the clerkly side of his makeup. This point is not only made explicitly but is reinforced by the very rhetorical organization of the digression/apologia which thus appears as implicit evidence of the narrator's clerkliness. The digression is divided into four sections in which the narrator speaks alternatively from an individual and from a general perspective. In Section 1 (vv. 101–16) the personal experience of the narrator is evoked as the authority for his declaration. If anyone should accuse him of cowardice he would not care because he says, "je vi des plus vaillans hommes" (v. 104) [I saw some very brave men] behave in the same manner. Section 2 (vv. 117–38) posits a generally valid opposition between clerc and chevalier, each of whom has an appropriate behavioral code: ". . . chevaliers acouardis / Et clers qui vuet estre hardis / Ne valent plein mon pong de paille" (vv. 133–35) [neither cowardly knights nor would-be brave clerks are worth anything at all]. It should be noted that this opposition will be exploited to define (in part) the relation between the poet-narrator and Amant in the second half of the *Fonteinne*. The third section of the digression (vv. 139–47) involves a return to the individual perspective:

> Et comment que je soie clers
> Rudes, nices et malapers,
> S'ay je esté, par mes deus fois,
> En tele place aucune fois
> Avec le bon Roy de Behaingne,
> Dont Dieus ait l'ame en sa compaigne!
> Que maugré mien hardis estoie,
> Car il n'i avoit lieu ne voie
> Ne destour ou fuïr sceusse. . . .

[Although I am an awkward, foolish, uncouth clerk, I have twice been brave in spite of myself in the presence of the good King of Bohemia — may his soul be with God in paradise — for there was never a place or a journey or a battle that could make him retreat.]

Although a clerc, the narrator has served with "le bon Roy de Behaingne" with whom he was brave in spite of himself. His clerkly identity thus appears as only one side of the narrator's character. Further, the personal anecdote from his extradiegetic past (complete with specific battle details) seems momentarily to conflate the narrator of the *Fonteinne* with Machaut the poète whose most illustrious patron was in fact John of Bohemia. (This point is made in other of Machaut's works both early and late — e.g., the *Behaingne* and the *Confort d'ami* — and may thus be viewed as a biographical element consistently employed by Machaut in the creation of his global poetic identity.) The narrator is thus abruptly distanced from his subject matter while at the same time gaining increased (temporal) depth and authority. The fourth section of the digression (vv. 156–88) involves a reassumption of the clerkly, didactic stance: "Je parle tout en general / Sans riens dire d'especial" (vv. 181–82) [I am speaking in general, without addressing particular cases]. The narrator answers possible accusations of boasting by positing as a generally valid behavioral rule that one should follow and imitate one's "signeur" (v. 162) in a battle situation. (Again there seems to be a certain amount of preparation for the relationship, within the context of the story line, between the poet-narrator and Amant — also a *signeur*.)

Returning to his subject matter, the narrator recounts how he was finally able to understand the words of the voice next door, that of a lover forced to leave his beloved against his will. The lover announces his intention of making a complainte in a speech (vv. 200–20) which serves to establish important parallels and differences between him and the narrator. Amant's language (employing standard topoi, to be sure) recalls that of the narrator speaking as lover in the Prologue. He too has a dame to whom his "fin cuer" (v. 202) [pure heart] belongs, and he will make a song out of his feeling ("sentement" [v. 220]) for her. However, not only is this feeling one of "dure dolour" (v. 211) [harsh suffering], in contrast to the narrator's "sentement joli" (v. 11) [joyful emotion], but it will function narratively in the dit while the narrator's will not. The narrator now prepares to act as scribe for an intercalated lyric poem which displays an extraordinary degree of technical mastery and which is the expression of the love experience of another character — Amant, the protagonist:

> Si que je pris mon escriptoire,
> Qui est entaillie d'ivoire,
> Et tous mes outils pour escrire
> La complainte qu'i voloit dire.
> (vv. 229–32)

[I took my inkstand of engraved ivory and all my implements in order to write down the complaint that he wanted to make.]

The "Complainte de l'Amant" exists simultaneously in two structural contexts. First, it is within the narrative structure of the *Fonteinne* where Amant as character provides both subject matter (his love experience, "mon sentement" [v. 220]) and articulation; the poet-narrator as character simply transcribes graphically Amant's expression of his experience. This configuration is emblematized in lines 233–34: "Si commença piteusement / Et je l'escri joieusement" [He began (to speak) sadly and I joyfully wrote it down]. The fact that the narrator transcribes the complainte of Amant also functions as a structural device by means of which the lyric poem (the love experience of the protagonist) is set into the narrative (the first-person account of the narrator). We have here a much more elaborate (and nuanced) development of the construct of narrator as witness than was to be found either in the *Behaingne* or in the *Lyon.*

Second, the complainte exists within the context of the oeuvre of Guillaume de Machaut where Amant as patron (le duc de Berry) provides subject matter (i.e., love experience) only, and Machaut the poète provides the poetic articulation of the experience. One may, I think, view this as a particularly rich exploitation on the part of Machaut of the limitations and restrictions inherent in his situation as court poet.[24] In a way that is both artful and highly self-conscious (on the level both of poetic diction and narrative form) these constraints are turned into resources.[25]

The contents of the complainte (vv. 235–1034) may be summarized briefly as follows. Amant begins with a description of his unhappy predicament (vv. 235–542): obliged to leave his beloved, he does not know if his love has been noticed or returned. An archetypal lyric situation is presented (with commented tenses) in a courtly diction which makes elegant use of the whole repertoire of standard amorous topoi. There is then a shift in discourse as Amant, speaking now as a clerkly narrator figure (and employing narrated tenses) recounts the story of Ceyx and Alcyone (vv. 543–698).[26] This Ovidian narrative is used not only to invest dreams with authority but serves as model and authorization for Amant's prayer to the god of sleep; Amant asks that Morpheus help him by revealing his love and suffering to his dame in a dream (vv. 699–882). The shifts in diction and attitude found in the complainte recall the various sides of the character of the narrator figure as he appeared in the Prologue. Not only is Amant thereby presented (implicitly) as a kind of permutation of the poet-narrator, but the presence of the common creator of both characters (Machaut the poète) is further intensified. Apt exploitation of linguistic, rhetorical, and structural parallels calls attention to the text as text, as poetic artifact, and (repeatedly) to the fact that it is Machaut who is articulating the love experience of his protagonist-patron. Further, the motif of the importance and truth of dreams underlying much of the complainte involves a complex exploitation of the *Roman de la rose* as subtext. When Amant hopes his dame will realize that "Songier souvent ne doit mie estre fable, / Einsois chose doit estre veritable" (vv. 783–84) [Often dreams are not fables but rather tell the truth], more is going on however than a simple transformation of one of the central motifs of the *Rose* for the purposes of the present lyric lament. In addition, this intertextual reference to the *Rose* functions structurally (as part of a network of such references) within the *Fonteinne* as a whole. To mention only one example of this functioning, it prepares for, and will be elaborated by, the poet-narrator's later commentary (vv. 1565–68) on the long dream that he has in the course of the narrative. A link between the poet-narrator and the lover-protagonist is thus suggested by purely literary means (i.e., a common intertextual presence in the direct discourse of both characters). A greater (and more subtle) overall structural cohesion results from this — a cohesion which includes a greater integration of the lyric and narrative verse forms employed in the *Fonteinne*. Machaut as poète figure thus becomes increasingly present in his text while the "literariness" of this latter is repeatedly emphasized. Thus, even as it is put into the mouth of Amant, the complainte is made to exist as an independent artistic creation, emanating from Machaut the poète, author of the dit as a whole and of the larger oeuvre in which the dit is situated. In this context, it is highly significant that the complainte poeticizes itself as a technical achievement: in the last strophe we find the boast: "Cent rimes ay mis dedans ceste rime" (v. 1021) [I have used one hundred rhymes in this poem]. This claim is the more impressive when we remember that the complainte (vv. 235–1034) comprises two hundred stanzas of four lines each, grouped by fours into strophes. Formal mastery, in an important sense, guarantees the status (and the discourse) of Machaut the professional court poet.

What follows the complainte may be described as the second narrative segment (vv. 1035–290). After having discovered that his transcription of the complainte has taken all night (the intercalated lyric being thus placed into narrative temporality), the narrator, speaking as a professional poet (but as character, i.e., within the context of the story line) judges the complainte:

> Et puis je lus de chief en chief
> La complainte qu'avoie escripte
> Pour vir s'il y avoit redite,
> Mais nes une n'en y trouvay;
> Et encor moult bien esprouvay
> Qu'il y avoit, dont j'eus merveilles,
> Cent rimes toutes despareilles.
> (vv. 1046–52)

[I then read from beginning to end the complaint I had written down to see if it contained any repeated rhymes, but I did not find a single one. Indeed, I realized that it contained one hundred dissimilar rhymes, which amazed me.]

The irony and wittiness of this judgment—picking up as it does the complainte's self-characterization—are evident. Further, this serves to highlight the distinction between the poet-narrator of the *Fonteinne* and Machaut the poète while simultaneously emphasizing the artifice—the fictionality—of the entire dit with its complex narrative configuration, even as the dit continues to unfold.

The narrator leaves his room to find the lover he has been listening to and the scene of the meeting between the narrator and Amant may be seen as a kind of dramatization of the court poet side of the narrator's character. There is a ritualized beginning as he kneels before his noble patron (v. 1214) who has him rise (v. 1226). In response to Amant's question the narrator replies (in a direct speech, vv. 1239–70, that opens with the vocative "Monsigneur") that he has undertaken his present journey specifically to find Amant, to whom he offers his love and his service. The social difference between the two characters (between court poet and princely patron) is incorporated into the narrator's extremely courtois speech[27] and thus helps to structure the relationship between the two from its inception. With an equal display of courtoisie, Amant warmly accepts the poet-narrator's offer and graciously thanks him for having ". . . a moy tout einsi vous donnez / Et ligement abandonnez" (vv. 1285–86) [thus wholeheartedly and loyally entered my service].

The third narrative segment (vv. 1291–542) begins with the poet-narrator and the lover-protagonist, whose bodies are emblematically linked, entering together into a locus amoenus. As if to establish from the outset the *Roman de la rose* as literary analogue to the present scene, the first sentence spoken in the garden contains the word "deduit" twice in the rhyme position (vv. 1297–98), recalling the proprietor of the enclosed garden in Guillaume de Lorris.

Straightaway Amant leads the narrator to a magnificent fountain which is elaborately described (vv. 1300–70). We have a descriptive set piece of the kind found in the *romans antiques*[28] but here filtered through a first-person consciousness (as in the *Rose*, e.g., in the description of the portraits outside the wall of the garden). The fountain is supported by an ivory pillar on which the story of Narcissus is sculpted so skillfully that it seems alive to the narrator (vv. 1310–12). Its marble surface bears the story of Helen's abduction by Paris (including Venus inflaming Helen with her "brandon qu'art sans fumee" [v. 1321] [torch that burns without smoking]) followed by scenes from the Trojan War. The surrounding plaisance is watered by the fountain, birdsong is everywhere (vv. 1355–60; cf. the *Rose*, vv. 641–75) and the whole is compared by the narrator to the "paradis terrestre" (v. 1369; cf. the *Rose*, v. 634). The fountain then is first presented descriptively — by the narrator. And motifs (even verbal reminiscences) from the *Rose* form, as it were, the visible building blocks of the description.

Next, the fountain is presented narratively — by Amant (vv. 1380–420). First, explaining that the garden "fu jadis li demours / De Cupido, le dieu d'amours" (vv. 1381–82) [was once the abode of Cupid, the god of love], he recounts how Venus had the ivory and marble sculpted by Pygmalion (vv. 1395–98). Then, at almost the precise midpoint of the dit (v. 1413) the fountain (and the poem) are named: *la Fonteinne amoureuse*, whose water causes those who drink to love; "Et si les faisoit amer si / Que pluseurs en ont esté mort, / Sans secours, de piteuse mort" (vv. 1418–20) [and it makes them love so much that many have died a piteous death without solace].

The structural importance of the midpoint in Old French romance frequently involves the identity of the hero who is there named or renamed.[29] By an adept exploitation of this romance convention, the "hero" of the *Fonteinne* is presented as the poetic text itself (emblematized by the fountain).[30] For, as should be evident from the preceding discussion, the fountain is indeed meant to serve as a kind of emblem for the dit whose name it shares. In this way the poem is invested with a profound (yet playful) self-referentiality.

Further, the fountain exists not only as an "object" in the narrative sequence of the *Fonteinne* but as a purely literary entity, created out of (by means of references to) what amounts to an almost omnipresent subtext, the *Roman de la rose.* This process of intertextual reference and transformation allows itself to be perceived as such. Having, for example, Pygmalion sculpt the story of Narcissus onto the fountain at the command of Venus involves an obvious conflation of the two Ovidian myths most explicitly employed (and reworked) by Guillaume de Lorris and Jean de Meun.[31] The fountain becomes, then, an emblem not only of the poetic text in which it figures (yielding a kind of structured circularity) but of the literary processes (intertextuality, generic transformation, etc.) which have produced the text.

An extremely adept and subtle literary consciousness is thus at work in this scene — one which seems to insist on its own presence in the text. What results is an implicit affirmation of the primacy of the relationship poet/text. It is the insistence on the primacy of this relationship that allows the narrative configuration of the poet-narrator as witness-participant (as used in a particular dit) to function within the context of the global poetic identity of the oeuvres complètes, that allows Machaut the poète to speak of the *Fonteinne* as his own "experience" and as forming part of his service to Amour (even though its ostensible subject matter is the love experience of someone else). For, as is explicitly demonstrated in the *Prologue,* the poète's service to Amour resides in his poetic activity.

The narrator declines to drink at the fountain, stating that ". . . la fonteinne ne son mestre / Ne porroient d'amours plus mettre / En mon cuer qu'il i en avoit" (vv. 1427–29) [neither the fountain nor its master could put any more love into my heart than was already there]. The lover component of the narrator's identity which is thus stressed (referring back to his dame, last mentioned in v. 12) serves to link him with Amant, who in his turn refuses to drink from the fountain.

In a long speech (vv. 1439–510) Amant tells of his love and impending exile and ends with a request that the narrator make a poem out of his (Amant's) unhappy situation:

> Pour ç'amis, je vous vueil prier
> Que tant vueilliez estudier
> Que de m'amour et de ma plainte
> Me faciés ou lay ou complainte.
> Car je say bien que la pratique
> Savez toute, et la theorique
> D'amour loial et de ses tours,
> Et ses assaus et ses estours
> Vous ont donné mainte frisson. . . .
>   (vv. 1501–9)

[Because of this, my friend, I beg you to please consider how you can make a lay or complainte for me out of my love and my lamenting. For I well know that you have a complete practical and theoretical knowledge of loyal love; and (love's) assaults and attacks have often made you tremble. . . .]

This request not only presents an integrated résumé of the three major components of the narrator's identity (clerc, lover, and professional court poet), but provides a model, within the context of the story line, of the extratextual situation (the poet/patron relationship) that lies behind the dit as a whole. The text thus incorporates (in a way which heightens its textuality, its existence as poetic artifact) the extratextual situation that is presented as having generated it.

The narrator then presents Amant with his own complainte: ". . . Sire, vostre requeste, / Tenez; vesla ci toute preste" (vv. 1519–20) [Sire, take what you have requested; here it is all ready]. He then proceeds to explain how he came to hear and record it (vv. 1535–42); in effect, the entire narrative progression of the first half of the *Fonteinne* is explicitly restated in summary form, along with the elegant fictional construct (i.e., that Amant is the poet of the complainte) around which it is built. The text thus reaffirms itself as text (the fiction, as fiction), and at the same time the narrative works to authorize its own content. This is indeed a scene of great ingenuity. Machaut the poète has of course already fulfilled the request that Amant the character (at once lover and patron) is presented as making; the complainte (as situated by the temporal structure of the dit) has already been written. The narrative structure of the *Fonteinne* thus serves as a means through which Machaut "lends" his poetic craft to the character of his patron, whose love experience is sung. The poet appears as intermediary, as the necessary interpreter of another's love, on two levels simultaneously: intranarrative (as the poète who has created the intercalated complainte) and extranarrative (as the poète who has created the *Fonteinne* as a whole).

At this point in the story line first Amant, then the narrator, fall asleep (an action which is motivated by mention of the preceding sleepless night, v. 1552). The focus is centered on the narrator who, just before sleep overtakes him, says, I "pris a penser a ma dame" (v. 1548) [began to think about my lady]. The long dream sequence that follows is presented from his perspective:

> En mon dormant songay un songe
> Que je ne tien pas pour mensonge,
> Einsois le tien a veritable
> Et bon, que qui le teingne a fable.
> (vv. 1565–68)

[And while I slept I had a dream which I do not consider to be a lie. Rather, I hold it to be true and good, no matter who regards it as a fable.]

The echoes of the opening of the *Rose* are of course obvious[32] and function, as has been previously remarked, to call attention to the textual presence of the poète figure, speaking through the narrator. Further, they serve to present the dream of the *Fonteinne* as in some sense a reversal of the dream of the *Rose* by inviting a comparison between the two. First, the *Fonteinne* reverses the narrative sequence found in the *Rose*: parc and fountain here precede the dream, for which they serve as a setting, rather than being, as in the *Rose*, part of the dream itself. Second, the *Fonteinne*, where the dream is only one part of a larger narrative structure which contains it, reverses the framework of the *Rose*, where dream and narrative are coterminous. As so often in the works of Machaut, the *Rose* is being fragmented and transformed for the purposes of a new (and much smaller) poem — but it is invoked in such a way as to serve itself as authorization for this process of transformation. For the narrator of the *Fonteinne* (combining narrated and commented tenses) is simultaneously affirming the "truth" of his dream within the narrative context of the dit and within the larger context of the vernacular poetic tradition embodied by the *Rose*, whose vocabulary he employs.

The dream sequence of the *Fonteinne* (vv. 1569–2518) may be seen as falling into two parts. The first, more purely narrative, is addressed to the poet-narrator. The second, more purely lyrical, is addressed to Amant, though presented from the perspective of the narrator, who functions as the witness to the entire dream.

The dream begins as Venus appears before the narrator, carrying a golden apple inscribed: "Donnee soit a la plus belle!" (v. 1603) [To be given to the most beautiful]. The narrator, reacting in good clerkly fashion, feels a strong desire to have this text glossed: "Et volontiers veïsse qu'elle / Me deïst la signefiance / De l'escripture et la substance" (vv. 1604–6) [I would have greatly liked for her to tell me the significance and the purport of the writing]. Venus procedes to fulfill the narrator's wish by recounting to him the story of the wedding of Peleus and the judgment of Paris (vv. 1633–2144). The explication of the golden apple is simultaneously a glossing of the fountain (which is thus again presented as a literary entity, as text) on whose surface, we remember, the story of "Venus, Paris et dame Heleinne" (v. 1314) was carved. As she narrates, the Goddess of Love seems to take on the aspect of a clerc. She cites written authority for her words (". . . se l'istoire ne ment" [v. 1898] [if the story does not lie]) and has the character Mercury, a secondary narrator in her story, do the same for the story of Paris' birth (". . . ce dit la lettre" [v. 1923] [so the text says]; ". . . se l'istoire ne ment" v. 1958). Venus's tale thus takes on an existence independent of its narrator — and is authorized by a seemingly impersonal clerkliness, which of course resides in the figure of the poète.

In the middle of Venus's narration is embedded an explicit indicator of the presence of Machaut the poète. Interrupting Mercury's story of the birth of Paris, Machaut proclaims a clerkly rather than lyric-based authority for the Ovidian narration in progress:

> Mais loange ne vueil ne gloire
> De ceste geste ou ceste hystoire,
> Qu'on scet bien que pas nez n'estoie
> Eins la fondation de Troie,
> Mais ce l'ay mot a mot escript,
> Si com veü l'ay en escript.
>
> (vv. 1989–94)

[But I want neither praise nor glory on account of this tale or this story, for it is obvious that I was not born before the foundation of Troy. But what I have written down here is taken word for word from a written source.]

Venus then resumes speaking and recounts how Paris chose her to receive the golden apple, declaring: "comme fin et loial amant / . . . tous mes jours la serviray" (vv. 2136–37) [I will serve her (Venus) all my life as a pure and loyal lover]. Venus closes her story by telling the narrator: "Or as response a ta pensee" (v. 2144) [I have now answered your request]. This is highly significant (especially given the context provided by the *Rose* references) in that narrative bereft of any interpretive discourse is thus presented as gloss, as a sufficient explication of the "signefiance" (v. 1605), the "substance" (v. 1606) of a given text. This point is all the more striking since Machaut's source for the Ovidian matière of Venus's speech (and he goes out of his way to call attention to the fact that he is working from a written source) is the *Ovide moralisé*,[33] in which narrative discourse is regularly interrupted by interpretive discourse.[34] Machaut has systematically and, it would seem, purposefully "demoralized" his source in a context in which an implicit thematization of the process of glossing and interpreting invests such a transformation with a particular significance.

The second part of the dream begins as Venus turns to the sleeping Amant (v. 2145), announcing that she has brought "sa dame et sa drue" (v. 2165) [his lady and sweetheart] to comfort him. Amant's dame then sits down next to her sleeping lover and speaks to him "Par la guise et par la maniere / Qui est escripte ci derriere" (vv. 2205–6) [In the following manner, as is written below].

What follows is the second intercalated lyric poem of the *Fonteinne* which, though directly spoken by the dame (as character), has been introduced as written object, as écriture, calling attention to its existence as a poetic artifact independent of the dit which contains it, as well as to its extradiegetic creator: Machaut the poet-author. The intercalated piece itself, entitled "Le Confort de l'amant et de la dame" (vv. 2207–494) is an extended declaration of love and fidelity in the face of the lovers' impending separation.

It is important to note that once again it is the love experience of Amant that is being given poetic articulation by Machaut, and that the two lyric set pieces of the *Fonteinne* (the loci both of the most intensely patterned language and of the most intense emotive experience) are linked by this fact as well as by means of structural symmetry and correspondences (e.g., Amant/dame as speakers; complainte/confort; first half of the dit/second half, etc.). The dream comes to a close as Amant's lady, having finished speaking, kisses her lover and exchanges rings with him before departing in the company of Venus.

The fourth narrative segment (vv. 2519–744) begins as Amant and the narrator awaken simultaneously to discover that they have dreamed the same dream, and that the ring given by the dame in the dream is "in reality" on Amant's finger:

> Car en l'eure nous esveillames
> Et tous deus un songe songames,
> Einsi com nous le nous comptames.
>   Si s'en merveille,
> Car l'annel en son doy trouvames.
>   (vv. 2519–23)

[For we awoke at that moment and both dreamed the same dream, as we recounted to each other. And we were astonished to find the ring on his finger.]

The interpenetration of dream and "reality" within the context of the dit (which, as poetic structure, contains both) is emphasized by the fact that the verse form used by the dame for the confort continues to be used by the narrator to recount the end of the dream and the awakening of the two dreamers, before he switches back to octosyllabic rhyming couplets. The formal overlapping of lyric and narrative verse also functions to heighten the text's self-presentation as text and thus may be seen as yet another trace of the presence of the poète embedded in the language of the dit.

After declaring his gratitude to Venus and to the God of Sleep, Amant recounts "his" dream in summary form to the narrator (vv. 2593–631), who swears that he has had the same dream (vv. 2632–40). The self-authentification process thus built into the narrative recalls (with similar implications) that already discussed in connection with the narrator's summary restatement of the complainte sequence (vv. 1535–42).

The narrator now intervenes from an extradiegetic perspective. Speaking as clerc (and employing commented tenses) he authenticates the multiple dream just described in the narrative by recounting an exemplum: one hundred Roman senators "qui tous cent un songe songerent" (v. 2647) [all one hundred of whom dreamed the same dream]. He first describes their dream (an apocalyptic vision of nine suns of different colors), then states that the dream has a "grant signefiance" (v. 2686) [important significance] which was explained by "la prophete et sage Sebille" (v. 2689) [the wise and prophetic Sibyl] who ". . . la verité de leur songe / Leur moustra sans nulle mensonge" (vv. 2693–94) [showed them the true meaning of their dream without lying]. The narrator concludes by citing his *auctoritas*, but explicitly refuses to include an explication of the dream:

> Quier en "l'Istoire des Rommains,"
> La le verras, ne plus ne mains,
> Car l'exposition seroit
> Trop longue, qui la te diroit.
> (vv. 2695–98)

[Look in The History of the Romans. There you will find it all, for it would take too long to give you the whole account (here).]

This intervention is an arresting example of the way in which the identity of the narrator as construct (overlapping as it does with that of Machaut the poète) operates: his extradiegetic, clerkly sapience is used to authenticate the "truth" of his narrative. In addition, there is a second (implicit) authentification — of dreams as having signefiance. This is at once structured and reinforced by the resonances with the *Rose*, especially in lines 2693–94, where we find the rhyme words "songe"/"mensonge." In this context Machaut's refusal to gloss the dream of the senators may perhaps be viewed as having a more general import. He seems to be doing here explicitly what he had done implicitly by demoralizing the narrative material taken from the *Ovide moralisé*. Part of the poetic use to which Machaut puts his sources in the *Fonteinne* seems to involve the implicit affirmation of poetic discourse as such, an endeavor deriving from, and authorized by, the *Rose*, whose presence in this text is so striking.

When Amant begins to express misgivings about the absence of his dame the narrator reminds him point by point of the contents of the dream (vv. 2704–20), and he becomes "tous reconfortez" (v. 2721) [entirely comforted]. After explaining that Amant is now effectively protected from the possible ravages of exile and Fortune, the narrator declares: "Ce fu la fin de son confort" (v. 2740) [Thus was he completely consoled].

The fifth (and final) narrative segment (vv. 2745–848) opens as a chevalier comes upon the protagonists in the garden and abruptly reimposes an "objective" temporality on the narrative: "vous avez ici esté / Bien la moitié d'un jour d'esté" (vv. 2750–52) [you have spent the better half of a summer day here]. Amant leaves the garden and, after spending the night in his castle, departs the next morning for the last leg of his journey into exile, accompanied by the narrator. As they travel Amant gives repeated evidence of his good spirits, of the fact that he is truly and effectively "conforté" (v. 2798), and ends by singing a rondel: "Eu païs ou ma dame maint" (vv. 2825–32) [In the land where my lady remains] from the deck of the ship that is to carry him away. Before they part at the seashore Amant rewards the narrator "liberalement et largement" (v. 2837) [freely and generously] for his service. The professional court poet component of the narrator's identity is thus adroitly exploited as the dit draws to an end, and the exemplary poet/patron relationship between the narrator and Amant receives an appropriate and functional emphasis in the closing lines of a poem whose Prologue had included a poeticization of the relationship between Machaut and the duc de Berry.

The *Fonteinne* concludes with a couplet in which a shift from narrated to commented tense operates to present the narrator (the particular "je" of this particular poem) as subsumed by the global poetic identity of the oeuvres complètes (the "je" of the poète): "Einsi parti. Je pris congié. / Dites moy, fu ce bien songié?" (vv. 2847–48) [And so I went away. I took my leave. Tell me, was this well dreamed?]. The "je" who employs the preterite (in v. 2847) is a character in this poem. The "je" who employs the present (in v. 2848) is the author of the poem addressing his audience ("Dites moy"), in which both his patron and his dame are presumably included.[35] The final word ("songié") seems to emblematize the conflation of these two "jes" by means of a suggestive polysemy coupled with the ambiguous antecedent of the pronoun "ce." Its meaning of "dreamed" refers to the dream in the garden — the product of the narrator. Its meaning of "thought up" refers to the *Fonteinne* in its entirety — the product of the poète. There is also the suggestion, resulting in part from the fact that *songier* has become semantically overcharged by means of the *Rose* references, that the whole of the *Fonteinne* is being referred to as a *songe*, as the dream of Machaut the poète.

This final expansion of the first-person voice behind the *Fonteinne* serves as an important closing signal, implicitly situating the work in the context of Machaut's oeuvre. One may perhaps even speak of a framing device, given the first line of the *Fonteinne*, where the poetic ego whose presence opens and explains the work seems to belong to Machaut the poète: "Pour moy deduire et soulacier" [In order to divert and amuse myself].[36]

A detailed consideration of the *Behaingne*, the *Lyon*, and the *Fonteinne* reveals a progressive development, an increasingly elaborate exploitation of the narrative stance in which the poet-narrator functions as witness-protagonist. In this context, the *Fonteinne* may be viewed as a culmination. As in the *Behaingne* and the *Lyon* on the level of narrative structure, the narrator figure of the *Fonteinne* operates as a device that allows the love experience of a third-person protagonist to be recounted in a first-person context: the narrator is the witness through whom both the complainte and the dream are presented. As in the *Lyon* on the level of plot the poet-narrator helps the lover protagonist of the *Fonteinne*, obtains "confort" for him. However, both the identity and function of the narrator figure are much more elaborately developed in the *Fonteinne* than in the two earlier dits. Not only is increased emphasis placed on his dual role (alternating between witness to his narration and participant in it), but there is consistent and artful exploitation of the distinction between the narrator's first-person voice and that of Machaut the poète, of which the narrator's voice is a permutation. This distinction allows for a great refinement of the construct of poet as "interpreter" of the love experience of someone else — utilized in the *Lyon* exclusively on the level of plot. The *Fonteinne* may in fact be seen as comprising two "collaborations" in which Amant's love experience is articulated simultaneously (but on different levels) by the narrator and the poète. As the narrator wrote down the complainte for Amant in the first half of the dit, so he dreams the dream for Amant in the second half. At the same time the organization and language of the text present Machaut the poète as the creator both of the complainte and of the dream.

v. Conclusion: Ramifications of Machaut's Achievement

The preceding discussion has sought to examine in detail both the nature and function of the innovative concept of poetic identity developed by Guillaume de Machaut. It has thus of necessity concentrated on Machaut's own artistic output. His *Prologue* and his seven long dits amoureux have been singled out as providing a textual corpus particularly well suited to the investigation at hand. At the same time this investigation has stressed Machaut's position as the culmination of a long series of developments in the history of OF literature by analyzing his self-conscious *remaniement* of the work of his poetic predecessors.

By way of conclusion, I would like to offer several suggestions regarding the broader ramifications of Machaut's achievement. On the one hand, this will involve an attempt to relate Machaut's concept of the poète to subsequent developments in medieval rhetorico-poetic theory, in particular to the notion of poetry as the *Seconde Rhétorique* that originated in late fourteenth-century France. On the other hand, this will involve a brief consideration of the ways in which Machaut's new kind of first-person, lyric-based poetic voice was to be developed and transformed by his successors, especially Deschamps, Froissart, and Villon.

The generation immediately following that of Guillaume de Machaut saw the start of a new and important development in medieval French poetic theory that was to continue into the first quarter of the sixteenth century: the principles of poetic composition in the vernacular were for the first time codified in a series of treatises, themselves written in French. The appearance of these treatises signaled nothing less than a new notion of the status of vernacular poetic activity, as is evidenced by the fact that they employed a new term to designate this activity: *La Seconde Rhétorique*.[1] The distinction that was thereby established vis-à-vis the *Première Rhétorique* (also a new term) was twofold: on the one hand, the Première Rhétorique was seen as concerned with Latin, to which the French vernacular was thus contrasted; in addition, the Première Rhétorique was seen as concerned with (rhetorical) prose, which was thus opposed to (vernacular) versification (though not necessarily to Latin metrics).[2]

By implication vernacular prosody was thus elevated to the level of Latin rhetorical theory, for the numerical designations Première and Seconde seem less to indicate a hierarchical distinction than to imply the basic similarity of two phenomena in a temporal sequence. Literary (and, indeed, linguistic) craftsmanship in the vernacular was presented as involving a system of rules to be learned — and thereby placed, at least implicitly, on a par with Latin. A new dimension of importance and dignity was thus bestowed upon the French vernacular as a literary medium and upon the specific poetic resources of the OF vernacular tradition, from rhyme considered in the abstract to the particular rhyme schemes and possibilities associated with specific formes fixes.[3]

The new kind of poetic identity developed by Guillaume de Machaut was closely linked to the new concept of vernacular poetry implied by the notion of the Seconde Rhétorique. Machaut's successful self-presentation as a poète, as a vernacular poeta, authorized the new concern with the rhetorical theory and practice of French vernacular poetry to be found in the treatises of the fourteenth and fifteenth centuries. At the same time, Machaut's equally successful self-presentation as an exemplum poetae provided particular poetic forms to be studied, cultivated, and imitated.

Illustrations of both of these aspects of Machaut's "decisive influence on the Second Rhetoric"[4] may be observed in the two earliest surviving treatises.[5] The first of these is Eustache Deschamps' *L'Art de dictier*, dated 1392. Written by Machaut's self-proclaimed disciple,[6] this enchiridion begins with a brief discussion of the seven liberal arts which is linked to a redefinition of the status of vernacular poetic discourse.[7] By far the larger part of Deschamps's treatise, however, is given over to a series of brief descriptive definitions of the major formes fixes, each followed by illustrative examples which are simultaneously presented as models to be imitated. One finds an implicit confirmation of Machaut's status as an exemplum poetae in the fact that his rondeaux are chosen by Deschamps to exemplify this forme fixe (which was, it should be noted, along with the ballade, to become the dominant lyric form in fifteenth-century France).[8]

The anonymous *Règles de la Seconde Rhétorique*, written between 1411 and 1432,[9] provides an explicit illustration of the importance of Machaut's identity as vernacular poeta for the theoretical tradition of the Second Rhetoric. The work begins with a list of exemplary vernacular poets whose works are presented as models to be imitated and who serve to *authorize* the poetic manual which follows. "Maistre Guillaume de Machault" is given a privileged, indeed, a pivotal position in this list as "le grant retthorique de nouvelle fourme, qui commencha toutes tailles nouvelles, et les parfais lays d'amours" [the great rhetorician of the new style, who originated all the new (poetic) forms and perfect amorous lays].[10]

Machaut's innovative concept of poetic identity thus provided, I would suggest, both impetus and authorization for subsequent developments in medieval French rhetorico-poetic theory. Similarly, the new kind of poète figure he created had significant consequences for subsequent developments in French literature.

Eustache Deschamps, as has been previously mentioned,[11] explicitly acknowledged Machaut as master and model. The younger writer, however, simultaneously extended and transformed the achievement of his predecessor.

First, Deschamps was conscious of himself as a poète, the creator of a unified (though heterogeneous) oeuvre. It is the strong sense of the presence of a single poetic identity — the global je of Eustache Deschamps — that provides a unifying principle for his numerous and varied literary works. This is true despite the fact that Deschamps does not succeed in reproducing, at the codicological level, the sense of ordered progression found in the great manuscripts of Machaut.[12] Indeed, this very failure may be seen as constituting part of Deschamps's identity as poète — a particular individual (more authentically a "person" than the conventional je of, say, the grand chant courtois, yet necessarily different from the "person" Guillaume de Machaut) linked to an oeuvre that is uniquely his own.

Deschamps thus builds on the first-person, lyric-based poetic voice established by Machaut. At the same time, he greatly expands the range of this voice, enlarging its vocabulary and diction. In addition to his elaborate employment of courtly conventions, Deschamps (always in a lyric context) makes extensive use of two other sets of attitudes and dictions: first, the moralizing, didactic register of the *sermon;* second, the humorous, "realistic" register of the *satire* (evincing what Poirion calls "une verve familière et anticourtoise"[13]).

If, however, Deschamps's oeuvre may be seen as involving an expansion of the discourse of the lyric-based poète, it also constitutes a kind of fragmentation of the newly strengthened lyric voice inherited from Machaut. An overwhelmingly large percentage of Deschamps's total poetic production is taken up by collections (largely unstructured) of various formes fixes: there is a proliferation of ballades, of rondeaux, of virelays, and of chançons royaux.[14] The smallest formal units of Deschamps's lyric poetry are thus invested with great importance. But the resulting fragmentation is not only "contained" by Deschamps's identity as poète, it serves in part to define that identity.

With Jean Froissart we have a further expansion of the possibilities inherent in the poète figure, the strengthened lyric je created by Guillaume de Machaut.[15] Poetry (i.e., verse) is abandoned (or perhaps dépassé) by the poète who is Jean Froissart; the lyric je is transferred into the witness figure of the chronicler. At the same time, poetic discourse is transformed into a new kind of historico-narrative discourse. Yet the sense of Froissart's presence as author figure can provide a unifying element for his varied literary output, which may thus be viewed as the oeuvre of a particular poète. Indeed, the chronological organization of his oeuvre reflects what must be seen as the progressive development of this poète.

First we have the corpus of Froissart's poetic works, both lyric and narrative[16] which was carefully arranged under the personal supervision of the poet himself in at least two surviving manuscripts (B.N., f. fr. 830 and 831).[17] Daniel Poirion describes "ces deux recueils" as presenting "les 'dittiers et traittiers amoureus et de moralité' classés selon un ordre logique et formel, analogue à celui de Machaut. . . . Il semble que les *dits* et les poèmes à l'intérieur de chaque section soient rangés par ordre chronologique. Froissart a donc voulu regrouper son oeuvre au terme de sa carrière poétique."[18]

The collection of his lyric-based poetry is thus itself presented as a record of the progressive "experience" of Froissart the poète. It is highly significant that the abandonment of poetry—a very conscious act on the part of Froissart—is also presented as part of this experience.[19] Froissart's global identity as author figure thus serves to link his poetic corpus with his *Chroniques*, as two distinct parts, two successive phases of a single oeuvre.[20] A considerable expansion (and strengthening) of Machaut's concept of the poète has been effected.[21]

The *Testament* of François Villon[22] may be viewed as a kind of culmination of the entire tradition of lyric-based poets originating with Machaut, but with its roots in the *Roman de la rose* and Rutebeuf. It is in the context of this tradition that Villon may be considered a poetic descendant of Machaut[23] and that Villon's own expansion and transformation of the lyric je may be seen as related to (even, in part, deriving from) Machaut's concept of poetic identity.

The *Testament* is a lyric-based single work, incorporating all sorts of permutations of the first-person voice. First, there are the shifts in persona effected by the poet-narrator who is in sequence (yet also simultaneously): a poor sinner ("le povre Villon"), an "amant martir" [martyr to love], a "bon follastre" [jolly, madcap fellow]. Second, there is the multiplicity of dictions exploited by the single voice of Villon the poète, which thereby provides the work with unity. Third, the first-person voice of the poet-narrator is transferred (or perhaps "lent") to a series of secondary characters: la Belle Heaulmiere (vv. 457–560, whose direct discourse, parallel in this respect to that of the poet-narrator, is first in *huitains*, then shifts to an intercalated forme fixe), Villon's "povre mere" [poor mother] (vv. 873–909), Ythier Merchant (vv. 978–89), Robert d'Estouteville (vv. 1378–405), and Jacques Cardon (vv. 1784–95).[24] Finally, there is the complex narrator-protagonist configuration. At the beginning of the *Testament* we are confronted with a temporal construct reminiscent of Guillaume de Lorris's Prologue to the *Rose*.[25] Villon, however, "reverses the procedure: his present is lyric; narrative (i.e., the past) is subordinated to the lyric present. Yet the same *dédoublement* prevails. . . ."[26] The je of the poet-narrator is thus "double" — both lyric and narrative. At the same time — and throughout the body of the *Testament* — this je contains, yet is contrasted with, an *il*, the third-person "povre Villon" (who may be seen as a "purely" narrative manifestation of the poet-protagonist).

The final working out of the implications of the narrator-protagonist configuration of the *Testament* occurs in the "Ballade de conclusion." The third-person "povre Villon" (associated with narrated tenses) seems effectively and definitively to be contained by the first-person voice of the poet-narrator (employing commented tenses exclusively):

> Icy se clost le testament
> Et finist du povre Villon.
> . . . en amours mourut martir;
> Ce jura il sur son coullon,
> Quant de ce monde voult partir.
>
> Et je croy bien que pas n'en ment. . .
> (vv. 1996–97, 2001–4)

[Here ends and finishes the testament of poor Villon. . . . he died a martyr to love, as he swore on his testicles when he left this world. And I well believe that he did not lie about this.]

"The narrator and he who died a martyr of love, though the 'same,' are (as in the *Rose*) poetically distinguished. The distinction is rendered explicit; the narrative *je* interferes in the past *fact* of the third-person Villon."[27]

There seems to be the further suggestion that the greatly strengthened lyric je of Villon the poète contains not only his various third- and first-person manifestations as they appear in the *Testament*, but the book itself, which is thus presented as the "experience" of this je. Villon the poète, then, will not "finist" as the *Testament* does.

At the same time, Villon's particular identity as poète, as author figure, provides the *Testament* with a special kind of unity. With Villon's greatly strengthened lyric voice, truly generic permutations, involving a series of different works (e.g., with Rutebeuf) no longer seem to be necessary. A single work (even a single work among many by the same poète/author) can now contain all. With the *Testament*, a new kind of (lyric-based) poetic summa has been created, which may, I would suggest, be viewed as deriving from Machaut's concept of the oeuvre of the poète.

Notes
Selected Bibliography
Index

Abbreviations
Used in the Notes
and Bibliography

CFMA	Classiques français du moyen âge
DA	*Le Dit de l'alerion*
DL	*Le Dit dou lyon*
DV	*Le Dit dou vergier*
FA	*La Fonteinne amoureuse*
JRB	*Le Jugement dou roy de Behaingne*
OF	Old French
RF	*Remede de Fortune*
SATF	Société des anciens textes français
SEDES	Société d'édition d'enseignement supérieur
TLF	Textes littéraires français
VD	*Le Voir-Dit*

Notes

Chapter I: Introduction:
Machaut and the Concept of *Poète*

1 See in particular Poirion's *Le Poète et le prince: L'Evolution du lyrisme courtois de Guillaume de Machaut à Charles d'Orléans* (Paris: Presses Universitaires de France, 1965).

2 It is most probable that Machaut's formal education took place at Paris and/or Reims in a necessarily ecclesiastical milieu. However, "il ne se destinait pas à la vie religieuse, ne reçut pas les ordres [and] demeura comme il le dit [in his *complainte* III] 'lais' ou 'clerc.'" (Armand Machabey, *Guillaume de Machault: La Vie et l'oeuvre musical* [Paris: Richard-Masse, 1955], 1, p. 20). Machaut's studies earned him the university title *Maître*.

3 For Machaut's poetic exploitation of his status as professional court poet see Chapters III and IV below. For a discussion of the import of the social gulf between the poet and his patrons see Poirion, *Poète*, pp. 192–205 and Jacqueline Cerquiglini, "Tension sociale et tension d'écriture au XIVème siècle: Les Dits de Guillaume de Machaut" in *Littérature et société au moyen âge. Actes du Colloque d'Amiens des 5 et 6 mai, 1978* (Paris: Champion, 1978), pp. 111–29.

4 Machabey, *Guillaume de Machault*, 1, p. 19. The four surviving papal bulls which grant Machaut various benefices (through King John's intercession) identify the poet's position in his royal patron's service as, successively, "clericus," "familiaris," and "domesticus" (1330); "domesticus," "familiaris," and "notarius" (1332); and "familiaris," "domesticus," and "secretarius" (1333 and 1335). See Antoine Thomas, "Extraits des archives du Vatican pour servir à l'histoire littéraire. III. Guillaume de Machaut," *Romania* 10 (1881), pp. 325–33.

5 Mention of Machaut's works is repeatedly made in inventories of the library of Charles V and that of Jean de Berry. See Machabey, *Guillaume de Machault*, 1, p. 68.

6 Facts of publication for all of the works mentioned in the following (selective) *état présent* of Machaut studies may be found in the Bibliography.

7 For the lyric poems set to music see, in addition to Ludwig and Schrade, Nigel Wilkins's edition of *La Louange des dames* (Edinburgh: Scottish Academic Press, 1972).

8 See Chapter III, n. 5, below.

9 Fourrier has also edited the *Dit du cerf blanc* (1979) which he considers (in contradistinction to Hoepffner and Chichmaref) to be an authentic work of Machaut. Though Fourrier marshals some important evidence, this attribution remains problematic. Publishing information for the Fourrier edition of these dits can be found in the Primary Sources section of the Bibliography under Jean Froissart, *"Dits" et "Debats."*

10 The following discussion is largely drawn from my "The Poetic Œuvre of Guillaume de Machaut: The Identity of Discourse and the Discourse of Identity," in *Machaut's World: Science and Art in the Fourteenth Century. Annals of the New York Academy of Sciences* 314 (Oct. 1978), pp. 219–33. See also my "Transformations of the Lyric 'Je': The Example of Guillaume de Machaut," *L'Esprit Créateur* 18 (1978), pp. 5–18.

11 Between the twelfth and fourteenth centuries the term *poète* as used in OF vernacular literature underwent a striking semantic development. The word is used in the twelfth century only to refer to classical antiquity, to the auctores and their world. Of its two principal meanings in this connection, the first is that of "seer." The *Französisches Etymologisches Wörterbuch (FEW)* gives the following definition: "un lettré, savant et sage, spéc. Grec ou Romain, considéré comme possédant des pouvoirs intellectuels extraordinaires" (9, p. 122); *Tobler-Lommatzsch* gives: "Weiser, Seher (vates); Priester" (8, p. 2058) for this meaning of *poète*. Of the eight illustrative citations that follow this definition in *Tobler-Lommatzsch*, seven are from the *Roman de Troie*. In addition, and more important for our purposes, the term *poète* as used in the twelfth century designates specifically the great poets of antiquity, the auctores. This meaning is the first one given in the *FEW*: "dans le vocabulaire des arts libéraux, auteur canonique servant de modèle d'expression en poésie." A look at *Tobler-Lommatzsch* reveals that the term was applied in this sense, either to a specific auctor or used with no explicit reference, simply as a means of citing

authority. Thus on the one hand we find Wace referring to Homer as a "poetes" (*Roman de Brut*, Ivor Arnold, ed. [Paris: SATF, 1938–40], 1, v. 1452). And in the early thirteenth century the term is used, in the *Roman de Dolopathos* (ca. 1222–25) to refer to Virgil (a character in the romance): "Onkes poetes ne fu tex, / S'il creust k'il ne fust c'uns Dex" (Charles Brunet and Anatole de Montaiglon, eds. [Paris: P. Jannet, 1856], p. 46). On the other hand we find in the *Münchener Brut* (Halle: Niemeyer, 1877), the term *poète* used to authenticate the parentage of Mars: "Filz fu Jovis, lo roi de Crete, / Si cum nos dient li pöete" (v. 3978). This kind of usage may still be found in *Li Livres dou tresor* of Brunetto Latini (Francis J. Carmody, ed., California Publications in Modern Philology 22 [Berkeley and Los Angeles: University of California Press, 1948]). It is important to note that neither Wace nor Benoît de Sainte-Maure use the term *poète* to refer to themselves or, indeed, to any contemporary vernacular writer of verses. The semantic field of the word is restricted to the auctores. The same restriction still applies to the word when it is used by Brunetto Latini. It is interesting to consider the prologue to Jakemes's *Roman du Castelain de Couci* in this regard, for in this late thirteenth-century narrative poem about the life of a late twelfth-century lyric poet, the term *poète* is not used to refer either to the narrator or to the protagonist. Rather we find the following terms employed: "menestrel" and "jongleour" (v. 31) — which are used pejoratively — "faiseur" and "trouver" (vv. 46, 47) — which are used positively (John E. Matzke and Maurice Delbouille, eds. [Paris: SATF, 1936]).

12 *Œuvres complètes de Eustache Deschamps*, A. Queux de Saint-Hilaire and Gaston Raynaud, eds. (Paris: SATF, 1878–1903), 3, pp. 259–60, *Ballade* no. 447.

13 Deschamps, *Œuvres complètes*, 1, pp. 245–46, *Ballade* no. 124.

14 The ensuing discussion is largely based on Karl D. Uitti, "The Clerkly Narrator Figure in Old French Hagiography and Romance," *Medioevo Romanzo* 2 (1975), pp. 394–408, and *Story, Myth and Celebration in Old French Narrative Poetry: 1050–1200* (Princeton: Princeton University Press), 1973, Chapters 1 (pp. 3–64) and 3 (pp. 128–231).

15 The edition used is the *texte critique* of Gaston Paris, *La Vie de Saint Alexis* (Paris: Champion, 1903), from which all quotations are taken.

16 See Uitti, "The Clerkly Narrator," pp. 398 ff. and *Story*, pp. 128 ff.

17 The most elaborate example of this is found in the Prologue to Part 3 of Wace, *Roman de Rou* (A. J. Holden, ed. [Paris: SATF, 1970], 1, pp. 161–167, vv. 1–166).

18 Benoît de Sainte-Maure, *Le Roman de Troie*, Léopold Constans, ed. (Paris: SATF, 1904–12), vv. 11 ff.

19 Wace's treatment of the death of King Arthur (in the *Roman de Brut*, vv. 13275 ff.) provides a good example of this distancing.

20 The edition used is Chrétien de Troyes, *Erec et Enide*, Mario Roques, ed. CFMA. (Paris: Champion, 1966).

21 Chrétien de Troyes, *Cligés*, Alexandre Micha, ed. CFMA. (Paris: Champion, 1970), vv. 1–44.

22 Cf. Michelle A. Freeman, "Chrétien's *Cligés:* A Close Reading of the Prologue," *Romanic Review* 67 (1976), pp. 89–101.

23 Chrétien de Troyes, *Le Chevalier au lion (Yvain)*, Mario Roques, ed. CFMA. (Paris: Champion, 1971), vv. 1–141.

24 The edition is Chrétien de Troyes, *Le Chevalier de la charrete (Lancelot)*, Mario Roques, ed. CFMA. (Paris: Champion, 1958).

25 Chrétien de Troyes, *Le Roman de Perceval ou le Conte du Graal*, William Roach, ed. TLF. (Geneva: Droz, 1959).

26 I take this term from Roger Dragonetti, *La Technique poétique des trouvères dans la chanson courtoise: Contribution à l'étude de la rhétorique médiévale* (Brugge: De Tempel), 1960. Of particular relevance to the present discussion are Chapter 1, Part 3 ("L'Argument de convenance dans la poésie courtoise des trouvères," pp. 21–30) and the Conclusion: "Essai d'interprétation de la poétique du Grand Chant courtois" (pp. 539–80). See also pp. 138–39.

27 For the import of the narrator-protagonist configuration in Guillaume de Lorris see Karl D. Uitti, "From *Clerc* to *Poète*: The Relevance of the *Romance of the Rose* to Machaut's World," in *Machaut's World: Science and Art in the Fourteenth Century*. Annals of the New York Academy of Sciences 314 (Oct. 1978), pp. 211–12. Other recent treatments of this issue include E. B. Vitz, "The *I* of the *Roman de la rose*," *Genre* 6 (1973), pp. 49–75; Daniel Poirion, *Le "Roman de la rose"* (Paris: Hatier, 1973), pp. 35 ff.; Paul Strohm, "Guillaume as Narrator and Lover in the *Roman de la rose*," *Romanic Review* 59 (1969), pp. 3–9.

28 For Jean de Meun as continuer/transformer of Guillaume de Lorris see Uitti, "From *Clerc* to *Poète*," pp. 210 ff. See in addition, Poirion, *"Rose,"* pp. 98–144 and "Narcisse et Pygmalion dans le *Roman de la rose*," University of North Carolina Studies in the Romance Languages and Literatures 92 (1970), pp. 153–65 in which an "opposition" is posited between Jean de Meun and Guillaume de Lorris. Paul Zumthor, to my mind incorrectly, regards Jean's continuation as a subversion of Guillaume's poem; see "Récit et anti-récit: *Le Roman de la rose*," *Medioevo Romanzo* 1 (1974), 5–24; "De Guillaume de Lorris à Jean de Meung," in *Etudes de langue et de littérature du moyen*

âge offertes à Félix Lecoy (Paris: Champion, 1973), pp. 609–20; and the *Essai de poétique médiévale* (Paris: Seuil, 1972), pp. 370–75.

29 Lines 10463 to 10650 in Guillaume de Lorris and Jean de Meun, *Le Roman de la rose*, Félix Lecoy, ed. (Paris: Champion, 1970–73). For the significance of the midpoint of the combined *Rose* texts (especially as it relates to the narrator-protagonist configuration), see the excellent analysis in Uitti, "From *Clerc* to *Poète*," pp. 212–14. See in addition Poirion, "*Rose*," pp. 3–4, 102.

30 For the notion of "poetic voice" as the basic unifying element in Rutebeuf's diverse oeuvre (which is thus presented as such) see Uitti, "The Clerkly Narrator," pp. 403–8. For a discussion of the first-person stance as a medieval literary convention and the generic implications of the use of this convention in Rutebeuf, see the important study by Nancy Freeman Regalado, *Poetic Patterns in Rutebeuf: A Study in Noncourtly Modes of the Thirteenth Century* (New Haven: Yale University Press, 1970), especially Chapter 5, "The Poet in His Poetry," pp. 255–311.

31 For this category of Rutebeuf's work see the superb edition of Edmond Faral and Julia Bastin, *Œuvres complètes de Rutebeuf* (Paris: Picard, 1959), 1, pp. 517–80. The question of the classification (generic or otherwise) of the various components of Rutebeuf's heterogeneous oeuvre is discussed briefly on pp. 220–21. See also Regalado, *Poetic Patterns*, pp. 6 ff.

32 Cf. in this regard Sarah Jane Williams's excellent article "An Author's Role in Fourteenth-Century Book Production: Guillaume de Machaut's 'livre ou je met toutes mes choses,'" *Romania* 90 (1969), pp. 433–54.

33 Cf. Elspeth Kennedy, "The Scribe as Editor," in *Mélanges de langue et de littérature du moyen âge et de la Renaissance offerts à Jean Frappier* (Geneva: Droz, 1970), 1, pp. 523–31.

34 I use the *sigla* first adopted by Hoepffner:
A–   Paris, B.N., f. fr. 1584
B–   Paris, B.N., f. fr. 1585
C–   Paris, B.N., f. fr. 1586
D–   Paris, B.N., f. fr. 1587
E–   Paris, B.N., f. fr. 9221
FG– Paris, B.N., f. fr. 22545, 22546
H–   Paris, B.N., f. fr. 881
J–   Paris, Bibl. de l'Arsenal, 5203
K–   Bern, Stadtbibl., 218
M–   Paris, B.N. f. fr. 843
P–   Paris, B.N., f. fr. 2166
In addition I adopt the following sigla of Ludwig:

Vg–   Previously owned by the Marquis de Vogüé, now at Wildenstein and Co., New York.

Morg.– New York, Pierpont Morgan Library, M. 396.

35 Williams, "An Author's Role," p. 447.

36 In the words of Ernest Hoepffner: "L'auteur, lorsqu'il écrivait ces vers [i.e., the *Prologue*] avait sous les yeux son oeuvre poétique tout entière, ou au moins à peu près terminée, et c'est sur l'ensemble de ses productions lyriques, sur ses dits, sur ses compositions musicales que porte le jugement qu'il émet dans le *Prologue*." Ernest Hoepffner, ed., *Œuvres de Guillaume de Machaut* (Paris: SATF, 1908–21), 1, p. liv. All quotations from the *Prologue* are taken from this edition.

Since the *Prologue* postdates much of Machaut's musical and poetic work, one should perhaps think in terms of a progressive development of his concept of poetic identity and a "retrospective" organization of his oeuvre.

37 It is important to note that the *Prologue* is found in its complete form in MSS *A* and *FG*, those which Hoepffner calls "les meilleurs manuscrits, qui sont en même temps les plus complets . . ." (1, p. lii), as well as in *Morg.* MSS *E* and *H* contain only the ballades of the *Prologue*, without the sequence of octosyllabic couplets.

38 Hoepffner, ed., *Œuvres*, 1, p. liv.

39 For a discussion of the significance of Nature's gifts in terms of Machaut's poetics see Douglas Kelly, *Medieval Imagination: Rhetoric and the Poetry of Courtly Love* (Madison: University of Wisconsin Press, 1978), pp. 4, 11–12.

40 A wide variety of terms has been applied to medieval writers—rather indiscriminately by modern critics, somewhat less so by the medieval writers themselves. We refer, for example, to Chrétien de Troyes as a "poet," but he would not have used such a term. Indeed, Chrétien does not have a single, all-inclusive term which serves to designate his poetic activity. Rather he uses different expressions to describe the particular aspects of that activity which are poetically relevant in a given work. Thus in the Prologue to *Erec et Enide* we find the declaration that "Crestïens de Troies . . . tret d'un conte d'avanture / une molt bele conjointure" (vv. 9, 13–14). In *Cligés* the vocabulary is somewhat different: "Crestïens comance son conte, / Si con li livres nos reconte" (vv. 43–44). With *Yvain* we find yet another variation: "Por ce me plest a reconter . . ." (v. 33), while in the Prologue to the *Charrete*, Chrétien, speaking in the first person, states: ". . . je . . . anprendrai . . . romans a feire . . ." (vv. 3, 2). Finally, in the Prologue to *Perceval* we find "Crestïens, qui entent et paine . . . A rimoier le meillor conte / Qui soit contez a cort roial" (vv. 62–65). The variety

of the expressions Chrétien makes use of in this context is striking. So also is the fact that he does not seem to feel it necessary to provide any kind of gloss on his name with respect to his professional identity.

Wace, in contradistinction to Chrétien, does provide a kind of professional gloss on his own name. We find at the beginning of the *Roman de Rou* the author identifying himself as "un clerc de Caen, qui out non Mestre Vace" (Part 1, v. 3). Both of these terms are significant and both are related to Wace's poetic enterprise in fundamental ways. *Maistre* is more than an ecclesiastical or academic title. The etymological sense of *magister*, "teacher," with all the authority such an identity involves, is very much present in Wace's use of the term and in the poetic stance he adopts. "Clerc" is perhaps an even more important word with respect to Wace's self-portrayal, as the Prologue to Part 3 of *Rou* makes evident (esp. vv. 8, 103, 141). Holden's gloss of the term as "un lettré savant" does not go far enough. For Wace the clerc, by his activity of reading and writing (the two seem to be inseparable) is the indispensible vehicle for the transmission of all cultural values. Without the activity of the clerc, mankind would have no memory, no knowledge of its own past. Wace's self-depiction as clerc thus makes use of the translatio studii topos to invest himself and his literary activity with tremendous importance. Yet the terms "clerc" and *maistre* as used by Wace also represent a kind of selectivity. It is only certain aspects of what we would regard as his overall literary or poetic activity that Wace chooses to valorize by so designating himself. Further, these are both terms whose primary meanings lie outside of the literary sphere. The degree to which they are to be applied to specifically literary activity varies according to the context.

The same is true for the term *jongleor*, widely used in the twelfth and thirteenth centuries. Faral's introductory description is particularly relevant in this connection:

Un jongleur est un être multiple: c'est un musicien, un poète, un saltimbanque; c'est une sorte d'intendant des plaisirs attaché à la cour des rois et des princes; c'est un vagabond qui erre sur les routes et donne des représentations dans les villages; c'est le vielleur qui, à l'étape, chante de "geste" aux pèlerins; c'est le charlatan qui amuse la foule aux carrefours; c'est l'auteur des "jeux" qui se jouent aux cours de fête, à la sortie de l'église; c'est le maître de danse qui fait "caroler" et baller les jeunes gens; c'est le "taboureur," c'est le sonneur de trompe et de "buisine" qui règle la marche des processions; c'est le conteur, le chanteur qui égaie les festins, les noces, les veillées; c'est l'écuyer qui voltige sur les chevaux; l'acrobate qui danse sur mains, qui jongle avec des couteaux, qui traverse des cerceaux à la course, qui mange du feu, qui se renverse et se désarticule; le bataleur qui parade et qui mime; le bouffon qui niaise et dit des balourdises; le jongleur, c'est tout cela, et autre choses encore.

(Edmond Faral, *Les Jongleurs en France au moyen âge* [Paris: Champion, 1910]. Quoted in Raleigh Morgan, "Old French 'jogleor' and Kindred Terms." *Romance Philology* 7 [1954], p. 283). The semantic field of *jongleor* thus was extremely wide — but did not at all correspond to that of our modern "poet."

Jongleor, clerc, maistre, trovëor — all are terms used by twelfth- and thirteenth-century poets to refer to their own poetic activity, or, more exactly, to certain aspects of it, for none of these terms takes into account the whole gamut of activities that we associate with the modern term "poet." Further, none of these terms serves as a real link between medieval poets and the poets of antiquity, the auctores. If Homer, in Benoît de Sainte-Maure's phrase, was a "clerc merveillos," (*Le Roman de Troie*, v. 45) the reverse was not true. Benoît was not a poète.

41 This decision, then, is largely a logistical one, taken in the interest of unity and economy. All three of the excluded narrative poems could, of course, be examined very fruitfully in conjunction with the dits amoureux to elaborate still further Machaut's concept of poetic identity and its relation to the oeuvre of the poète. In addition to the great individual value each of the three possesses in this context, suggestive links and groupings with the other dits are manifold. The *Jugement dou roy de Navarre* is a palinode to the *Jugement dou roy de Behaingne*. The *Confort d'ami* and the *Jugement dou roy de Navarre* share a common inscribed patron. The authoritative advisor stance of the *Confort d'ami* reappears in fragmentary form in both the *Fonteinne amoureuse* and the *Voir-Dit*. The codicological juxtaposition of the *Voir-Dit* and the *Prise d'Alexandrie* raises questions concerning the relation between poetic and historical truth as well as the status of the poet as truth teller. These and other aspects of Machaut's well-nigh inexhaustible oeuvre must await future treatment.

42 See Hoepffner, ed., *Œuvres*, 1, pp. lv–lvi, lix, lxiv–lxvi; 2, pp. i–iii, liv, lxiii–lxiv; 3, pp. i–ii, xxviii–xxx. It is only the pairing of the *Jugement dou roy de Behaingne* and the *Jugement dou roy de Navarre* that Hoepffner regards as resulting from considerations other than chronology.

The chart below shows the order of the ten longer narrative poems in *A*, accompanied by (approximate) dates of composition when possible:

Dit dou vergier	
Jugement dou roy de Behaingne	(before 1346)
Jugement dou roy de Navarre	(1349)
Remede de Fortune	(before 1342?)
Dit dou lyon	(1342)
Dit de l'alerion	(before 1349?)
Confort d'ami	(1357)
Fonteinne amoureuse	(1360–61)
Voir-Dit	(1363–65)
Prise d'Alexandrie	(1369–71)

It is important to note that the increasingly complex use Machaut makes of the two narrator-protagonist configurations to be studied in Chapters II–IV involves a pattern of alternation.

43 Uitti, *Story;* Kelly, *Medieval Imagination* and *"Sens" and "Conjoincture"* in *The "Chevalier de la charette"* (The Hague: Mouton, 1966); Gérard Genette, *Figures II* (Paris: Seuil, 1969), esp. *"Frontières du récit"* (pp. 49–69), and *Figures III* (Paris: Seuil, 1972), esp. *"Discours du récit"* (pp. 67–273). I make particular use of the terminological opposition "diegetic/extradiegetic," derived from *Figures* III, pp. 238–41 and 280, where "diégèse" is defined "dans l'usage courant" as "l'univers spatio-temporel désigné par le récit" and "diégétique" as "qui se rapporte ou appartient à l'histoire."

44 Harald Weinrich, *Tempus — besprochene und erzählte Welt* (Stuttgart: W. Kohlhammer, 1965; 2d ed., 1971); French translation: *Le Temps,* Michèle Lacoste, trans. (Paris: Seuil, 1973).

45 Emile Benveniste, "Les Relations de temps dans le verbe français," *Bulletin de la Société de Linguistique* 54 (1959), reprinted in Benveniste, *Problèmes de linguistique générale* (Paris: Gallimard, 1966), pp. 237–50.

Chapter II: Poet-Narrator as Lover-Protagonist: Early Poems.

1 All quotations from the *DV,* the *RF,* and the *DA* are taken from Hoepffner's edition.

2 See Hoepffner, ed., *Œuvres,* 1, pp. liii–lvi.

3 In this connection, Hoepffner judged the *DV* to be a rather poor "imitation" of the *Rose* (*Œuvres,* 1, pp. lvi–lvii). This is, I think, to miss the point. Recent criticism has been somewhat more charitable. James Wimsatt (*Chaucer and the French Love Poets: The Literary Background of "The Book of the Duchess"* [Chapel Hill: University of North Carolina Press, 1968], pp. 75–76) finds that Machaut in the *DV* "initiates a new kind of *dit amoureux,* one step further away than its predeces-

sors from the *Roman de la Rose* in that he unifies the narrative and reduces or eliminates the allegory. . . ." William Calin (*A Poet at the Fountain: Essays on the Narrative Verse of Guillaume de Machaut* [Lexington: University of Kentucky Press, 1974], pp. 23–38) provides a detailed and often insightful consideration of the *DV*'s relationship to the *Rose*, but judges Machaut's work to be a "failure" (p. 24). Kelly (*Medieval Imagination*, pp. 96 ff.) seems to regard the *DV* primarily as an example of the first stage in the development of Machaut's concept of fin'amors (in which desire and hope are still able to coexist).

4 The evocation of spring at the beginning of the *DV* recalls in detail the opening of the dream sequence in the *Rose*. Highly relevant to the significance of this topic in Guillaume de Lorris and in Machaut is its poetic function within the generic system of the grand chant courtois, discussed by Peter Dembowski in his important article "Vocabulary of Old French Courtly Lyrics — Difficulties and Hidden Difficulties," *Critical Inquiry* 2 (1976), pp. 763–79. See esp. his explication of the fundamental link, in courtly lyric, between the themes of seasonal renewal, of the "reawakening of the urge to make poetry" and of the "ever-returning desire to love" (pp. 770–71).

5 The extended deployment of this topos recalls both the diction and the "ideology" of twelfth- and thirteenth-century *artes amandi* (both in Latin and in the vernacular). See esp. the *De amore* of Andreas Capellanus (the 1st, 2nd, 3rd, and 6th dialogues of Book 1, *Trattato d'amore. Andreae Capellani regii francorum "De Amore libri tres." Testo latino del sec. XII con due traduzioni toscane inedite del sec. XIV,* S. Battaglia, ed. [Roma: Perella, 1947], pp. 24–80, 128–46) and the late thirteenth-century French translation/adaptation by Drouart la Vache *Li livres d'amours de Drouart la Vache,* Robert Bossuat, ed. [Paris: Champion, 1926], pp. 16–66, 84–93).

6 Without going into the complex and often-debated issue of allegory in the *Rose*, I would like, for the purposes of the present study, simply to distinguish between the use of personification characters (which the *Rose*, of course, employs extensively) and the opposition between text and gloss as two qualitatively different systems of discourse. While the *Rose* refers to this opposition (both Guillaume de Lorris and Jean de Meun promise to gloss the dream), it does not function as part of the poetic discourse of the *Rose* (the dream is not glossed) as it does, for example, in the *Ovide moralisé* (see Harald Weinrich, "Structures narratives du mythe," *Poétique* 1 [1970], p. 30).

7 Calin, *Poet*, pp. 23–25, 36–38, remarks on the split between the lyric love experience of the narrator and that of the abstract "archetypal Lover of whom the God of Love speaks" (p. 37).

8 This opposition will no longer be functional (at least not in the same way) in certain of Machaut's later dits — in particular, the *RF* and the *VD* — where the narrator-protagonist is depicted as both lover and poet.

9 For a discussion of the literary significance of this topic see Roger Dragonetti, "Trois motifs de la lyrique courtoise confrontés avec les *Arts d'aimer*," *Romanica Gandensia* 7 (1959), pp. 19 ff.

10 Hoepffner, ed., *Œuvres; 1*, p. lviii.

11 A similar (though more elaborate) construct is employed at the end of the dream sequence of the *FA*, vv. 2527–698.

12 That this was a recognized poetic procedure may be seen from the closing lines of Jean de Condé's *La Messe des oiseaux*, Jacques Ribard, ed. (Genève: Droz, 1970):

> Ceste amours nule fin ne prent;
> Ele est si pure et affinee
> Ke mais ne puet estre finee.
> Or prions a Dieu de cuer fin
> Que de la vraie amour sans fin
> Esprendre nous cuers finement.
> Chi prent mes contes finement.

See also the closing lines of Rutebeuf's *Vie de Sainte Elysabel*, v. 2, 2183–86.

13 Esp. vv. 1–86. Cf. Uitti, "From *Clerc* to *Poète*," pp. 211–12.

14 Kelly astutely points out that this initial description of the dame in the *RF* "converts the real lady into an Imagination. . . . The physical lady is abstracted, fragmented, and unified in the idea of *bonté* that emanates through her various attributes." (*Medieval Imagination*, p. 101). The kind of "sublimation" effected by this "abstraction of the lady as her qualities" may be seen as a result of the love service of the poète.

15 The *Dit de la panthère* perhaps serves as an intermediary. See E. Hoepffner, "Les Poésies lyriques du *Dit de la panthère* de Nicole de Margival," *Romania* 53 (1920), pp. 210–16, 225–26. The possible significance of the *Dit de la panthère* for the overall structure and meaning of the *RF* will be discussed below.

16 For the lay as a technical achievement see Hoepffner, ed., *Œuvres*, 2, pp. xxxvii–xxxviii. For a rhetorical and thematic analysis of the lay see Kelly, *Medieval Imagination*, 102–3.

17 The rhyme *songe/mensonge* in OF is of course much earlier than the *Rose*, going back at least to the *Roman d'Enéas* (see Renate Blumenfeld, "Remarques sur *Songe/Mensonge*," *Romania* 101 [1980], pp. 385–90). However, the sustained intertextual presence of the *Rose* in the

RF (as in the *VD*) provides a context in which this rhyme functions to recall vv. 1–2 of Guillaume de Lorris's poem.

18 Boethius, *The Consolation of Philosophy*, H. F. Stewart and E. K. Rand, eds. (Cambridge, Mass.: Harvard University Press, 1968), Book 1, 1–3 Metr. and 1–3 Pr. See Hoepffner, ed., *Œuvres*, 2, pp. xxi–xxii.

19 In this connection, it is significant that the narrator is first identified as L'Amant in the two passages that frame the chanson roial of the bele dame. From this point on he is consistently referred to by this title (in MSS *AFG*).

20 For the nature and function of the proverb as discourse in late medieval literary texts see Jacqueline and Bernard Cerquiglini, "L'Écriture proverbiale," *Revue des Sciences Humaines* 163 (1976), pp. 359–75.

21 For a consideration of the significance (structural and otherwise) of the midpoint in romance see Uitti, *Story*, pp. 179, 201 and "From *Clerc* to *Poète*," pp. 212–13.

22 See Hoepffner's detailed and astute consideration of the *Consolation* as Machaut's source in *Œuvres*, 2, pp. xxiv–xxx. The possibility that Machaut's knowledge of Boethius was to some degree mediated by Jean de Meun's prose translation of the *Consolation* must, however, be taken into account. Hoepffner's rejection of this possibility is based on incomplete manuscript information (see V. L. Dedeck-Héry, "The Manuscripts of the Translation of Boethius' *Consolatio* by Jean de Meun," *Speculum* 15 [1940], pp. 432–43) and on unfamiliarity with Jean de Meun's text (first edited by Dedeck-Héry in *Medieval Studies* 14 [1952], pp. 165–275).

23 Hoepffner quite rightly points out, however, that Machaut "use librement des éléments qu'il emprunte à son modèle, les transposant à son gré, les modifiant selon les besoins de sa cause, les amplifiant ou laissant de côté ce qui ne pouvait lui être utile et ajoutant par contre, quand bon lui semblait" *Œuvres*, 2, pp. xxii–xxiii.

24 Machaut's use of this standard construct of trouvère lyric also seems reminiscent of the description of Jean de Meun by Amors at the midpoint of the conjoined *Rose* texts:

> je l' [Jean] afubleré de mes eles
> et li chanteré notes teles
> que, puis qu'il sera hors d'enfance,
> endoctrinez de ma sciance,
> si fleütera noz paroles . . .
> (vv. 10, 607–11)

Thanks to Amors, Jean will become a "bird."

25 The grounds for Machaut's consistent preference for the generic term "chanson baladée" rather than "virelay" are discussed by Poirion in *Poète*, pp. 327-8.

26 Kelly (*Medieval Imagination*, pp. 100-105, 130-37) views the *RF* as the first of Machaut's poems in which his new conception of fin'amors is set forth in detail. The dit's "fundamental idea" is, in Kelly's terms, "the primacy and sufficiency of hope in love" which is presented "schematically" in the lay and developed "systematically" in the speeches of Esperence (p. 102). This cogent interpretation of the thematic content of the *RF* is, to my mind, highly relevant to Machaut's self-presentation as poète in the dit and to the related presentation of love as poetic subject matter. However, the opposition between Amant (the narrator-protagonist) and Machaut (the poète-author) that is built in to the structure of the dit must be taken into account in a consideration of the work qua amorous doctrine. This opposition allows the final representation of Amant's situation as a lover to be insolubly ambiguous (not positive, as Kelly implies, pp. 136-37), while at the same time Machaut's "sublimation of courtly love" remains intact as poetic "ideology."

27 It is interesting to note that this concluding maxim is reminiscent of the Venus and Adonis sequence in the *Rose*, esp. vv. 15, 721-34.

28 The fact that Amant's belief in the truth of his lady's words is visibly shown to depend not on the truthfulness of their content but rather on the identity of their enunciator raises an important question with regard to Machaut's concept of the "truthfulness" of poetic discourse. This question will be one of the central concerns of the *VD* (see esp. p. 151, n. 88 above).

29 It is interesting to note in this connection that at the beginning of Jean de Meun's section of the *Rose* (vv. 4029-68) Amant, also left with little except hope ("esperance"), declares himself dissatisfied and questions her value, for: "S'el [Esperance] est cortoise et debonere / el n'est de nule riens certeine" (vv. 4040-41).

30 For the didactic function of the intercalated lyrics of the *RF* see Hoepffner, ed., *Œuvres*, 2, pp. xxxiv-liv (esp. xxxv-liv); Machabey, *Guillaume de Machault*, 1, pp. 50-51; Daniel Poirion, *Le Moyen âge II: 1300-1480* (Paris: Arthaud, 1971), pp. 192-94; Calin, *Poet*, p. 70.

31 For an important discussion of the progressive development of this tradition, esp. with reference to first-person narration, see G. B. Gybbon-Monypenny's important article "Guillaume de Machaut's

Erotic 'Autobiography': Precedents for the Form of the *Voir-Dit*," in *Studies in Medieval Literature and Languages in Memory of Frederick Whitehead* (Manchester: Manchester University Press, 1973), pp. 133–52. As we shall see in Chapter III, an elaborate exploitation of several sets of possibilities inherent in this tradition was to be effected by Machaut in the *VD*. In the *RF* we have an expansion of the range of this tradition accomplished by transposing it into what might be called the fourteenth-century didactic register: the set of intercalated lyrics are presented as exempla forming together an ars poetica. At the same time Machaut is transforming a specific literary model from within this tradition: the *Dit de la panthère*, where the idea of using intercalated lyrics as poetic exempla appears, as it were, in embryo (see Hoepffner, "Les Poésies lyriques," esp. pp. 226–30).

32 In this respect it is revealing to compare the *RF* (written before 1349) in which an ars poetica is fully integrated into (indeed presented by means of) a narrative poem, with the *Art de dictier* (written in 1392) of Machaut's disciple Eustache Deschamps. In the later work we have a rhetorico-poetic treatise written in expository, didactic prose in which lyric poems (sometimes incomplete) are presented as illustrations of compositional rules. Machaut's single, all-inclusive poetic discourse (deriving from his identity as poète) is no longer felt to be sufficient for the purposes of writing "about" poetry. In addition, the ars poetica that was (perhaps necessarily) implicit in Machaut becomes explicit in Deschamps.

33 See esp. Gustaf Holmér, ed., *Traduction en vieux français du "De arte venandi cum avibus" de l'empereur Frédéric II de Hohenstaufen* (Lund, Sweden: Bloms, 1960) and Gace de la Buigne, *Le Roman des deduis*, Ake Blomquist, ed., (Karlshamn, Sweden: Johanssons, 1951).

34 This creates a pattern similar to that described by Harald Weinrich in the *Ovide moralisé*. See "Structures narratives," p. 30. Machaut, however, exploits this pattern in an exclusively first-person context.

35 This "je" thus contains the other two as the dit as a whole contains the two registers.

36 Note that the technical vocabulary of the falconry manuals is employed to describe this process.

37 Based on Vincent de Beauvais, *Speculum naturale* (Venice edition, 1591), Chapter 21, and Thomas de Cantimpré. Cited in Hoepffner, ed., *Œuvres*, 2, p. lxviii.

38 Similarly, the self-authorizing poetic activity of the poète "contains" both the lyric authorization (based on experience) and clerkly authorization (based on "bookishness") by presenting both as *literary*

constructs — as fictions — which function *within* the poetic economy of the *DA*.

39 The uncourtly advice which the narrator-protagonist receives after the loss of each of his four raptores recalls the voice of Ovid in the *Remedia amoris*. Cf. esp. v. 462: "Successore novo vincitur omnis amor."

40 For the structure of the *DA* as well as a consideration of the work's "technique of alternation of letter and gloss" see Kelly, *Medieval Imagination*, pp. 151-53.

41 Hoepffner (*Œuvres*, 2, p. lxix) is unable to identify a written source for this anecdote.

42 There seems to be a parallel between the construct keepers/alerion and that of Bel Accueil/rose (i.e., spokesman-guardian/object of desire which cannot speak) in Guillaume de Lorris.

43 In addition, the fact that "parer"/"comparer" form a thrice repeated annominatio further emphasizes the presence of the poète and his identity as verbal craftsman. From this perspective the entire dit seems to be implicitly presented, in rhetorical terms, as a poetico-linguistic structure, deriving from the poète figure who appears to overlap with the je of vv. 2821-30. (See also vv. 1197-98, 3245-6 and 3305-6 where the same rhyme recurs).

44 Hoepffner (*Œuvres*, 2, p. lxix) discounts what he considers to be superficial correspondences in Alexander Neckham and Vincent de Beauvais, positing an oral source (as indeed Machaut's text explicitly affirms in vv. 3398-400).

45 It is thus metaphoric discourse as such that is emphasized rather than a particular metaphoric system. In this respect Machaut's poem contrasts significantly with, e.g., the first-person *Prise amoureuse* of Jehans Acars de Hesdin (written in 1332, *Gesselschaft für Romanische Literatur* 22, E. Hoepffner, ed. [1910], 1-59) in which the love experience is presented "allegorically" by means of a single hunting episode which functions as a unified and consistent metaphoric system. For the tradition of the allegorical love hunt in medieval French literature (from its beginning with the mid-thirteenth century *Dis dou cerf amoureus*) see Marcelle Thiébaux, *The Stag of Love: The Chase in Medieval Literature* (Ithaca: Cornell University Press, 1974), pp. 144-66.

46 Calin convincingly regards the very narrative premise of the *DA* as subversive in this regard since "by assimilating *fin'amor* to hawking, Machaut undermines traditional courtly doctrine . . ." (*Poet*, p. 105; see also pp. 106-8).

47 It is of interest to note that Raison compares the narrator-protagonist's

situation to that of a lover whose *bien amée* has behaved dishonorably, and makes an identical recommendation for the hypothetical lover and the narrator-protagonist, thus anticipating the final conflation of the two registers.

Chapter III: Poet-Narrator as Lover-Protagonist: *Le Voir-Dit*.

1 See Poiron, *Poète*, pp. 199 ff.

2 Gybbon-Monypenny ("Precedents," pp. 149–51) suggests that the *VD* may be viewed, formally speaking, as the *Roman du Castelain de Couci* told in the first person.

3 The autobiographical first-person narrator will be referred to as "Guillaume" for the purposes of the present study, although he is not explicitly named within the context of the *VD* itself. The final intercalated lyric poem in the work (pp. 369–70) is a rondeau-anagram by Toute-Belle containing her lover's name which when resolved (pp. xxi–xxii; 369–70) gives "Guillaume."

4 This claim of truthfulness (made repeatedly and, of course, incorporated into the very title of the poem) has led to a good deal of scholarly debate. The two extreme positions are represented by Georg Hanf ("Ueber Guillaume de Machauts *Voir Dit*," *Zeitschrift für romanische Philologie* 22 [1898], pp. 145–96), who argues that the *VD* is purely fictional, and Walter Eichelberg (*Dichtung und Wahrheit in Machauts "Voir Dit"* [Frankfurt am Main: Duren, 1935]), who argues that the work is in the main "historically true," i.e., that the major events of the plot and all the inserted letters are biographically authentic. (Cf. also Calin's perceptive discussion of this issue, *Poet*, pp. 166–72.) While not unproductive, this controversy appears to me to be ultimately insoluble and to a large extent inappropriate. Rather than attempting to establish the degree to which the events of the story represent historico-biographical "facts," I will concentrate on examining how Machaut's claim of truthfulness may be said to function in the *VD* and how the "working out" of the poem determines what is meant by "truth."

5 My discussion of the narrative structure of the *VD* necessarily takes into account the limitations imposed by the edition used, *Le Livre du voir-dit*, Paulin Paris, ed. (Paris: Société des Bibliophiles Français, 1875). Unless otherwise noted, all quotations are taken from this edition. A new edition announced some time ago by Paul Imbs is still awaited. The P. Paris edition omits a 265 line sequence (Polyphemus's song to Galatea, which would have followed v. 7215, p. 294), subsequently published by Antoine Thomas ("Guillaume de Machaut et l'*Ovide moralisé*," [*Romania* 41 (1912)], pp. 384–89). Further, P. Paris

"left out other passages of a descriptive or allegorical nature, without telling the reader" (Calin, *Poet,* p. 17). Certain of these "coupures" were also noted and criticized by Thomas, pp. 383–84. There is even an error in numbering 600 lines (pp. 272–73) noted by Calin (*Poet,* p. 165), giving the edition 8,437 lines rather than the 9,037 it appears to contain. However, in spite of the edition's obvious inadequacies, Calin asserts that "Paris's deletions do not affect the plot in a significant way" (*Poet,* p. 17). In addition, he finds the text of the forty-six intercalated prose letters to be reliable, stating that "to the best of my knowledge P. Paris cut not one line from the epistles" (*Poet,* p. 176). For certain particularly important passages (esp. the Prologue, the midpoint sequence, and the Epilogue) I have consulted a microfilm of MS *A.*

6 Calin, *Poet,* pp. 200–201.

7 The word "aventure" is significant in this context, for it serves to imply that the first-person narrative in the *VD* is in some sense a romance, indeed a courtly romance in light of the next two lines: "Que ne fu villaine ne sure; / Ains fu courtoise et agréable." Machaut's exploitation of the romance genre and of courtliness within the poetic economy of the *VD* will become evident as the story progresses.

8 By means of historical and temporal references as well as by the dates on Letters 27–45, Machaut establishes a chronology of sorts for the *VD* which has enabled scholars to assign dates to the major events of the story. Guillaume is first contacted by Toute-Belle in late summer of 1362. He sets out on his journey to visit her around the end of April 1363 and takes his final leave c. June 20, 1363, after which he returns directly to Reims. The lovers' correspondence continues (with one long interruption) until November 1363, at which point a period of estrangement begins that is to last (punctuated by a few intermittent letters) until the fall of 1364, when Guillaume is visited by Toute-Belle's confessor. Reconciliation between the lovers takes place by letter during the spring of 1365. See Hanf, "Ueber Guillaume de Machauts *Voir Dit,*" pp. 170–92; Vladimir Chichmaref, ed., *Guillaume de Machaut: Poésies lyriques* (Paris: Champion, 1909), 1, pp. liii–lxiv; Machabey, *Guillaume de Machault* 1, pp. 56–62; Calin, *Poet,* pp. 173–74. It must be stressed, however, that this chronology is hypothetical and can be considered as valid only as a kind of general outline. For Machaut does not assign a specific year for any of the "events" or letters in the *VD* and, indeed, his "true story" contains numerous chronological inconsistencies (especially with regard to the dates on Letters 39–44) which are insoluble. A detailed and consistent

chronological structure simply cannot be derived on the basis of textual evidence. In fact, the text works to subvert any endeavor of this kind. This fact has, of course, long been recognized by scholars who have reacted to it in a variety of ways. Chichmaref attempts to resolve the contradictions by revising and correcting "faulty" dates while Hanf uses them to buttress his argument that the *VD* is a work of pure fiction. Eichelberg proposes a biographical explanation, and Calin finds the arguments of both Hanf and Eichelberg to be inconclusive.

This inescapably problematic aspect of the chronology of the *VD* may perhaps be seen as fitting into the system of self-authentication that is explicitly established at several points in the work: the "truth" of the subject matter being guaranteed by the (repetitive and "contradictory") form of the text and this form being justified by the "truth" of the subject matter. This seems to be at least a plausible assumption given Machaut's ability to maintain an internally consistent chronology in the *Prise d'Alexandrie* (written after the *VD*).

9 The technical excellence of Toute-Belle's rondeau is explicitly noted by Guillaume (vv. 151–54) and technical excellence will be a feature of her lyrics throughout the *VD*. Indeed both Hanf ("Ueber Guillaume de Machauts *Voir Dit*," pp. 160–67) and Calin (*Poet*, p. 171) have argued from this fact that all the intercalated lyrics of the poem, whether ascribed to Guillaume or Toute-Belle, must have been written by Machaut himself. This would, of course, have important implications for the "truthfulness" of the *VD* and for the relationship between Machaut the poète (author of the work as a whole as well as of the larger oeuvre in which it participates) and Guillaume the narrator-protagonist (a poetic construct "contained" by the poète figure). Sarah Jane Williams ("The Lady, the Lyrics and the Letters," *Early Music* 5 [1977], pp. 463–64) finds that certain of the lyrics attributed to Toute-Belle can in fact be differentiated from Machaut's work on technical grounds, concluding that a small number of Toute-Belle's poems must be the production of Machaut's historically "real" dame "Péronne d'Armentières". Williams concedes however that "while one cannot easily make out its exact limits, I suspect Péronne's oeuvre to be a rather slender one, which Machaut did his best to supplement in the course of putting the *VD* together."

10 ". . . over half of the *Voir Dit*'s lyrics form pairs, or companion pieces, with related subjects, rhymes, and verse forms. (Nowhere else in Machaut's works can such a concentration of paired lyrics be found.) Machaut sets the pattern in replying to his lady's poetic overture, as he will reply to the rondeau in her first letter, with a rondeau of exactly the same form, rhymes, and meter. Each time he calls atten-

tion to the procedure in the accompanying text, noting that his answer is 'En tel maniere et en tel rime, / Com elle en son Rondelet
rime' (p. 18)." Williams, "Lady," p. 465.

11 Paris, ed., *Voir-Dit*, p. 13.

12 The *VD* contains forty-six intercalated prose letters which function
collectively both as an important structuring element (at times played
off against the larger narrative structure of the *VD* as a whole) and as
a guarantee of the poem's authenticity, its "truth." The order of the
early letters and their relation to the narrative passages in which they
are set has given rise to problems of interpretation. Williams ("Lady,"
p. 463), referring to a later passage (*VD*, pp. 202–3) in which the narrator, in the process of compiling the *VD*, states that he is having
trouble arranging the letters in proper order, assumes that "the early
letters gave him [i.e., Machaut] a great deal of trouble. He managed
to write a series of them into the text in the wrong order, linking
them with the verses surrounding them in a way that defies satisfactory re-arrangement." Williams takes this as evidence for the nonfic-
tional, historico-biographical origin of the letters: "Machaut, whose
poetry is usually both conventional and highly organized, surely did
not deliberately create such disorder and confusion for his readers.
Whatever editorial changes he made before the *Voir Dit* was put into
final form, it is easier for us to believe in the authenticity of the letters,
or of most of them, than for us to suppose they are wholly imaginary."
("Lady," p. 463. Cf. also Williams, "An Author's Role," p. 439 and
Eichelberg, *Dichtung und Wahrheit*, pp. 36 ff.). P. Paris, whose basic
assumption about the letters is the same as that of Williams, attempts
to remedy the "confusion" by reordering the early letters (as he explains somewhat opaquely in his note, *Voir-Dit*, p. 387). The following chart illustrates his editorial solution to this "problem." Arabic
numerals designate the MS position of the letters and Roman numerals indicate the position in which they are found in the Paris edition:

MSS AGE	Paris ed.
1	I
2	IV
3	V
4	VI
5	VII
6	II
7	III
8	VIII

It should be emphasized that the letters in question are in the *same*
order in MSS *AGE*. (I am grateful to Dr. Lawrence Earp for having

brought these facts to my attention.) There is thus a very real possibility that their apparent "confusion" may be intended to function as part of the program of self-authentification in evidence throughout the *VD* (see pp. 98–99, 110).

13 Brownlee, "The Poetic Œuvre," p. 223.

14 Remy de Gourmont, "Le Roman de Guillaume de Machaut et de Peronne d'Armentières," *Promenades Littéraires*, 5th series (Paris: Mercure de France, 1913), pp. 7–37.

15 Poirion, *Poète*, p. 200. See also Paris, ed., *Voir-Dit*, p. 25, n. 2.

16 Williams, "An Author's Role," p. 453. Cf. also Williams, "Lady," p. 464 and Calin, *Poet*, p. 171. Poirion (*Poète*, p. 200) cites several other examples of this process: "La ballade: 'Gent corps, faitis, cointe, apert et joly' [*VD*, p. 152] que Machaut prétend avoir fait 'nouvellement / A son tresdous commandement' [vv. 3609–10] se trouve au début de *La Louange des Dames* [bal. no. 5] dans tous les manuscrits, ce qui suggère une date de composition bien antérieure. Et d'autres poèmes de la collection se trouvent étrangement dispersés tout au long de *La Louange*" [numbers 161, 178, 180, 194, 199, 227, 231, 237, and 239 are listed in Poirion's n. 27].

17 See Williams, "An Author's Role," pp. 466, 453–54.

18 Poirion (*Poète*, p. 200) astutely observes that "sur le plan littéraire le poète n'a pu jouer franchement le jeu de la vérité. Le rapport entre le roman vécu et les 'choses' lyriques n'est pas aussi direct qu'il voudrait le faire croire."

19 This fits in with the *VD*'s program of secularization of religious vocabulary which is consistently employed in a courtly amorous context. What results involves neither a metaphorical (nor allegorical) dimension added to the narrative nor any trivialization of the religious register but rather a sustained playfulness and a rhetorical enrichment, a "thickening" of Machaut's courtly discourse.

20 As we shall see, the different perspectives (protagonist/beloved: narrator/reader) built into this formal configuration can be played off against each other. See esp. Letter 41 (pp. 313–15) as contrasted with its preceding narrative "explanation" (p. 313).

21 This recalls the formal configuration of lyric verse and narrative prose (= *ragioni*) passages in the *Vita Nuova* (minus the *divisioni*) and the juxtaposition of vida and *canso* (minus the *razo*) in thirteenth- and fourteenth-century troubadour *chansonniers*. Cf. G. B. Gybbon-Monypenny, "Precedents," and "Autobiography in the *Libro de buen amor* in the Light of Some Literary Comparisons," *Bulletin of Hispanic Studies* 34 (1957), pp. 63–78.

22 The working out of the desir/esperance dialectic will be one of the

central narrative (and thematic) motifs of the *VD*. See Kelly, *Medieval Imagination*, p. 147.

23 See Guillaume's Letter 41 (pp. 313–15) in which he does the same thing to Toute-Belle. This initial losengier episode serves as a kind of thematic and structural authorization for a much more elaborate exploitation of this motif in Part 2 of the *VD*.

24 Thus there are far fewer lyric pieces in Part 2 of the *VD* where they seem to have been replaced by clerkly intercalations.

25 This is the only name that is explicitly used for Guillaume's dame in the entire course of the *VD*. The work does, however, contain two anagrams of her name: the first, in the form of a rondeau (pp. 266–67) gives "Peronne"; the second (vv. 9014–30) gives "Peronne d'Armentiere" (Paris, ed., *Voir-Dit*, pp. xx–xxiii; p. 266, n. 3; p. 370, n. 1). Paris's solution to these anagrams has been almost universally accepted by subsequent scholarship and seems to be further validated by Eustache Deschamps's Ballades 447 ("Apres Machaut qui tant vous [Péronne, v. 16] a amé," *Œuvres complètes*, 3, pp. 259–60) and 493 (refrain: "Recevoy moy: j'ay falli a Peronne," *Œuvres complètes*, 3, pp. 318–19). Paris goes on to identify the Péronne of the *VD* with one Peronelle d'Unchair, dame d'Armentières and daughter of Jean de Conflans, but this hypothesis, though certainly plausible (and widely accepted) cannot be regarded as definitive. Even if it could, however, its value for a reading of the *VD* would be minimal since, as Calin (*Poet*, p. 171) quite rightly observes, the exact relationship between this historical personage and the author of the *VD* will never be known. Thus the question of whether or to what degree Toute-Belle (or Péronne) corresponds to a specific historical prototype is not only insoluble but unproductive (one is reminded of the debates over the historical existence of Beatrice and Laura).

26 This scene is perhaps meant to be reminiscent of Amant's entering into the service of Amors in the *Rose* of Guillaume de Lorris. In any case the commingling of religious and feudal terminology in the context of courtly diction may be seen as part of the process of "rhetorical enrichment" discussed in note 19 above.

27 Cf. Pygmalion in the *Rose*, vv. 20, 907–82 and in the *Ovide moralisé*, Book 10, vv. 972–89.

28 The first and most conventional of the three exchanges of love tokens in Part 1 of the *VD* — an exchange of rings ("verges") — has already taken place. See pp. 29, 54.

29 Here "livre" apparently means narrative poem or dit as opposed to lyric forme fixe (see Williams, "An Author's Role," pp. 438 ff.). For the second principal meaning of the term see note 30 below.

30 Williams, "An Author's Role," p. 450, cogently explains that the word "livre" in this context, as later in the *VD* (Letter 33, p. 259), means something like Machaut's oeuvres complètes: "his personal copy (perhaps partly autograph) of his works, left unbound, to which he added new works as he finished them, grouping new lyrics with other lyrics, a musical composition or narrative poem with others of its kind, and from time to time supervising an 'edition' of a single copy to be made for one of his patrons."

31 Guillaume sets out on his journey around the end of April 1363. See n. 8 above; also, Calin, *Poet*, p. 173, and Chichmaref, ed., *Poésies lyriques*, 1, pp. lvii–lviii.

32 See Williams, "Lady," p. 465.

33 It is interesting to note that this first meeting has involved the first two steps of the *gradus amoris: visus* and *alloquium* (see Lionel J. Friedman, "Gradus amoris," *Romance Philology* 19 [1965–66], pp. 167–77). A distorted version of this medieval commonplace has in fact been set in motion and will function as a structuring element in the episode dealing with the progression of the love affair.

34 This is the third step of the gradus amoris as utilized by the *VD: osculum*. Not only is Guillaume's identity as courtly lover undercut by the fact that he achieves this gradus by means of an intermediary (i.e., his secretary) but, as we shall see, the osculum step is "diluted"— taking place in two parts (see n. 37 below).

35 This is in accord with Toute-Belle's consistent presentation as a Laura who "creates herself" (see p. 97 and n. 14 above).

36 This rondeau (item 148 in the *Louange des dames* and 4 in the section of the rondeaux set to music in *A* and in the Chichmaref edition) is singled out for special mention by Williams ("Lady," see n. 9 above) as having been composed independently of the *VD*. It thus serves as a particularly visible sign of the presence of Machaut the poète. At the same time, however, the rondeau functions narratively in the context of the story line of the *VD*, where it is carefully presented as having been generated by a particular episode of Guillaume the protagonist's love experience. The same intercalated lyric may thus be seen as evidence of the "poetic success" of both the narrator-protagonist of the *VD* and the poète who is the work's author.

37 This is the second part of the osculum step of Guillaume's gradus amoris. Again, it is Toute-Belle who acts as initiator while Guillaume acts as a passive, timid recipient. At the same time, Machaut continues his programmatic utilization of religious terminology in an amorous context: "le pais" of v. 2666 refers to the *Pax Dei*, the paten that is kissed during the Mass (see Paris, ed., *Voir-Dit*, p. 110, n. 3).

38 Kelly, *Medieval Imagination*, pp. 121-54.

39 The presence of Machaut the poète in this passage is signaled by an extratextual reference to contemporary historical events, especially the open hostility between Charles le Mauvais, king of Navarre (one of Machaut's most important patrons during the 1350s) and the House of France. This conflict finally obliged Machaut to take sides in favor of the royal family, effectively breaking with his former patron after 1357 (see Chichmaref, ed., *Poésies lyriques* 1, p. xlviii; Machabey, *Guillaume de Machault*, 1, p. 49). Further, the narrative verse passage under consideration was probably written after the death of Jean II (April 8, 1364) and thus at a time when the duke of Normandy of the *VD* would have already become Charles V (crowned at Reims on May 19, 1364).

40 All of this takes place on June 12, 1363. See Paris, ed., *Voir-Dit*, p. 143, n. 3; Chichmaref, ed., *Poésies lyriques*, 1, p. lviii; Machabey, *Guillaume de Machault*, 1, p. 59; Calin, *Poet*, p. 173.

41 Chichmaref, ed., *Poésies lyriques*, 1, p. lviii, n. 3.

42 This constitutes the fourth step of Guillaume's gradus amoris: *contactus* or *amplexus*.

43 Cf. Chichmaref, ed., *Poésies lyriques*, 1, p. lix and Machabey, *Guillaume de Machault*, 1, p. 59.

44 Dated c. June 20, 1363. Cf. Calin, *Poet*, p. 173; Machabey, *Guillaume de Machault*, 1, p. 60; Chichmaref, ed., *Poésies lyriques*, 1, p. lix.

45 This appearance of Venus, somewhat out of place among the conventions of courtly lyric, is perhaps meant to recall the *Rose* and the role played in the earlier poem by the goddess of love. This connection would seem to be confirmed by the fact that the *VD*'s exploitation of religious vocabulary in a secular, amorous context reaches its culmination in the Venus sequence. At the same time, as in the *Rose*, Venus here is associated with (female) sexuality.

46 The lovers have thus achieved some kind of physical intimacy, but scholarly interpretations of the exact sexual significance of this episode vary greatly. Cf. Paris, ed., *Voir-Dit*, p. 160, n. 1; Poirion, *Poète*, pp. 529-30 and *Le Moyen âge*, p. 193; Calin, *Poet*, pp. 189-91; Kelly, *Medieval Imagination*, p. 147. In fact, Machaut has structured the scene so that the precise nature of the final step in Guillaume's gradus amoris (the *factum*) remains elegantly and insolubly ambiguous.

47 The "self-created Laura" motif is stressed as Toute-Belle declares that her honor can only increase as a result of Guillaume's poetic activity: "Par vos dis ne me puet descroistre, / Ainsois ne fait toudis qu'acroistre" (vv. 3897-98).

48 "L'Archeprestre et ses Bretons," v. 3959, identified as Arnaud de Cer-

voles, one of the most feared captains of the Grande-Compagnie which was terrorizing the countryside of Champagne and Burgundy during the years 1360–65. Cf. Paris, ed., *Voir-Dit*, p. 68, n. 1; p. 167, n. 1; and Chichmaref, ed., *Poésies lyriques*, 1, pp. lv–lvi.

49 This is perhaps intended to recall the midpoint of the *Rose* where Amors speaks at length of the work in which he is a character.

50 See Kelly, *Medieval Imagination*, pp. 130–37, 146–47, esp. n. 59.

51 This process of self-quotation has been seen to operate elsewhere in the *VD* with a similar result. Cf. pp. 103–4 above.

52 See, in this context, Poirion, *Poète*, pp. 196–205 and Cerquiglini, "Tension," pp. 122–27.

53 See, e.g., Hanf, "Ueber Guillaume de Machauts *Voir Dit*," pp. 195–96. Calin (*Poet*, p. 201) disagrees with earlier critical opinion, and, to my mind quite rightly, affirms the importance of Part 2 for the work as a whole. Yet, with regard to narrative structure he states that "in the second half of the *VD* artistic 'composition' is less overt" than in the first half.

54 An important consequence of Guillaume's poetic treatment of their love affair has already begun to make itself felt: Toute-Belle's public renown: "car je ne suis en compagnie que on ne parole tousjours de vous . . . brief, chascuns vous tient comme la fleur des dames" (p. 191). Toute-Belle is thus shown as in the process of being transformed into a Laura figure by the power of Guillaume's poetry.

55 Cf. n. 12 above.

56 Cf. Letter 17 where the making of the *VD* is first mentioned and pp. 114–15 above.

57 Letter 27 is thus the first of the letters to be dated, and all subsequent letters (with the exception of 46, the very last letter in the work) will also include dates, although from Letter 39 on, the dating becomes hopelessly confused and inconsistent. See notes 8 and 12 above.

58 The source for this narrative, which is not cited in the *VD*, has been demonstrated to be the *Ovide moralisé*. See Cornelis de Boer, "Guillaume de Machaut et l'*Ovide moralisé*," *Romania* 43 (1914), pp. 339–41. As is usual with Machaut's utilization of this source, the religious, allegorical interpretation attached to the Ovidian narrative is omitted — indeed in this case it may be said to be subverted.

59 In this first dream, the (silent) ymage functions as an emblem of Toute-Belle. Thus, the "behavior" of the ymage concretizes (or dramatizes) Toute-Belle's emotional condition, just described in terms of the color code in which blue signifies fidelity and green signifies change/newness: "En lieu de bleu [Toute-Belle] vestit vert" (v. 4929). This metaphoric

"description" is then literally applied to, projected upon, the ymage. This entire construct will be radically and strategically transformed in the second dream sequence (see pp. 145-47 below).

60 It is interesting to note that the lover's reaction is simultaneously that of the clerc, as Guillaume, observing the symbolic changes in Toute-Belle's ymage immediately thinks of the following:

> . . . des ymages
> Qu'avoit fait Virgiles li sages,
> Qui aus Rommains le chief tournoient
> Quant leurs subjés se reveloient.
> (vv. 4942-45)

61 Both Paris (*Voir-Dit*, p. 242, n. 3) and Williams ("Lady," p. 464) attribute this to Machaut.

62 One of which involves a knowledge of the text of the *VD* that Toute-Belle the character could not possess at this point in the narrative: "A Semiramis/M'as comparée" (vv. 5570-71).

63 There is even a kind of clerkly coda appended to the complainte (vv. 5907-34) in which Guillaume uses the story of the deification of Julius Caesar (for which a bookish authority is cited: "l'istoire des Romains," v. 5919) as the basis for a rhetorically elegant louange of his dame.

64 For an illuminating discussion of the term "livre" as employed in this passage, see Williams, "An Author's Role," pp. 433-54.

65 The description stresses the physical aspect of the book—the *VD*'s status as manuscript:

> Toutevoie j'y envoiay,
> Et ce livre moult fort loiay
> En bonne toile bien cirée,
> Que la lettre n'en fust gastée.
> (vv. 5975-78)

66 Rather than designating two qualitatively different elements of the *VD* (as Paris, *Voir-Dit*, p. 262, n. 1 assumes), Machaut seems to be emphasizing the "truthful" nature of his poetic discourse *as poetic discourse*.

67 This seems to be at variance with Kelly's formulation of the "new conception of *fin'amors*" to which all of Machaut's dits after the *RF* "adhere more or less explicitly" and according to which "love is self-sufficient and not dependent on desire" (*Medieval Imagination*, pp. 144, 147). However, once we distinguish between Machaut the poète

and his various first-person personae (including Guillaume of the *VD*) Kelly's interpretation appears more valid than ever. It is the poète's service to Amour, i.e., the act of making poetry, that is not dependent on desire, or indeed on the love experience as such. It is thus love as poetic subject matter that is "self-sufficient." The failure of the *VD*'s narrator-protagonist *qua lover* (including his inability to master Desir) only serves to emphasize this point.

68 Note that the sequence of emotive and mental processes is: *complaindre/plaindre-penser-ymaginer*.

69 On p. 273 of the Paris edition (*Voir-Dit*) v. 6104 is printed as v. 6704. Since this 600-line error in numbering will continue for the rest of the work, for the sake of convenience I will identify direct quotations by the printed verse numbers, along with page references when appropriate.

70 Linked by Friedrich Ludwig, ed. (*Guillaume de Machaut: Musikalische Werke* [Leipzig, 1928] 2, p. 69) to "der Bretone Thomas Paien [who] lehrte als berühmter Jurist im 3. Viertel des 14. Jahr. an der Sorbonne."

71 Cf. Williams, "Lady," p. 466.

72 This contrasts with (indeed, reverses) the secretary's behavior in Part 1, where he functioned (enthusiastically) as a successful intermediary between the two lovers (see, e.g., pp. 108, 111 above). Once again, Part 2 of the *VD* works to subvert Part 1.

73 Attested in contemporary chronicles, cf. Chichmaref, ed., *Poésies lyriques*, 1, p. lxii, and Machabey, *Guillaume de Machault*, 1, p. 61.

74 Machaut bases his reworking of this myth on the version found in the *Ovide moralisé*; cf. Boer, "Machaut," pp. 336-38.

75 This 264-line sequence (including a brief introduction and conclusion) is almost entirely omitted from the Paris edition (where it would have started at v. 7200), but was edited and published in its entirety by Antoine Thomas (cf. n. 5 above) who also established the *Ovide moralisé* as its source. Calin (*Poet*, pp. 180-81, 195) notes suggestive parallels between this elaborate treatment of the unsuccessful love affair of the one-eyed giant who sings a lyric poem and the poet-lover Guillaume, the "borgne vallet" of Toute-Belle.

76 Poirion (*Poète*, pp. 199-200) views this passage as a particularly striking illustration of Guillaume's inappropriateness for the role of courtly lover: the fundamental distinction, inherent in Machaut's sociohistorical condition, between aristocratic patron and clerc-poet. It should be noted, however, that Machaut is able to turn this (sociohistorical) restraint into a (poetic) resource by making it function poetically within the economy of the *VD*.

77 Chichmaref, (*Poésies lyriques*, 1, p. lxiii) gives February/March 1364 for the date of Toute-Belle's letter.

78 See p. 103 above for a discussion of Toute-Belle's earlier employment of the same "strategy," which involves, quite simply, the systematic refusal to commit to writing sincere doubts about the validity of the partner's love. An epistolary confrontation is thus avoided while a serious "experiential" doubt is allowed to exist.

79 The second dream is thus set in motion (as was the first) by the ymage. Even as this parallel works to recall the first dream, however, it serves to underscore several important transformations. First, the ymage is no longer mute, but highly articulate. Second, the ymage is no longer an emblem of Toute-Belle, but a different "character." Third, while the question of the "truth" of the first dream centered on the ymage, in the second dream the focus is on Toute-Belle's own behavior. An important progression is thus suggested as the impossibility (or irrelevance) of ascertaining Toute-Belle's "true" affective state is made increasingly explicit.

80 Based on that found in Book 2 of the *Ovide moralisé*; cf. Boer, "Machaut," pp. 341–42.

81 It is important to note that Guillaume the narrator intervenes at this point to qualify the judgment of Guillaume the protagonist:

> Mais pas ne m'a tenu convent,
> Car sa convenance est tout vent;
> S'il est voirs ce qu'on m'en a dit.
> Autrement ne di-je en mon dit.
> (vv. 8227–30, pp. 332–33)

82 This represents a poeticization of the construct of clerkly citation of bookish authority, since the *VD*'s description of Fortune is not derived from either Fulgentius or Livy; cf. Paris, ed., *Voir-Dit* p. 333, n. 1.

83 The conventional language of traditional clerkly misogyny at this point in the text is significant:

> . . . en semblance
> De femme, pour son inconstance:
> Car c'est chose assez veritable,
> Que trop est femme variable.
> (vv. 8245–48, p. 333)

84 "A la fin du mois d'octobre, [1364]" according to Chichmaref, ed., *Poésies lyriques*, 2, p. lxiii, n. 1. Cf. my note 8 above.

85 The confessor employs a more generalized clerkly authority, "en escript sa figure hé," v. 8655, in place of Guillaume's specific citation of Livy.

86
> Cinc personnes, si com vous dites,
> Grandes, moyennes et petites,
> Vous ont chanté de Toute-Belle
> Une chanson qui n'est pas belle,
> Ne gracieuse à recorder.
>   (vv. 8764–68, p. 356)

87 The formal arrangement of this part of the confessor's comparison — five stanzas of ten octosyllabic lines, each ending with the refrain "Et tout par legierement croire" — recalls Guillaume's earlier treatment of Fortune's five circles. This formal parallelism may be seen as a sign of Machaut the poète.

88 It is significant that Guillaume's belief results not from having discovered the "truth" about Toute-Belle's actions, but rather from literary factors. The confessor's portrait of Fortune effectively implies that Guillaume's non-courtly behavior and discourse must necessarily exclude him from playing the role of lover in terms of the literary conventions that define that role.

Furthermore, it is only the source of the confessor's message (i.e., Toute-Belle) and not its content (i.e., Toute-Belle's innocence) whose authenticity has been established (cf. vv. 8598–610). Jacqueline Cerquiglini astutely considers that "Machaut donne ici, de manière emblématique, la clé de sa conception de la vérité du langage. . . . La parole . . . n'est vraie que comme faire, comme acte. Le voir dit, la paole vraie, ce sera alors l'écriture du *Voir Dit*. Le texte, le Dit comme genre atteste le dit, la parole. Le *Voir Dit* ne dit que la vérité de son écriture, la vérité du poète, il ne dit rien sur la sincérité de la dame." ("Syntaxe et syncope: Langage du corps et écriture chez Guillaume de Machaut," *Langue Française* 40 [Dec. 1978], p. 40).

89 Williams, "An Author's Role," p. 441.

90 Cf. Chichmaref, ed., *Poésies lyriques*, 1, p. lxiii, n. 1; Machabey, *Guillaume de Machault*, 1, pp. 61–62.

91 As Calin persuasively argues, in *Poet*, pp. 192–94.

92 Cf. Calin's perceptive concluding remarks on this subject which stress the fact that ". . . whatever his success or failure as a lover, the Narrator's status as an artist is never left in doubt" (*Poet*, p. 199). Cf. in addition J. Cerquiglini's important observations: "Tout, dans cet amour, est placé sous le signe de la littérature. . . . Plus que l'histoire d'un amour le *Voir Dit* se révèle bien être l'histoire de l'écriture d'un livre. Echec de l'amant-clerc, réussite du poète . . ." ("Tension," p. 126).

Chapter IV: Poet-Narrator as Witness-Participant

1 All quotations from the *JRB*, the *DL*, and the *FA* are taken from the Hoepffner edition.

2 In this respect it is significant that the initial appearance of a first-person verb form involves a tense from Weinrich's narrated world: "m'acesmay" (v. 10).

3 Calin (*Poet*, pp. 47-50), in discussing the narrative configuration of the *JRB* asserts that "Machaut's originality lies in the creation of an I-narrator who witnesses the story but does not himself play a leading role in it" (p. 48). Hoepffner (*Œuvres*, 1, pp. lx-lxiii) considers this aspect of the *JRB* to be rather a development of generic possibilities inherent in the "débat amoureux" (a narrative form dating from the twelfth century and related to the lyric *jeux-parti*) and singles out Machaut's transformation of the purely passive witness-narrator of the earlier form (as found, e.g., in "Blancheflour et Florence," [Paul Meyer, ed., *Romania* 37 (1908), pp. 221-34] dating from the second half of the thirteenth century) into a narrator figure who is alternately witness and participant as "un nouveau trait bien caractéristique de l'oeuvre de Guillaume. Il ne reste pas témoin impassible de l'aventure; il prend lui-même part à l'action" (1, p. lxi). Hoepffner elsewhere (*Œuvres*, 3, pp. xxxi-xxxii) adduces an additional generic model for the *JRB*: the "chansons à personnages" with their conventionalized situation in which the poet first overhears, then confronts, the lover. Machaut expands and transforms this lyric construct (dating from "l'ancienne paraphrase française du *Cantique des Cantiques*") by employing it in a new, narrative context. A further development of this process, in which the initial lyric situation is significantly elaborated, will be found in the *FA*.

4 It is noteworthy that a grammatical rhyme serves to provide a link between the first words of the narrator in this passage and the last words of the chevalier: "je ne *fais*" (v. 1184, emphasis added).

5 This suggestive reference was first noticed by Jean Frappier in "*La Chastelaine de Vergi*, Marguerite de Navarre et Bandello," *Publications de la Faculté des Lettres de Strasbourg* 105 (1945), pp. 106-7: "Certes ce petit chien [in the *JRB*] n'est pas si bien 'afaitié' que celui de la châtelaine de Vergi, mais lui aussi joue à sa façon un rôle d'intermédiaire, et il ne semble pas impossible que dans ce passage Guillaume de Machaut ait ingénieusement adapté et transposé dans un autre ton le conte du XIIIe siècle." Calin (*Poet*, p. 49) follows Frappier in considering the "petit chien" of the *JRB* as a playful subversion of the "chienet afetié" of the *Chastelaine de Vergi*, but adduces (uncon-

vincingly and somewhat gratuitously) Petit-crû and Husdent as additional analogues.

6 An interesting indication of the shift in the relationship between the narrator and the two "protagonists" that has taken place between the Introduction and the second major narrative segment (a shift explained by the narrator's transformation from witness into participant) is provided by the shift from third- to second-person pronouns (referring to the chevalier and the dame) in parallel passages. Thus, e.g.: "Lors me boutay par dedans la fueillie / Si embrunchiez qu'*il* ne me *virent mie*" (vv. 53-54, emphasis added) is retold as "Je regarday / Le plus fueillu dou brueil; si m'i boutay / Car de *vous* faire anui moult me doubtay" (vv. 1280-82, emphasis added).

7 Cf. Hoepffner, ed., *Œuvres*, 1, lxii.

8 See Ernest Hoepffner, "Anagramme und Rätselgedichte bei Guillaume de Machaut," *Zeitschrift für romanische Philologie* 30 (1906), p. 405.

9 Cf. Hoepffner, ed., *Œuvres*, 2, p. lx.

10 This rhetorical procedure is, as Hoepffner remarks in *Œuvres*, 2, p. lxii, reminiscent of *Li Bestiares d'amours* of Richard de Fornival ("*Li Bestaires d'amours*" di Maistre Richart de Fornival e "*Li Response du Bestaire,*" Cesare Segre, ed., Documenti di filologia 2 [Milan and Naples: Ricciardi, 1957]) in which learned and/or marvelous accounts of animal behavior are repeatedly interpreted in an amorous, first-person context for the express purpose of moving Richard's dame. Machaut seems deliberately to be recalling the earlier work in order to stress, from the outset, the predominance of the lover over the clerc in the identity of the narrator figure of the *DL*. The fact that this is suggested by means of an adept intertextual reference implies the presence of an author figure — Machaut the poète — whose literary orientation, a manifestly clerkly trait, serves to differentiate him from his first-person narrator.

11 Belonging, in the words of Hoepffner (*Œuvres*, 2, pp. lviii-lix) "en propre à ce genre de romans d'aventures."

12 It is significant in this connection to note that Yvain is explicitly transformed from chevalier into amant in Machaut's *Motet V* (*Poésies lyriques*, Chichmaref, ed., 1, p. 491): "Et c'est tout cler que monsignour Yvon / Par bien servir, non pas par vasselage, / Conquist l'amour dou grant lion sauvage" (vv. 26-28).

13 For a discussion of *Yvain* as a model for the *DL* along with some of the literary implications of this filiation for Machaut's poem, cf. Hoepffner, ed., *Œuvres*, 2, pp. lviii-lxi. Calin (*Poet*, p. 83) in considering the narrator-lion construct of the *DL* asserts that "Machaut

took the idea from *Yvain"* but does not examine the function of this visibly literary model within the context of Machaut's work, declaring simply that "the *DL* animal's friendship is gratuitous."

14 Calin, *Poet*, pp. 78–79.

15 Cf. Uitti, *Story*, pp. 206–17 and Jean Frappier, *Chrétien de Troyes et le mythe du Graal* (Paris: SEDES, 1972), pp. 138–41.

16 Hoepffner, ed., *Œuvres*, 2, p. lix.

17 Hoepffner (*Œuvres*, 2, pp. lvii–lviii) finds the chevalier's speech to be "le morceau le plus original du poème" with "aucun précédent" in earlier vernacular poetry.

18 Further authority in this connection results from an implicit correspondence with one of the key literary models for the *DL*. We recall that Chrétien's *Chevalier au lyon* receives its title only as part of the poem's conclusion, v. 6804 in Mario Roques's edition of 6808 lines.

19 There is no possessive pronoun specifying to whom the "sentement joli" belongs — thus leaving both its character and its relation to the narrator figure somewhat ambiguous; similarly with the "vray cuer." In addition there is a suggestive ambiguity in "faite . . . de vray cuer" where the "de" can mean both "out of" and "by means of."

20 Hoepffner (*Œuvres*, 3, pp. xxvi–xxvii) resolves the anagram into: "Guillaumes de Machaut and Je(h)ans duc (de) Berry e Overgne."

21 Cf. Regalado, *Poetic Patterns*, pp. 190–91, 205 ff. and Uitti, "The Clerkly Narrator," pp. 403–8.

22 Hoepffner (*Œuvres*, 3, p. 253) implicitly recognizes this when he remarks that "l'entassement de rimes sur les racines *las, li* et *lai* des vers 1–32 marque dès le début le souci artistique qui domine le poète dans cette pièce."

23 There is perhaps an intended inversion of the opening of Guillaume de Lorris's narrative with Machaut's "Il n'a pas lonc temps que j'estoie / En un lit ou pas ne dormoie" (vv. 61–62). First, Machaut's first-person narrator is situated in the recent past, as opposed to the separation of five years between the time of experience and the time of writing in the *Rose*. Second, Machaut's insomnia followed by an aural experience which is not a dream seems to invert the framework in which the poet-narrator of the *Rose* ". . . me dormoie mout forment / et vi un songe en mon dormant" (vv. 25–26). The presence in the *FA* of reworked motifs from the *Rose* becomes increasingly explicit as the dit unfolds until this process itself seems to be thematized — and to serve as another indication of the presence of the poète figure in the text.

24 Cf. Poirion, *Poète*, p. 194: "Notre poète, 'comis' aux chansons amoureuses va se tourner vers les princes, et se faire l'interprète de leurs

rêves et de leurs désirs." Also pp. 197 ff., esp., "La fonction du poète n'est pas d'être le héros mais l'interprète de l'amour. . . . Machaut compose selon son sentiment personnel, et d'après les intérêts d'autrui." Cf. also Poirion, *Le Moyen âge*, esp. pp. 71-94, 191-96.

25 The poet-narrator (as character) posing as the scribe for the complainte contrasts strikingly with the poète (the global poetic identity behind the oeuvres complètes) who, as master poetic craftsman, articulates the complainte. This automatic contrast functions to give an elegant artificiality to the narrator-as-scribe pose which results in an artfully implicit compliment to Amant the Patron being embedded in the very narrative structure of the *FA*, while at the same time providing yet another affirmation of Machaut's poetic mastery.

26 Machaut's source appears to be the *Ovide moralisé*. See Hoepffner, ed., *Œuvres*, 3, p. xxxiv and *Ovide moralisé*, ed., Cornelis de Boer, Verhandelingen der Koninklijke Akademie van Wetenschappen te Amsterdam. Afdeeling Letterkunde, n.s. 15, 21, 30, 37, 43 (Amsterdam: Müller, 1915-38), Book 11, vv. 2996-3787. It is important to note that Machaut "demoralizes" the story for the purposes of his own poetic text.

27 This involves an elaboration of suggestions made by the narrator early in the work, vv. 117-38, 156-88.

28 Cf., e.g., the description of Camille's tomb in the *Roman d'Enéas*, Salverda de Grave, ed. CFMA. (Paris: Champion, 1968-73), vv. 7531-7718.

29 Cf. Uitti, *Story*, pp. 179, 201.

30 This also involves, on the part of Machaut, a further development of Jean de Meun's exploitation of this structural convention of romance; near the midpoint of the conjoined *Rose* texts, the *work* is renamed the "Miroër aus Amoureus" (v. 10621).

31 Cf. Poirion, "Narcisse et Pygmalion," pp. 153-65. It should be noted in this regard that Jean de Meun's reworking of the (Ovidian) Pygmalion story is simultaneously a response to Guillaume de Lorris's reworking of the Narcissus story, to which (unlike the Ovidian original) it makes explicit reference; see the *Rose*, vv. 20846-58.

32 Cf. esp. vv. 1-4: "Aucunes genz dient qu'en songes / n'a se fables non et mençonges / mais l'en puet tex songes songier / qui ne sont mie mençongier."

33 Cf. Hoepffner, ed., *Œuvres*, 3, pp. xxxiv-v and *Ovide moralisé*, Boer, ed., 1, pp. 37-39.

34 See Weinrich, "Structures narratives," pp. 30-31.

35 Cf. the "il" / "je" opposition in the "Ballade de conclusion" of Villon's

Testament, Jean Rychner and Albert Henry, eds. (Geneva: Droz, 1974), 1 (Texte), vv. 1996–2023 and 2 (Commentaire), p. 275.

36 It is interesting that v. 1 of the *FA* is also a reminiscence of the *Jugement dou roy de Navarre*, vv. 493–94. Cf. Hoepffner, ed., *Œuvres*, 3, p. 253.

Chapter V: Conclusion: Ramifications of Machaut's Achievement

1 It should be emphasized that the arts de Seconde Rhétorique were primarily designed to "provide the nobility with the rudiments of verse writing in French. As such they were by and large manuals for amateurs" (Kelly, *Medieval Imagination*, p. 3; cf. also Poirion, *Le Moyen âge*, pp. 65 ff.). It was, however, at the courts of these aristocratic "amateurs" that much of the most intense poetic activity of the fourteenth and fifteenth centuries took place in France. The lettered French nobility not only participated directly in this activity, but at times were themselves responsible for some of its most dazzling achievements, as in the cases of René d'Anjou and Charles d'Orléans.

2 On the distinction between the Première and the Seconde Rhétorique cf. Ernest Langlois, ed. *Recueil d'arts de Seconde Rhétorique* (Paris: Imprimerie Nationale, 1902), pp. i–ii and Warner F. Patterson, *Three Centuries of French Poetic Theory: A Critical History of the Chief Arts of Poetry in France (1328–1630)* (Ann Arbor: University of Michigan Press, 1935), 1, pp. 3–12. It should be noted that the two aspects of the distinction between the Première and the Seconde Rhétorique were not always clearly articulated as such. Rather, a degree of overlapping prevailed between the opposition Latin/vernacular and the opposition prose/verse.

3 For an interesting discussion of the complex development of the limits of the semantic field of the word *rime* in French see Paul Zumthor, "Du rythme à la rime," in *Langue, Texte, Énigme* (Paris: Seuil, 1975), pp. 125–43.

4 Kelly, *Medieval Imagination*, p. 3.

5 Langlois (*Recueil d'arts*, p. v) considers that "très probablement il a existé, de la seconde moitié du XIVe siècle, et surtout du XVe, des Arts de Seconde Rhétorique que nous ne connaissons pas."

6 For Deschamps's depiction of his relationship to Machaut see his Ballades 123, 124, 127, 447, 493, and 1474, as well as his Lay 306 ["Le Lay amoureux"], all in Deschamps, *Œuvres complètes*, Saint-Hilaire and Raynaud, eds. Cf. also Chapter I, pp. 7 ff. above.

7 This redefinition involves primarily an explicit separation of poetry as a purely verbal art form from music (with which it was previously associated in theoretical writings) and a valorization of the former at the expense of the latter. Cf. Roger Dragonetti, "'La Poesie . . . ceste musique naturelle.' Essai d'exégèse d'un passage de l'*Art de dictier* d'Eustache Deschamps*," in *Fin du moyen âge et Renaissance: Mélanges de philologie française offerts à Robert Guiette* (Antwerp: Nederlandische Boekhandel, 1961), pp. 49–64. For a more general discussion of the separation of music and poetry in the Second Rhetoric see Kelly, *Medieval Imagination*, pp. 239–56.

8 It is significant that the other exemplary lyric pieces to be found in the *Art de dictier* all come from Deschamps's own poetic production.

9 Cf. Langlois, ed., *Recueil d'arts*, p. xxviii. I consider this work to be the second oldest of the surviving arts de Seconde Rhétorique even though it is preceded in Langlois's *Recueil* by the *Des Rimes* (1405) of Jacques Legrand. Legrand's text is not, properly speaking, a treatise at all, being but a single chapter excerpted from a larger work, the *Archiloge Sophie*, itself a French adaptation of Legrand's earlier Latin work, the *Sophologium*.

10 Langlois, ed., *Recueil d'arts*, p. 12.

11 Cf. n. 6, above.

12 Cf. Poirion, *Poète*, pp. 218–19 for an incisive discussion of the organization of the MSS of Deschamps's works, esp. B.N., f. fr. 840.

13 Poirion, *Poète*, p. 229.

14 Poirion (*Poète*, p. 218) finds that "les proportions de l'oeuvre: 1500 pièces totalisant 82,000 vers sont surprenantes."

15 Froissart makes no explicit mention of Machaut, but numerous instances of direct "influence" have been demonstrated. Cf. Jakob Geiselhardt, *Machaut und Froissart. Ihre literarischen Beziehungen* (Jena, Germany: Weida i. Th., 1914) and B. J. Whiting, "Froissart as Poet," *Mediaeval Studies* 8 (1946), pp. 189–216. Cf. in addition the introductions to Anthime Fourrier's excellent editions of Froissart's *L'Espinette amoureuse* (Paris: Klincksieck, 1963), *La Prison amoureuse* (Paris: Klincksieck, 1974), and *Le Joli Buisson de Jonece* (Geneva: Droz, 1975).

16 For an overall consideration of Froissart's achievement as a poet see Peter Dembowski's important article "La Position de Froissart-poète dans l'histoire littéraire: Bilan provisoire," *Travaux de Linguistique et de Littérature* 16 (1978), 131–47.

17 It is important to note that Froissart's long Arthurian romance, *Méliador*, is the only one of his works in verse that is not included

in these two codices (the principal MS for *Méliador* being B.N., f. fr. 12557). A special "generic" status thus seems to be assigned to *Méliador* which, qua romance, constitutes a separate category of Froissart's oeuvre, perceived as such by the poet himself. The visible chronology of the composition of *Méliador* (cf. Dembowski, "La Position de Froissart-poète," pp. 134, 138, 142) would serve to reinforce the impression of the progressive development of Froissart the poète conveyed by B.N., f. fr. 830 and 831.

18 Poirion, *Poète*, p. 206.

19 Cf. Michelle A. Freeman's penetrating analysis, "Froissart's *Le Joli Buisson de Jonece:* A Farewell to Poetry?" in *Machaut's World: Science and Art in the Fourteenth Century.* Annals of the New York Academy of Sciences 314 (Oct. 1978), pp. 235–47.

20 Given the special position of *Méliador,* a tripartate division of Froissart's oeuvre (into "les poésies, le roman et les *Chroniques*") is also possible, as Dembowski ("La Position de Froissart-poète," p. 143) suggestively remarks.

21 It is perhaps significant in this context that Machaut's last literary work — the *Prise d'Alexandrie* — involved his utilization, for the first time, of the stance of epic chronicler and recounted (though in verse) contemporary historical events.

22 All references are to the Rychner-Henry edition.

23 Direct influence seems unlikely. John L. La Monte ("The 'Roy de Chippre' in François Villon's 'Ballade des seigneurs du temps jadis,'" *Romanic Review* 23 [1932], pp. 48–53) has argued that v. 369 of the *Testament* contains a reference to Pierre Ier de Lusignan, the protagonist of Machaut's *La Prise d'Alexandrie,* but Rychner and Henry (*Testament,* 2, 57–58) offer convincing (though not, perhaps, conclusive) counterarguments.

24 For the last four examples cf. the perceptive "observation générale" of Rychner and Henry (*Testament,* 2, 248): "dans les cas . . . où le poèm inséré dans le *Testament* constitue véritablement un legs de Villon . . . le poète prête sa voix au légataire, qui s'exprime à la première personne."

25 See Rychner-Henry, eds., *Testament,* 2, p. 14.

26 Karl D. Uitti, "A Note on Villon's Poetics," *Romance Philology* 30 (1976–77), p. 192.

27 Uitti, "Note on Villon," p. 192. Cf. in addition the illuminating comments of Rychner-Henry, eds., *Testament,* 2, p. 275.

Selected
Bibliography

Primary Sources

Acart de Hesdin, Jehan. *La Prise amoureuse.* Ed. Ernest Hoepffner. Gesellschaft für romanische Philologie 22. Dresden: Niemeyer, 1910.

Andreas Capellanus. *The Art of Courtly Love.* Trans. John J. Parry. New York: Columbia University Press, 1941.

Andreas Capellanus. *Trattato d'amore. Andrae Capellani regii francorum "De Amore libri tres." Testo latino del sec. XII con due traduzioni toscane inedite del sec. XIV.* Ed. S. Battaglia. Rome: Perella, 1947.

Benoît de Sainte-Maure. *Le Roman de Troie.* 6 vols. Ed. Léopold Constans. SATF. Paris: Firmin Didot, 1904–12.

"Blancheflour et Florence." Ed. Paul Meyer. *Romania* 37 (1908), 221–34.

Boethius. *The Theological Tractates. The Consolation of Philosophy.* Ed. H. F. Stewart and E. K. Rand. Cambridge, Mass.: Harvard University Press, 1968, pp. 128–411.

Buigne, Gace de la. *Le Roman des deduis.* Ed. Ake Blomquist. Karlshamn, 1951.

La Chastelaine de Vergi. 2d ed. Ed. Frederick Whitehead. Manchester: Manchester University Press, 1951.

Chrétien de Troyes. *Le Chevalier au lion (Yvain).* Ed. Mario Roques. CFMA. Paris: Champion, 1971.

Chrétien de Troyes. *Le Chevalier de la charrete (Lancelot).* Ed. Mario Roques. CFMA. Paris: Champion, 1958.

Chrétien de Troyes. *Cligés.* Ed. Alexandre Micha. CFMA. Paris: Champion, 1970.

Chrétien de Troyes. *Erec et Enide.* Ed. Mario Roques. CFMA. Paris: Champion, 1966.

Chrétien de Troyes. *Le Roman de Perceval ou le Conte del Graal*. Ed. William Roach. TLF. Geneva: Droz, 1959.

Condé, Jean de. *La Messe des oiseaux*. Ed. Jacques Ribard. TLF. Geneva: Droz, 1970.

Dancus Rex, Guillelmus Falconarius, Gerardus Falconarius. Ed. Gunnar Tilander. Cynegetica 9. Lund, Sweden: Bloms, 1963.

Deschamps, Eustache, *Œuvres complètes de Eustache Deschamps*. 11 vols. Ed. A. Queux de Saint-Hilaire and Gaston Raynaud. SATF. Paris: Firmin Didot, 1878–1903.

Drouart la Vache. *Li Livres d'amours*. Ed. Robert Bossuat. Paris: Champion, 1926.

Fornival, Richart de. *"Li Bestaires d'amours" di Maistre Richart de Fornival e "Li Response du Bestaire."* Ed. Cesare Segre. Documenti di filologia 2. Milan and Naples: Ricciardi, 1957.

Froissart, Jean. *"Dits" et "Debats."* Avec en appendice quelques poèmes de Guillaume de Machaut. Ed. Anthime Fourrier. TLF. Geneva: Droz, 1979.

Froissart, Jean. *L'Espinette amoureuse*. Ed. Anthime Fourrier. Paris: Klincksieck, 1963.

Froissart, Jean. *Le Joli Buisson de Jonece*. Ed. Anthime Fourrier. TLF. Geneva: Droz, 1975.

Froissart, Jean. *La Prison amoureuse*. Ed. Anthime Fourrier. Paris: Klincksieck, 1974.

Jakemes. *Le Roman du Castelain de Couci et de la Dame de Fayel*. Ed. John E. Matzke and Maurice Delbouille. SATF. Paris: SATF, 1936.

Langlois, Ernest, ed. *Recueil d'arts de Seconde Rhétorique*. Paris: Imprimerie Nationale, 1902.

Latini, Brunetto. *Li Livres dou tresor*. Ed. Francis J. Carmody. California Publications in Modern Philology 22. Berkeley and Los Angeles: University of California Press, 1948.

Lorris, Guillaume de, and Jean de Meun. *Le Roman de la rose*. 3 vols. Ed. Félix Lecoy. CFMA. Paris: Champion, 1965–70.

Machaut, Guillaume de. *"Le Dit de la harpe."* Ed. Karl Young. In *Essays in Honor of Albert Feuillerat*, pp. 1–20. Ed. Henri M. Peyre. New Haven: Yale University Press, 1943.

Machaut, Guillaume de. *Guillaume de Machaut: Musikalische Werke*. 4 vols. Ed. Friedrich Ludwig. Leipzig: Breitkopf und Härtel, 1926–54.

Machaut, Guillaume de. *Guillaume de Machaut: Poésies lyriques*. 2 vols. Ed. Vladimir Chichmaref. Paris: Champion, 1909.

Machaut, Guillaume de. *Le Livre du voir-dit*. Ed. Paulin Paris. Paris: Société des bibliophiles françois, 1875.

Machaut, Guillaume de. *La Louange des dames*. Ed. Nigel Wilkins. Edinburgh: Scottish Academic Press, 1972.

Machaut, Guillaume de. *The Marguerite Poetry of Guillaume de Machaut*. Ed. James Wimsatt. University of North Carolina Studies in the Romance Languages and Literatures 87. Chapel Hill: University of North Carolina Press, 1970.

Machaut, Guillaume de. *Œuvres de Guillaume de Machaut*. 3 vols. Ed. Ernest Hoepffner. SATF. Paris: Firmin Didot, 1908-21.

Machaut, Guillaume de. *Les Œuvres de Guillaume de Machaut*. Ed. Prosper Tarbé. Reims and Paris: Techener, 1849.

Machaut, Guillaume de. *Polyphonic Music of the Fourteenth Century*. Vols. 2 and 3, *The Works of Guillaume de Machaut*. Ed. Leo Schrade. Monaco: Editions de l'oiseau-lyre, 1956.

Machaut, Guillaume de. *La Prise d'Alexandrie ou Chronique du roi Pierre de Lusignan*. Ed. M. Louis de Mas Latrie. Geneva: Fick, 1877.

Margival, Nicole de. *Le Dit de la panthère d'amours*. Ed. Henry A. Todd. SATF. Paris: Firmin Didot, 1883.

L'Ovide moralisé. Ed. Cornelis de Boer. Verhandelingen der Koninklijke Akademie van Wetenschappen te Amsterdam. Afdeeling Letterkunde, n.s. 15, 21, 30, 37, 43. Amsterdam: Müller, 1915-38.

Le Roman de Dolopathos. Ed. Charles Brunet and Anatole de Montaiglon. Paris: P. Jannet, 1856.

Le Roman d'Enéas. 2 vols. Ed. Salverda de Grave. CFMA. Paris: Champion, 1968-73.

Rutebeuf. *Œuvres complètes de Rutebeuf*. 2 vols. Ed. Edmond Faral and Julia Bastin. Paris: Picard, 1956-60.

Traduction en vieux français du "De arte venandi cum avibus" de l'empereur Frédéric II de Hohenstaufen. Ed. Gustaf Holmér. Lund, Sweden: Bloms, 1960.

Traductions en vieux français de "Dancus Rex" et "Guillelmus Falconarius." Ed. Gunnar Tilander. Cynegetica 12. Karlshamn: Johanssons, 1965.

La Vie de Saint Alexis. Ed. Gaston Paris. CFMA. Paris: Champion, 1903.

Villon, François. *Le Testament Villon*. 2 vols. Ed. Jean Rychner and Albert Henry. TLF. Geneva: Droz, 1974.

Wace. *Le Roman de Brut*. 2 vols. Ed. Ivor Arnold. SATF. Paris: SATF, 1938-40.

Wace. *Le Roman de Rou*. 3 vols. Ed. A. J. Holden. SATF. Paris: SATF, 1970-72.

Scholarship

Benveniste, Emile. *Problèmes de linguistique générale*. Vol. 1. Paris: Gallimard, 1966.

Boer, Cornelis de. "Guillaume de Machaut et *L'Ovide moralisé.*" *Romania* 43 (1914), 335–52.

Brownlee, Kevin. "The Poetic Œuvre of Guillaume de Machaut: The Identity of Discourse and the Discourse of Identity." In *Machaut's World: Science and Art in the Fourteenth Century.* Ed. Madeleine Pelner Cosman and Bruce Chandler, pp. 219–33. Annals of the New York Academy of Sciences 314 (Oct. 1978).

Brownlee, Kevin. "Transformations of the Lyric 'Je': The Example of Guillaume de Machaut." *L'Esprit Créateur* 18 (1978), 5–18.

Calin, William. *A Poet at the Fountain: Essays on the Narrative Verse of Guillaume de Machaut.* Lexington: University of Kentucky Press, 1974.

Calin, William. "A Reading of Machaut's *Jugement dou roy de Navarre.*" *Modern Language Review* 66 (1971), 294–97.

Cerquiglini, Jacqueline. "Le Montage des formes: L'Exemple de Guillaume de Machaut." *Perspectives Médiévales* 3 (1977), 23–27.

Cerquiglini, Jacqueline. "Syntaxe et syncope: Language du corps et écriture chez Guillaume de Machaut." *Langue Française* 40 (Dec. 1978), 60–74.

Cerquiglini, Jacqueline. "Tension sociale et tension d'écriture au XIVème siècle: Les Dits de Guillaume de Machaut." In *Littérature et Société au Moyen Age. Actes du Colloque d'Amiens des 5 et 6 mai, 1978.* Ed. Danielle Buschinger, pp. 111–29. Paris: Champion, 1978.

Dembowski, Peter. "La Position de Froissart-poète dans l'histoire littéraire: Bilan provisoire." *Travaux de Linguistique et de Littérature* 16 (1978), 131–47.

Dembowski, Peter. "Vocabulary of Old French Courtly Lyrics: Difficulties and Hidden Difficulties." *Critical Inquiry* 2 (1976), 763–79.

Dragonetti, Roger. "'La Poesie . . . ceste musique naturelle.' Essai d'exégèse d'un passage de l'*Art de dictier* d'Eustache Deschamps." In *Fin du moyen âge et Renaissance: Mélanges de philologie française offerts à Robert Guiette.* Ed. Guy de Poerck, Maurice Piron, Louis Mourin, et al., pp. 49–64. Antwerp: Nederlandische Boekhandel, 1961.

Dragonetti, Roger. *La Technique poétique des trouvères dans la chanson courtoise: Contribution à l'étude de la rhétorique médiévale.* Brugge: De Tempel, 1960.

Dragonetti, Roger. "Trois motifs de la lyrique courtoise confrontés avec les *Arts d'aimer* (Contribution à l'étude de la thématologie courtoise)." *Romanica Gandensia* 7 (1959), 5–48.

Eichelberg, Walter. *Dichtung und Wahrheit in Machauts "Voir Dit."* Frankfurt am Main: Düren, 1935.

Faral, Edmond. *Les Jongleurs en France au moyen âge.* Paris: Champion, 1910.

Frappier, Jean. "*La Chastelaine de Vergi,* Marguerite de Navarre et Bandello." *Publications de la Faculté des Lettres de l'Université de Strasbourg* 105 (1945), 89–150.

Frappier, Jean. *Chrétien de Troyes et le mythe du Graal.* Paris: SEDES, 1972.

Freeman, Michelle A. "Chrétien's *Cligés:* A Close Reading of the Prologue." *Romanic Review* 67 (1976), 89–101.

Freeman, Michelle A. "Froissart's *Le Joli Buisson de Jonece:* A Farewell to Poetry?" In *Machaut's World: Science and Art in the Fourteenth Century.* Ed. Madeleine Pelner Cosman and Bruce Chandler, pp. 235–47. Annals of the New York Academy of Sciences 314 (Oct. 1978).

Freeman, Michelle A. "Problems in Romance Composition: Ovid, Chrétien de Troyes and the *Romance of the Rose.*" *Romance Philology* 30 (1976–77), 158–68.

Friedman, Lionel J. "Gradus amoris." *Romance Philology* 19 (1965–66), 167–77.

Geiselhardt, Jakob. *Machaut und Froissart. Ihre literarischen Beziehungen.* Jena, Germany: Weida i. Th., 1914.

Genette, Gérard. *Figures II.* Paris: Seuil, 1969.

Genette, Gérard. *Figures III.* Paris: Seuil, 1972.

Gourment, Remy de. "Le Roman de Guillaume de Machaut et de Peronne d'Armentières." *Promenades Littéraires.* 5th series. Paris: Mercure de France, 1913, pp. 7–37.

Günther, Ursula. "Chronologie und Stil der Kompositionen Guillaume de Machauts." *Acta Musicologia* 35 (1963), 96–114.

Gybbon-Monypenny, G. B. "Autobiography in the *Libro de buen amor* in the Light of Some Literary Comparisons." *Bulletin of Hispanic Studies* 34 (1957), 63–78.

Gybbon-Monypenny, G. B. "Guillaume de Machaut's Erotic 'Autobiography': Precedents for the Form of the *Voir-Dit.*" In *Studies in Medieval Literature and Languages in Memory of Frederick Whitehead.* Ed. W. Rothwell, W. R. J. Barron, David Blamires, et al., pp. 133–52. Manchester: Manchester University Press, 1973.

Hanf, Georg. "Ueber Guillaume de Machauts *Voir Dit.*" *Zeitschrift für romanische Philologie* 22 (1898), 145–96.

Hoepffner, Ernest. "Anagramme und Rätselgedichte bei Guillaume de Machaut." *Zeitschrift für romanische Philologie* 30 (1906), 401–13.

Hoepffner, Ernest. "Die Balladen des Dichters Jehan de la Mote." *Zeitschrift für romanische Philologie* 35 (1911), 153–66.

Hoepffner, Ernest. "Chrestien de Troyes und Guillaume de Machaut." *Zeitschrift für romanische Philologie* 39 (1917–19), 627–29.

Hoepffner, Ernest. "La Chronologie des pastourelles de Froissart." In *Mélanges Offerts à M. Emile Picot.* Ed. Henri Omont, et al., pp. 27–42. Vol. 2. Paris: Morgand, 1913.

Hoepffner, Ernest. "Les Poésies lyriques du *Dit de la panthère* de Nicole de Margival." *Romania* 53 (1920), 204–30.

Kelly, Douglas. "Courtly Love in Perspective: The Hierarchy of Love in Andreas Capellanus." *Traditio* 24 (1968), 119–47.

Kelly, Douglas. *Medieval Imagination: Rhetoric and the Poetry of Courtly Love.* Madison: University of Wisconsin Press, 1978.

Kelly, Douglas. "*Sens*" and "*Conjoincture*" in the "*Chevalier de la charrette.*" The Hague: Mouton, 1966.

Kelly, Douglas. "*Translatio Studii:* Translation, Adaptation, and Allegory in Medieval French Literature." *Philological Quarterly* 57 (1978), 287–310.

Kennedy, Elspeth. "The Scribe as Editor." In *Mélanges de langue et de littérature du moyen âge et de la Renaissance offerts à Jean Frappier.* Vol. 1, pp. 523–31. Geneva: Droz, 1970.

La Monte, John L. "The 'Roy de Chippre' in François Villon's 'Ballade des seigneurs du temps jadis.'" *Romanic Review* 23 (1932), 48–53.

Laurie, I. S. "Deschamps and the Lyric as Natural Music." *The Modern Language Review* 59 (1964), 561–70.

Lubienski-Bodenham, H. "The Origins of the Fifteenth-Century View of Poetry as 'Seconde Rhétorique.'" *The Modern Language Review* 74 (1979), 26–38.

Machabey, Armand. *Guillaume de Machault: La Vie et l'oeuvre musical.* 2 vols. Paris: Richard-Masse, 1955.

Patterson, Warner F. *Three Centuries of French Poetic Theory: A Critical History of the Chief Arts of Poetry in France (1328–1630).* 2 vols. Ann Arbor: University of Michigan Press, 1935.

Poirion, Daniel. "The Imaginary Universe of Guillaume de Machaut." In *Machaut's World: Science and Art in the Fourteenth Century.* Ed. Madeleine Pelner Cosman and Bruce Chandler, pp. 199–206. Annals of the New York Academy of Sciences, 314 (Oct. 1978).

Poirion, Daniel. *Le Moyen âge. II: 1300–1480.* Paris: Arthaud, 1971.

Poirion, Daniel. "Narcisse et Pygmalion dans le *Roman de la rose.*" In *Essays in Honor of Louis Francis Solano.* Ed. Raymond J. Cormier and Urban T. Holmes, pp. 153–65. University of North Carolina Studies in the Romance Languages and Literatures 92. Chapel Hill: University of North Carolina Press, 1970.

Poirion, Daniel. *Le Poète et le prince: L'Évolution du lyrisme courtois de Guillaume de Machaut à Charles d'Orléans.* Paris: Presses Universitaires de France, 1965.

Poirion, Daniel. *Le "Roman de la Rose."* Paris: Hatier, 1973.

Reaney, Gilbert. "A Chronology of the Ballades, Rondeaux and Virelais

Set to Music by Guillaume de Machaut." *Musica Disciplina* 6 (1952), 33–38.

Reaney, Gilbert. "The Development of the Rondeau, Virelai and Ballade Forms from Adam de la Hale to Guillaume de Machaut." In *Festschrift Karl Gustav Fellerer*. Ed. Heinrich Hüschen, pp. 421–27. Regensburg: Bosse, 1962.

Reaney, Gilbert. *Guillaume de Machaut*. London and New York: Oxford University Press, 1971.

Reaney, Gilbert. "Guillaume de Machaut: Lyric Poet." *Music and Letters* 39 (1958), 38–51.

Reaney, Gilbert. "The *Lais* of Guillaume de Machaut and Their Background." *Proceedings of the Royal Musical Association* 82 (1955–56), 15–32.

Reaney, Gilbert. "The Poetic Form of Machaut's Musical Works: I. The Ballades, Rondeaux and Virelais." *Musica Disciplina* 13 (1959), 25–41.

Reaney, Gilbert. "Towards a Chronology of Machaut's Musical Works." *Musica Disciplina* 21 (1967), 87–96.

Regalado, Nancy F. *Poetic Patterns in Rutebeuf: A Study in Noncourtly Poetic Modes of the Thirteenth Century*. New Haven: Yale University Press, 1970.

Strohm, Paul. "Guillaume as Narrator and Lover in the *Roman de la rose*." *Romanic Review* 59 (1969), 3–9.

Suchier, Hermann. "Das Anagramm in Machauts Voir Dit." *Zeitschrift für romanische Philologie* 21 (1897), 541–45.

Thomas, Antoine. "Guillaume de Machaut et *l'Ovide moralisé*." *Romania* 41 (1912), 382–400.

Uitti, Karl D. "The Clerkly Narrator Figure in Old French Hagiography and Romance." *Medioevo Romanzo* 2 (1975), 394–408.

Uitti, Karl D. "From *Clerc* to *Poète*: The Relevance of the *Romance of the Rose* to Machaut's World." In *Machaut's World: Science and Art in the Fourteenth Century*. Ed. Madeleine Pelner Cosman and Bruce Chandler, pp. 206–16. Annals of the New York Academy of Sciences 314 (Oct. 1978).

Uitti, Karl D. "Literary Discourse: Some Definitions and Approaches." In *Patterns of Literary Style*. Ed. Joseph Strelka, pp. 198–216. University Park: Pennsylvania State University Press, 1971.

Uitti, Karl D. "A Note on Villon's Poetics." *Romance Philology* 30 (1976–77), 187–92.

Uitti, Karl D. "Remarks on Old French Narrative: Courtly Love and Poetic Form (I)." *Romance Philology* 26 (1972–73), 77–93.

Uitti, Karl D. "Remarks on Old French Narrative: Courtly Love and Poetic Form (II)." *Romance Philology* 28 (1974-75), 190-99.

Uitti, Karl D. *Story, Myth and Celebration in Old French Narrative Poetry: 1050-1200.* Princeton: Princeton University Press, 1973.

Vitz, E. B. "The *I* of the *Roman de la rose.*" *Genre* 6 (1973), 49-75.

Weinrich, Harald. "Structures narratives du mythe." *Poétique* 1 (1970), 25-34.

Weinrich, Harald. *Le Temps.* Trans. Michèle Lacoste. Paris: Seuil, 1973.

Weinrich, Harald. *Tempus — besprochene und erzählte Welt.* Stuttgart: W. Kohlhammer, 1964; 2d ed. 1971.

Weinrich, Harald. "Tense and Time." *Archivum linguisticum,* n.s. 1 (1970), 31-41.

Whiting, B. J. "Froissart as Poet." *Mediaeval Studies* 8 (1946), 189-216.

Williams, Sarah Jane. "An Author's Role in Fourteenth-Century Book Production: Guillaume de Machaut's 'livre ou je met toutes mes choses.'" *Romania* 90 (1969), 433-54.

Williams, Sarah Jane. "The Lady, the Lyrics and the Letters." *Early Music* 5 (1977), 462-68.

Williams, Sarah Jane. "Machaut's Self-Awareness as Author and Producer." In *Machaut's World: Science and Art in the Fourteenth Century.* Ed. Madeleine Pelner Cosman and Bruce Chandler, pp. 189-97. Annals of the New York Academy of Sciences, 314 (Oct. 1978).

Wimsatt, James I. *Chaucer and the French Love Poets: The Literary Background of the "Book of the Duchess."* Chapel Hill: University of North Carolina Press, 1968.

Zumthor, Paul. "Autobiography in the Middle Ages?" *Genre* 6 (1973), 29-48.

Zumthor, Paul. *Essai de poétique médiévale.* Paris: Seuil, 1972.

Zumthor, Paul. "De Guillaume de Lorris à Jean de Meung." In *Etudes de langue et de littérature du moyen âge offerts à Félix Lecoy,* pp. 608-20. Paris: Champion, 1973.

Zumthor, Paul. "Récit et anti-récit: Le *Roman de la rose.*" *Medioevo Romanzo* 1 (1974), 5-24.

Zumthor, Paul. "Du Rythme à la rime." In *Langue, Texte, Énigme.* Paris: Seuil, 1975, pp. 125-43.

Index

Abbreviatio, 27, 159
Abelard, 98
Alcyone, 194
Amant: character in *Rose*, 19, 42
Amant couart topic, 32, 41, 113
Amédée VI, Count of Savoy, 4
Amors: character in *Rose*, 13, 19, 230*n*24
Amour: as personification character, 17,
  18, 19, 21, 29–37 passim, 71–73, 75,
  77–78, 79–80, 84, 89, 91, 166, 168;
  service of, 17, 18, 19, 21, 37, 41, 55,
  61–63, 68, 82, 85, 96, 157, 170, 187,
  189, 198, 243*n*67; affective state, 40–
  47 passim, 55, 62, 139, 183; men-
  tioned, 65, 66, 74, 81, 83, 90, 92, 93,
  143, 148. *See also* God of Love
Amplificatio, 96
Anagram: signature, 60, 92, 156, 186,
  188–89
Anaphora, 175
Andreas Capellanus: *De amore*, 228*n*5
Annominatio, 14, 35, 121, 154, 175, 190
Apollo, 147
Arnaud de Cervoles, Archpriest of Vé-
  lines, 127, 241*n*48
Ars amandi, 38, 63, 65, 67, 68, 70–71,
  82, 228*n*5
Ars poetica, 38, 63, 232*n*31

Artus de Bretagne, 102
Attemprance, 29, 123
Aubade, 120
Auctor, 7, 8, 44, 65, 104, 133, 220*n*11
Audience, 9, 10, 92, 129, 166, 172
Aventure, 90, 96, 174, 189

Baladelle, 52
Ballade, 7, 8, 16, 41, 101, 102, 103, 124,
  140, 151, 210, 211, 224*n*37
Bel Acueil: character in *Rose*, 86, 233*n*42
Benoît de Sainte-Maure: *Roman de
  Troie*, 10, 220*n*11, 226*n*40
Benveniste, Emile, 23
Biauté, 166
Birdsong, 53–54, 158–59, 172–73, 174,
  197
Boethius: *Consolation of Philosophy*,
  42, 43, 45, 46, 50–52
Bon-avis, 123–24
Bonne of Luxembourg, 4

Calin, William, 5, 6, 177, 227*n*3, 228*n*7,
  233*n*46, 242*n*53, 244*n*75, 246*n*92
Canens, 143
Celer, 29
Cerquiglini, Jacqueline, 219*n*3, 230*n*20,
  246*n*88, 246*n*92

Ceyx, 194
Chanson baladée, 55, 102. *See also* Virelay
Chanson roial, 46–47, 211
Charles d'Orléans, 6, 251n1
Charles II, King of Navarre: patron of Machaut, 4, 21, 241n39
Charles V, King of France: patron of Machaut, 4, 114, 118, 220n5, 241n39; as dauphin (Duke of Normandy), 114, 115, 116–18, 132–33, 144
Chastelain de Couci, 12
Chastelaine de Vergi, 139, 161, 247n5
Chevalerie, 4, 106
Chichmaref, Vladimir, 5, 101, 235n8
Chrétien de Troyes: *Yvain*, 11, 176, 224n40, 249n18; *Perceval*, 11, 180, 224n40; *Erec et Enide*, 11, 181, 224n40; *Charrete*, 11, 224n40; *Cligés*, 11, 224n40; mentioned, 11, 174, 180, 181, 224n40
Clerkly narrator figure, 3, 9, 10, 11, 12
Circe, 142, 143
Codex, 3, 15, 16, 25, 36, 137
Complainte, 43, 128, 135, 136, 193–96, 199, 200, 207
Confort-d'ami, 123–24
Conon de Béthune, 12
Coronis, 147
Courtly love, 6, 115. *See also* Fin'amors
Courtoisie: quality of, 4, 196; personification character, 164–65, 166
Crécy, battle of, 4
Crécy, town of, 116
Cruautez, 30

Dangier (Dongier), 30, 75, 121, 138, 141
David, 18
Deduit: character in *Rose*, 42, 55, 159, 197
Dembowski, Peter F., 228n4, 252n16, 252n17, 253n20
Desir, 29, 30, 76, 103, 112, 124–25, 128, 130, 131, 139, 166, 231n36
Deschamps, Eustache: ballades, 7–8, 9,

18, 20; as poète, 208, 210–11; *Art de dictier*, 209–10, 232n32, 252n8
Dit de l'alerion: narrator-protagonist, 63–64, 67–68, 71, 88, 90–93; metaphoric discourse, 64, 66–67, 76, 77, 82, 87, 89–91; exemplarity, 64, 67, 92; narrative structure, 64, 72–73, 80, 85, 88, 92; esprivier, 65, 66–72; alerion, 65, 73–79, 89–92; aigle, 65, 80–85; gerfaut, 65, 85–88; register, 65–66, 91; intercalated exempla, 74, 83; mentioned, 21, 24, 150. *See also* Amour; Ars amandi; Falconry manual; Fin'amors; Locus amoenus
Dit dou lyon: narrator figure, 171, 173, 175, 180, 182, 186–88; generic models, 172, 174, 176–77, 180, 181, 183, 187; narrative structure, 172, 174, 177, 182–86 passim; temporality, 172, 184, 185; lion (as lover), 176–80, 182–85; chevalier, speech of, 181–82; mentioned, 21, 157, 190, 194, 206, 207. *See also* Chrétien de Troyes; Losengier; Margival, Nicole de; Romance
Dit dou vergier: codicological status, 24–26, 35–36; narrator-protagonist, 26–27, 31–32, 33, 34–35; narrative structure, 26, 28, 29, 32, 33, 34; *Roman de la Rose* (as model), 27–28, 29, 30, 31, 36; dream-vision, 28–34; God of Love (speeches of), 28–33; love experience, 30–32; mentioned, 21, 45, 48, 93. *See also* Amant couart topic; Guillaume de Lorris; Locus amoenus
Dit amoureux, 7, 93, 208, 227n3
Doubtance, 30
Dous Penser. *See* Penser
Dous Plaisir (Douce Plaisance), 29, 75, 121
Dragonetti, Roger, 222n26, 229n9, 252n7
Durbui, Castle of, 162, 163, 169
Durtez, 30

Eichelberg, Walter, 234n4, 235n8
Erec, 181

Esperance. *See* Esperence
Esperence (Esperance, Espoir): as simple personification, 29, 30, 78, 90,
  111, 130; as authority figure, 46,
  49–54, 55–57 passim, 93, 123–28; in
  love, 103, 125–26, 231*n26*; mentioned, 136. *See also* Desir
Espoir. *See* Esperence
Exemplum poetae, 8, 63

Falconry manual: as genre, 66, 67–91
  passim
Fin'amors, 6, 65, 66, 72, 80, 84, 85, 107,
  110, 113, 125, 179. *See also* Courtly
  love
Fonteinne amoureuse: Amant (as protagonist), 188–89, 193, 194, 196, 199,
  202–3, 205, 206, 207; narrative structure, 188, 195, 196, 201, 203, 205; narrator figure, 188–93, 195–96, 199, 201,
  204–5, 206, 207; "Complainte de
  l'Amant," 193–95, 199–200; dreams,
  194–95, 200–205, 206, 207; fountain,
  197–99; "Confort de l'Amant et de la
  Dame," 203; mentioned, 21, 28, 106–
  7, 135, 147–48, 157, 226*n41*. *See also*
  Anagram; Jean de Berry; Morpheus;
  Roman de la Rose; Venus
Forme fixe, 41, 103, 209, 210, 211, 213
Fortune: as abstraction, 43, 44, 45, 50,
  51, 74, 148, 154; image of, 148–49,
  151–52
Fourrier, Anthime, 5, 220*n9*
Franchise, 29, 166
Fran Voloir. *See* Voloir
Frappier, Jean, 247*n5*
Freeman, Michelle A., 222*n22*, 253*n19*
Friedman, Lionel J., 240*n33*
Froissart, Jean, 208, 211–12, 252*n17*
Fulgentius, 148

Genette, Gérard, 22, 227*n43*
God of Love, 28, 29, 30, 31, 32–33, 34,
  82, 183, 197. *See also* Amour
Gourmont, Remy de, 98
Grace, 29, 75

Gradus amoris, 128, 240*n33*, 240*n34*,
  240*n37*, 241*n42*, 241*n46*
Grand chant courtois, 3, 11, 12, 188
Guillaume de Lorris: *Roman de la Rose*,
  12–13, 14, 19, 28, 86, 197, 198, 213,
  228*n6*, 249*n23*; mentioned, 8, 156.
  See also Jean de Meun; *Roman de la
  Rose*
Guillaume Longue Espée, 74
Guillemette: Péronne's cousin, 119
Gybbon-Monypenny, G. B., 231*n31*,
  234*n2*

Hagiography, 3, 9–10, 11
Hanf, Georg, 234*n4*, 235*n8*
Hardiesse, 166
Hebe, 131, 148
Helen of Troy, 139, 197, 201
Heloïse, 98
Henry, Albert, 251*n35*, 253*n24*
Hoepffner, Ernest, 5, 16, 22, 25, 34, 180,
  181, 224*n36*, 230*n23*, 247*n3*, 248*n10*
Honneur, 75, 121, 164–65, 166
Honte, 30, 111, 112, 124

Imbs, Paul, 5
Iolaus, 131, 148

Jakemes: *Roman du Castelain de Couci*,
  221*n11*, 234*n2*
Jean II, King of France, 4, 136
Jean de Berry, 4, 194, 206, 220*n5*
Jean de Luxembourg, King of Bohemia:
  patron of Machaut, 4, 163, 192,
  219*n4*; character in dit amoureux,
  162–64, 165–69
Jean de Meun: *Roman de la Rose*, 13,
  17, 19, 198, 228*n6*, 250*n30*; translator
  of Boethius, 230*n22*; mentioned, 8,
  156. *See also* Guillaume de Lorris;
  Roman de la Rose
Jeunesse, 166, 168
Josephus, 133
Jugement dou roy de Behaingne: narrative structure, 158, 159, 160, 164, 169;
  narrator figure, 158–59, 160, 161, 162,

Jugement dou roy de Behaingne (cont.)
164, 165, 167, 170, 171; dame (as lover), 159–60, 168–69; chevalier (as lover), 160, 166, 168–69; personification characters, 165–66, 168; judgment scene, 167–68; love, 168, 171; signature, 169–70; generic analogues, 247*n3*; mentioned, 21, 157, 190, 192, 194, 206, 207, 226*n41*. *See also* Chastelaine de Vergi; Durbui, Castle of; Jean de Luxembourg; Locus amoenus; Raison; *Roman de la Rose*
Jugement dou roy de Navarre. See Machaut, Guillaume de

Kelly, Douglas, 6, 22, 115, 125, 224*n39*, 228*n3*, 229*n14*, 231*n26*, 243*n67*
King Arthur, 11

Lady Philosophy, 46, 48, 51
Lancelot, 12, 106, 139, 181
Largesse, 166
Laura, 98, 239*n25*, 241*n47*, 242*n54*
Lay, 41–42, 43, 105, 124, 127. *See also* Machaut, Guillaume de
Leander, 139
Leësse, 166
Livy, 148
Locus amoenus, 66, 92, 110, 197, 205. *See also* Plaisance; Vergier
Loiauté, 29, 166, 168
Losengier, 104, 141, 143, 144, 152, 239*n23. See also* Médisant
Louange, 40, 95, 105
Louis IX, King of France, 74
Ludwig, Friedrich, 5, 223*n34*, 244*n70*
Lyric je: defined, 11–12

Machabey, Armand, 5, 235*n8*
Machaut, Guillaume de: career, 4; *Prise d'Alexandrie*, 4, 5, 21, 22, 226*n41*, 236*n8*, 253*n21*; manuscripts, 4, 16, 24, 25, 101, 107, 123, 140, 164, 170, 211, 223*n34*, 224*n37*; *Dit de la fleur de lis et de la Marguerite*, 5; *Dit de la harpe*, 5; *Dit de la Marguerite*, 5;

Dit de la Rose, 5; music, 5, 101, 105; *Jugement dou roy de Navarre*, 15, 21, 22, 127, 226*n41*, 251*n36*; oeuvre, concept of, 15, 48; *Prologue*, 16–19, 20, 24, 25–26, 36, 198, 208, 224*n36*, 224*n37*; *Confort d'ami*, 21, 22, 132, 192, 226*n41*; chronology (of works), 22, 226*n42*; *Louange des dames*, 101, 238*n16. See also Dit de l'alerion*; *Dit dou lyon*; *Dit dou vergier*; *Fonteinne amoureuse*; *Jugement dou roy de Behaingne*; *Remede de Fortune*; *Voir-Dit*
Malebouche, 138, 141
Margival, Nicole de: *Dit de la panthère d'amours*, 176–77, 183, 232*n31*
Mas Latrie, Louis de, 5
Médisant, 58, 83, 146, 147. *See also* Losengier
Mercury, 201–2
Merencolie, 130
Mesure, 123
Morpheus, 148, 194
Music, 5, 12, 101, 105. *See also* Machaut, Guillaume de

Narcissus, 197, 198
Nature: as personification character, 16, 17, 19, 172; as abstraction, 37, 65
Noblesse, 166

Orpheus, 18
Ovid, 8, 133, 233*n39*
Ovide moralisé, 202, 205, 228*n6*, 242*n58*, 250*n26*
Ovidian conventions, 29, 30, 41, 46, 69, 101, 109, 135, 142–43, 147, 175, 194, 198, 202

Pacience, 50
Paien, Thomas, 140, 244*n70*
Pais, 75
Paour, 30, 112
Paranomasia, 14
Paris: as exemplary lover, 139, 197; judgment of, 201, 202

Paris, Paulin, 5, 98, 155, 234n5, 237n12, 244n69
Paris, France, 119, 123, 219n2
Peleus, 201
Penser (Dous Penser), 29, 30, 166
Perceval, 180, 181
Péronne d'Armentières: and Deschamps, 7–8; her poetry, 236n9; her identity, 239n25; mentioned, 101, 138. See also Voir-Dit
Petrarch, 20, 98
Picus, 143
Pierre de Lusignan, King of Cyprus: patron of Machaut, 4, 21
Pitié, 29
Plaisance: as locus amoenus, 42, 45, 54, 55, 66, 158, 180, 182. See also Locus amoenus; Vergier
Poeta, 18, 20
Poirion, Daniel, 3, 5, 101, 211, 212, 238n16, 238n18, 244n76, 249n24
Polyphemus, 143, 244n75
Prière, 55
Prouesse, 166
Pygmalion, 197, 198
Pyramus, 139

Raison, 75, 89, 93, 138, 166, 167–68
Reader, 56, 98, 101, 103, 121, 129, 138, 146, 160, 166, 168, 173, 188
Reaney, Gilbert, 5
Regalado, Nancy Freeman, 223n30, 249n21
Règles de la Seconde Rhétorique, 210
Reims, France, 123, 125, 128, 219n2
Remede de Fortune: narrative structure, 37–38, 39, 42–43, 45, 48, 49, 52, 54, 60; narrator-protagonist, 37–38, 39–41, 60–62; didacticism, 37–39, 57, 58, 59, 60, 63; Roman de la Rose (as model), 39, 40, 41, 45, 53–54, 55; intercalated lyrics, 41–42, 43–45, 46–47, 51–52, 54, 55–56, 57; lyric inspiration, 41, 43, 47; Consolation of Philosophy (as model), 42, 45–46, 48, 50–52; Fortune, 43–44, 50–52; dream-vision

(trance), 45–48; Esperence (as character), 45–52, 54, 57; truth, 58–59; mentioned, 6, 21, 24, 93, 105, 127, 231n26. See also Ars amandi; Ars poetica; Lady Philosophy
René d'Anjou, 6, 251n1
Richard de Fornival: Li Bestiares d'amours, 248n10
Richesse, 166
Robert, Duke de Bar, 136
Romance: as genre, 3, 9–12, 49, 198; roman d'aventures, 174, 180, 187; roman antique, 198. See also Chrétien de Troyes; Dit dou lyon; Roman de la Rose
Roman de Lancelot, 102
Roman de la Rose: as tradition, 3, 6, 9, 20, 23, 212; structure, 12, 13, 14; and Machaut's poète figure, 17, 19–20; as textual model for Machaut, 23, 27–32 passim, 36, 39–42, 45, 48, 49, 53, 55, 96–98, 134, 138, 158–59, 173, 189, 194–95, 197–98, 200–201, 202, 205, 206, 228n4, 228n6, 230n24, 249n23, 250n30; mentioned, 8, 102, 213. See also Guillaume de Lorris; Jean de Meun
Rondeau (rondel), 41, 97–98, 100, 109, 112, 113, 124, 138, 154, 205, 210, 211, 236n9, 240n36
Rondelet, 57, 116
Rutebeuf, 14, 190, 212, 214
Rychner, Jean, 251n35, 253n24

Saint-Denis, France, 119
Schrade, Leo, 5
Seconde Rhétorique, 208–9, 210
Semiramis, 130, 131, 148, 243n62
Souffissance, 50, 121
Souvenir, 29, 30

Thibaut de Champagne, 12
Thisbe, 139
Tousac, Pierre, 139
Translatio imperii, 10, 11
Translatio studii, 10, 11, 225n40

Tristan, 106
Trojan War, 165, 197

Uitti, Karl D., 12, 22, 213, 221n14, 222n27, 223n30

Valerius Maximus, 130
Venus, 105, 120–21, 153, 197, 198, 201, 202–4
Vergier: as locus amoenus, 26, 27, 34, 89, 91, 92, 97, 110, 112, 113, 163, 173–74, 181, 184, 186. See also Locus amoenus; Plaisance
Vie de Saint Alexis, 9–10
Villon, François: Testament, 212–14; "Ballade de conclusion," 213; mentioned, 4, 208
Virelay, 41, 55, 56, 109, 124, 211, 231n25. See also Chanson baladée
Voir-Dit: narrator-protagonist, 94–96, 98–100, 104–5, 106–8, 118, 128, 130, 140, 141, 145, 149–50, 156; narrative structure, 95, 96–97, 101, 103–4, 107–8, 114, 118, 122–23, 127–28, 131, 137, 141, 145, 150, 154, 156, 234n5; truth (as theme), 95, 99, 109, 111, 121–22, 123, 126–27, 131, 134, 137–38, 146, 147; chronology (including letters), 97, 101, 111, 118–20, 130–31, 153, 235n8, 237n12; intercalated lyrics, 97–98, 101–2, 103, 109, 112, 135, 140, 236n9, 236n10; naming, 99–100, 105,

138, 154; ymage, 100, 105, 106, 129, 132–34, 146–48, 242n59, 245n79; pilgrimage, 106, 108, 113–14, 118–19; patrons (and public), 107, 113, 114–16, 118, 129, 132, 136, 143–44; book (as theme), 116, 127, 129–31, 134–35, 136–39, 140–41, 150, 152–53, 154; "Lay d'Esperance," 124–27, 128; dreams, 132–34, 146–48; autobiography, question of, 234n4, 235n8, 236n9, 237n12; mentioned, 5, 15, 21, 93. See also Charles V; Desir; Esperence; Fin'amors; Fortune; Gradus amoris; Losengier; Péronne d'Armentières; Roman de la Rose; Venus
Voloir (Fran Voloir, Volenté), 29, 30, 76, 166

Wace: as poet, 10–11, 221n11, 225n40; Roman de Brut, 221n11, 222n19; Roman de Rou, 221n17, 225n40
Weinrich, Harald, 22–23, 34, 65–66, 163, 190, 228n6, 247n2
Williams, Sarah Jane, 223n32, 237n12, 240n30, 240n36
Wimsatt, James, 5, 227n3

Young, Karl, 5
Yvain, 176, 181, 248n12

Zumthor, Paul, 222n28, 251n3

COMPOSED BY METRICOMP
GRUNDY CENTER, IOWA
MANUFACTURED BY MALLOY LITHOGRAPHING, INC.
ANN ARBOR, MICHIGAN
TEXT AND DISPLAY LINES ARE SET IN PALATINO

Library of Congress Cataloging in Publication Data
Brownlee, Kevin.
Poetic identity in Guillaume de Machaut.
Bibliography: pp. 255–262.
Includes index.
1. Guillaume, de Machaut, ca. 1300–1377 — Criticism
and interpretation. 2. Narrative poetry, French — History
and criticism. 3. First person narrative. 4. Self in
literature. 5. Poets in literature. I. Title.
PC1483.G5B7 1984   841'.1   83-14498
ISBN 0-229-09200-3